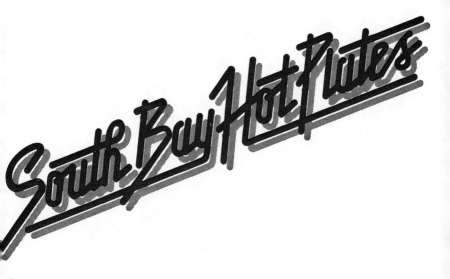

South Bay Hot Plates

J. Izzo Jr.

A CANDID COLLECTION
OF RESTAURANT REVIEWS BY
SAN JOSE'S #1 RESTAURANT CRITIC

Single Copy Orders: $5.95 plus Postage and Handling.

Send to: JK WEST PUBLICATIONS
            P. O. Box 18758
            San Jose, California 95158

Cover concept and design: *Rick Tharp Did It, Los Gatos*
Photography: *Sollecito Photography, Sunnyvale*
Retouching: *Littlejohn's, Los Gatos*
Typesetting: *Terry's Type, Campbell*
Layout: *Joseph Mangelli, San Jose*

STAFF

Editor . . . . *Kristine Estrada*

Production Manager . . . . *Joseph Mangelli*

Graphic Design . . . . *Joseph Mangelli*

Technical Advisor . . . . *Charles Magonia*

Research . . . . *Edward Butler*
Debra Estrada
Robert Michels

CONTENTS

ACKNOWLEDGEMENTS

I would like to thank the following editors at the **SAN JOSE MERCURY AND NEWS** for their help and instruction in the field of good reporting.

Jennie Buckner
Robert Cochnar
Bob Drews
Sandy Flickner
David Frazier
Iris Frost
Robert Ingle
Jim Mitchell
Soundra Noda
John Parkin
Mary Phillips
Al Pierleone
Zeke Wigglesworth

NOTES

Joseph Izzo Jr. has researched and evaluated 167 restaurants in the Bay Area. He has visited all restaurants as an unannounced, paying customer and has not been influenced, persuaded, or pressured by any motivation or consideration other than to present fair, honest reviews. SOUTH BAY HOT PLATES was designed to guide and assist the customer in choosing a restaurant best suited to his/her taste and pocketbook.

PRICE SYSTEM

Because menu prices are subject to constant change, Joseph Izzo Jr. selected to categorize the restaurants into 3 price ranges: BARGAIN; MODERATE; EXPENSIVE.

> BARGAIN: Majority of entrees $5 and Under
> MODERATE: Majority of entrees between $6 and $10
> EXPENSIVE: Majority of entrees over $10.

KEY TO RESTAURANT RATINGS: The following rating system takes into consideration five major aspects of dining: PRICE or VALUE; PORTION; QUALITY OF FOOD AND PREPARATION; AMBIENCE; SERVICE.

> ★★★★★ The Best
> ★★★★ EXCELLENT
> ★★★ GOOD
> ★★ FAIR
> ★ Mediocre and Below

WHEELCHAIR ACCESS

FULL WHEELCHAIR ACCESS: Includes designated parking for handicapped drivers, ramps for architectural changes in elevation, wide lavatory stalls and handrails, and aisles wide enough for navigation.

LIMITED WHEELCHAIR ACCESS: Indicates that a wheelchair will fit into some part of the dining

NOTES

area of the restaurant. There may be steps, inaccessible lavatory facilities and inconvenient parking to contend with.

NON-SMOKING SECTIONS

In San Jose the Non-Smoking Ordinance requires that a restaurant with a seating capacity of 100 or more must provide a non-smoking section. Other cities and towns have smoking ordinances with varying seating capacities. In the heading of each review, the smoking section policy will be indicated by NON-SMOKING SECTION *OR* NO NON-SMOKING SECTION. It must also be noted that just because a restaurant claims to have a non-smoking section, it doesn't mean that this section will be free from second hand smoke. Proper ventilation is most important in determining the degree of smoke in a restaurant.

CREDIT CARDS

Most restaurants accept credit cards. In the heading of each review, they will be indicated by the following abbreviations:

AE   AMERICAN EXPRESS
MC   MASTER CARD
V   Visa

If a restaurant takes all of the above 3, plus either CARTE BLANCHE and/or DINERS CLUB, the heading will indicate ALL MAJOR CREDIT CARDS.

INTRODUCTION

Life without good food, is a life without spirit.

Dining out is one of the highest forms of entertainment. The purpose of a good restaurant is to serve you, the patron, and to make your time away from home an enjoyable experience, a relaxing break from the grind and woes of daily existence.

The *BEST* restaurants are those where the owners (who are, in many cases, the chefs) have made a firm commitment to make their establishment the best it can possibly be. A good owner hangs in for the duration and refuses to shift around from restaurant to restaurant, seeking profit rather than serving the patron to the best of his/her abilities. In the long run, the commited owner is usually the one who makes the most money.

When it comes to *SELECTING* a restaurant, trust your cravings. If you want a pizza, eat a pizza. If you want a greasy hamburger, don't be talked into sushi. Remember, dining out is *your* entertainment, your good time. It's also your money that will be spent, so follow where your hunger sends you and nine times out of ten, you'll go home with a smile. Take over-zealous recommendations with a grain of salt. What one person simply adores, could be the very antithesis of what you want.

Always study the menu. *BEWARE* of long winded listings, offering so many dishes you become dizzy with indecision. The great majority of chefs would rather deal with a limited menu so they can concentrate their attention and talent on a few dishes, rather than wasting their talent on many. When forced to prepare many items, a chef can lose focus and may be forced to cut corners to justify the extensiveness of the menu. He becomes a slave to the menu, not a master of his craft. Beware also of the waiter or waitress who claims that *EVERYTHING* on the menu is a specialty.

In the Modern Age of restaurant going, we are faced with a great influx of ethnic cuisines. Instead of the basics, like Italian, French, Chinese, Mexican, and of course, American,

INTRODUCTION

you can now take your palate on a journey to such places as Thailand, Morocco, Indonesia, the Middle East, and landmarks beyond. Don't be afraid to *EXPERIMENT* occasionally. Too many of us miss out on tasting excellent foods because of bogus, preconceived notions about exotic cuisines.

When troubled by a foreign phrase you don't understand or by a tricky or vague translation, you should always request of your waiter or waitress a complete description. If he cannot describe a dish with some accuracy, he did not do his homework. The best dining establishments are usually the most honest and sincere, with trained waiters and waitresses who know the food they are serving. It is your right to know as much about a dish as you want.

Nouvelle Cuisine has been highly touted by many gastronomes in the past few years. When I was in Paris, I had the opportunity to speak with Claude Deligne, Head Chef at Taillevent, one of the world's greatest French restaurants highlighting Nouvelle Cuisine. He said that Nouvelle Cuisine was "a natural outgrowth of what the people wanted." His customers demanded lighter foods, so sauces became lighter, foods became lighter, the whole experience of dining out no longer left one feeling leaden or uncomfortable. According to Deligne, one of the major factors that distinguishes Nouvelle from Classic cuisine is the absence of flour in the sauces. Sauces are naturally thickened in Nouvelle Cuisine, and meats and produce are almost always local products, insuring immediate freshness.

Deligne also warned of the "Abuses" in the preparation of Nouvelle Cuisine. Some restaurants claim to serve it, but have no idea about the importance of culinary balance and the keen attention to every detail. The theory behind taste, texture, visual presentation must be fully understood before Nouvelle Cuisine can be accomplished in its purest form. A great chef is one who has trained and studied in the classic mode, who has achieved, through arduous work, the mastery of food preparation and presentation.

INTRODUCTION

The *ORDERING* of meat and fish depends again on personal tastes. If you prefer meat well done, by all means, order it that way; you have to eat it. Be aware, though, that according to many food experts, quality cuts of beef (beef from the heart of the tenderloin or filet) should be cooked rare or, at most, medium rare for full flavor and tenderness. Lamb tenderloin should also be ordered rare. When lamb is overcooked, it tends to lose its natural juices, its rich, distinctive flavor, and its unique, textural quality.

Be aware, too, that the best seafood is served very simply. Fish has often been ruined at the hands of a cook who doesn't understand its delicacy. Ask about the preparation when you order. Seafood is best grilled quickly over a hot, clean fire, poached carefully, or sauteed for a short time in a very gentle sauce. Over saucing or applying heavy sauces can destroy fish; it can ruin any dish. The freshest fish is usually the best in flavor and in texture. Many restaurants offer blackboards listing seasonal catches. It is my recommendation that you order only the freshest items available.

I am not given to the belief that *PROVIMI VEAL* is the *ONLY* veal to eat. There are many varieties that can be equally satisfying and less expensive. A calf is weaned on milk for the first six to eight weeks of life. When butchered during this state, the meat has a tendency to be very white in color, milky in flavor, and delicate in texture. I enjoy good "milk-fed" veal. Quality cannot be argued with. However, it must be noted that after six to eight weeks, most calves will begin to eat grass. This colors the flesh and slightly toughens the meat. When prepared in a stew, breaded and pan fried (Veal Milanese and Wienerschnitzel), or even oven roasted, this type of heartier veal can also be good eating, not only in flavor, but in texture as well.

As for *PASTA*, I am sold on it being boiled to the point of texture called *AL DENTE*. **Al Dente** translates "To the Tooth." When prepared to this degree, pasta offers a slight resistance to the bite. In Italy, pasta comes to the table in

INTRODUCTION

this manner without the patron having to ask for it. When overcooked, pasta loses its natural texture and tantalizing semolina flavor.

When unhappy about your dinner, the service, or any aspect of the dining experience, it is your right to *COMPLAIN*. If meat is not cooked to your specifications – send it back, but don't eat half of it before notifying the waiter. This goes for wine as well. If it's sour, speak up when you taste it, not after you have polished off half the bottle.

It is always important to exercise discretion when complaining. It will do you and your guests no good to blow up at the table and make a scene. If a waiter or waitress is being difficult, you can excuse yourself from the table and quietly discuss the matter. It may seem like a lot of trouble, but it can also save an evening out from being a total disaster. If all fails, tell the manager. Your complaints should be translated as constructive criticism. Then, if that doesn't work, a very effective way in dealing with such a problem is to write a letter to *ACTION LINE* in the **SAN JOSE MERCURY AND NEWS**. But, by all means, don't make a fool out of yourself.

Many restaurants today are stocking their cellars with extensive selections of fine French and California wines. Some of these wines can be very pricy and can turn an average priced meal into a financial setback. The best thing to do is to study up on wines so that you can select a vintage that will best suit your taste and your pocketbook. By no means should you feel that House wines be avoided. Restaurants today carry some fine House wines that go well with almost any dish of your choosing.

When drinking wine, it is common knowledge that white wines go better with lighter foods, like fish and chicken, while red wine compliments heartier foods, like beef and pasta dishes with heavy tomato sauces.

TIPPING is and has always been a controversial subject. The current rate of gratuity is 15%. Not 10%. Not 5%. If the service has been adequate, be fair and tip according to the norm. If the service is below average, reduce the tip. It is my personal opinion that to leave no tip at all is an expression of poor taste. Don't let the waiter or waitress get so far out of control that you are placed in a situation where you leave nothing on the table.

When it comes to making *RESERVATIONS*, it is important to inform the host when making the reservation of personal needs. If you desire a *NON-SMOKING SECTION*, tell the host that you want a table in a well ventilated area, free from secondhand smoke. If you are in a *WHEELCHAIR*, require a table comfortably spaced with ample room for navigation. If a restaurant cannot adequately reserve a table according to your personal specifications, go elsewhere.

If you have made a reservation and find that you must *CANCEL*, it is common courtesy to inform the restaurant as soon as possible to avoid their loss of business.

In Closing, if I were to give one piece of advice that precedes all the others, I can only say that when dining out remember that it is your hard-earned money and you should get the most out of it. Enjoy yourself. *YOU DESERVE IT.*

Joseph Izzo, Jr.

ADAM'S RIB ★★
BBQ Ribs

Price Range: Bargain

2590 Portola Drive, Santa Cruz	Master Charge – Visa
Phone: (408) 476-5010	No Reservations
Hours: 11:30 a.m.–9 p.m., Daily	No Non-Smoking Section
Take Out	Limited Wheelchair Access

Adam's Rib has become Santa Cruz's heart throb barbecued rib place. The store is very small with only three tables inside, about 4 or 5 outside along the patio. Most of the business here is take-out which people who live in the Cruz are more than willing to do. Adam's Rib is doing a wonderful business.

Both pork and beef ribs are offered. The meat is barbecued in a brick chimney stove under a slow wood blaze. The pork ribs come out extremely tender with plenty of juicy, sweet pork meat to set your teeth firmly into. The beef ribs are large and require some extended motor activity with the choppers. The meat, however, is very flavorful, especially when smeared with Adam's special sauce. The sauce is a deep rust in color with a spicy, slightly sweet flavor.

Adam's ribs make good party food. Ribs are the type of handy edibles that can make a beer bash in a '59 Chevy a full coarse dining adventure. Acquire plenty of napkins. The ordeal will be messy.

ACAPULCO ★★★
Mexican

Price Range: Moderate

2305 S. Winchester Blvd., San Jose	Master Charge – Visa
Phone: (408) 374-5500	Reser. Recommended
Hours: 11 a.m.–10 p.m., Sun–Thurs.	Non-Smoking Section
11 a.m.–11 p.m., Fri. & Sat.	Full Wheelchair Access
Full Bar	

I don't understand the management at the San Jose branch of Acapulco. The food is very good, but the service, despite numerous complaints, still stinks. The waiters and waitresses are consistently slow, forgetful, and aloof. On more than one occasion, my guest and I simply walked out because nobody even came to our table to say hello, or God forbid, take an order. If you want to sit at one of those romantic booths, sequestered and private, odds are you will be forgotten, unless one of the busboys spot you. I recommend you make yourself clearly visible, cough a lot, chortle, and guffaw.

Once you are served, however, things improve immensely. One of my favorite dishes here is Carnitas. This festive, roasted pork dish is prepared with exceptional savor by the chefs. A large platter of pork chunks seasoned sparingly is presented. With the pork you receive three dressings: raw cilantro, a chunky salsa salad, raw diced onions, plus jalapenos if you ask for them. Also included are long, crisp scallions, avocado slices, rice, beans, and tortillas. Carnitas is fun to eat and emphasizes natural flavors without depending on sauces or heavy spices.

Empanada Verde is another fine Mexican specialty at Acapulco. A large, flour tortilla is fried to a semi-puffed form. This slightly crisp tort is then filled with a spicy chile verde (pork in green chile), monterey jack cheese, and mashed pinto beans, then folded over once. The empanada can be eaten as an appetizer or as an entree.

Acapulco's menu is extensive, listing mostly gourmet Mexican items, created by Chef Ramon, plus the usual commonalities like taco, enchilada, burrito, chile relleno, and those boring combination dishes. Tacos are well made, with at least three meat fillings to choose from. I like the shredded beef with green peppers.

The atmosphere is comfortable and Mexican elegant with colorful serapes on the ceiling, brass, and stained glass. It becomes crowded during the typical peak hours and lounge waits can be long. So call ahead.

ADRIATIC ★★★★★   **Price Range: Expensive**
Continental

14583 Big Basin Way, Saratoga	All Major Credit Cards
Phone: (408) 867-3110	Reservations Required
Hours: 6–10 p.m., Mon.–Sat.	No Non-Smoking Section
Extensive Wine List	Limited Wheelchair Access

I rate Adriatic one of the best restaurants in the South Bay. All my dining experiences here have been thoroughly satisfying. Ed Begovic and his wife, Nada, uphold consistency and excellence of cuisine as their highest attributes. Each patron becomes an honored guest in the hands of the Begovics, who go out of their way to insure satisfaction.

Adriatic is a small restaurant with an interior of subtle elegance etched in white lace and royal blue. Ceilings are high and ventilation is excellent. Non-smokers will not have to worry about second hand smoke. Tables are few, though spaced comfortably for maximum privacy. Adriatic is a romantic restaurant, a place where you will feel inspired to put on a fine suit or new dress.

The cuisine is an innovative style of continental flavored with the spice and allure of the Balkans, the homeland of the Begovics. Having been here on several occasions, I have had the opportunity to taste many dishes on the menu, which always highlight the freshest seasonal produce and the finest cuts of meat and poultry.

A notable appetizer includes the delicious Balkan sausage, Cheuapcici. These sausages are made from a delicate blending of lamb, veal, and beef tenderloin, lightly seasoned, and soaked in Radenska, Yugoslav mineral water. They are simply grilled and served with a fresh vegetable garni. I love to eat cheuapcici with pepperinccini, (pickled peppers). Also, Prawns Florentine are worth a pre-entree indulging. Large gulf prawns are prepared in a saute of olive oil, garlic and capers and set on a bed of spinach.

The one entree that I order almost every time I come here is Veal with Morilles. Medallions of milk-fed provimi veal are dipped in egg, then sauteed in a delicate brown sauce flavored with the wild French Morel mushrooms. The medallions are finished on one end with melted cheese. Delectable.

When spring lamb is in season, which is only in spring time, ask Mr. Begovic for a special lamb creation. Otherwise, the lamb tenderloin en croute is a fine example of Chef Nada's culinary expertise. Adriatic was the first restaurant to serve fresh quails. This provocative poultry dish is one of the most original to be served in a continental restaurant. The quails are always fresh, the meat of these dainty birds tender and game sweet.

Desserts vary from night to night, though there are a few which can be enjoyed all the time, like the dessert crepes. The one I like is the crepe filled with walnuts and covered with chocolate sauce. When Amaretto torte is available – by all means order it. The flavor of Amaretto is strong and clears the olfactory of any impurities.

Adriatic's wine list enjoys a strong California influence with several top line vintages offered, such as Freemark Abbey, Martin Rey, and Grgich-Hills.

ALDO'S ★★★

Price Range: Bargain

Breakfast and Lunch

Santa Cruz Yacht Harbor, Santa Cruz	Cash Only
Phone: 426-3736	No Reservations
Hours: 7 a.m.–4 p.m., Daily	No Non-Smoking Section
Beer and Wine	Limited Wheelchair Access

Aldo's still looks like a fish and tackle shop. But remains the heart throb breakfast and lunch spot for local Santa Cruzeans. When the morning light hits your eyes on a cruel and painful spectrum, Aldo's is there to pull you through with hearty grub and noisy breakfast chatter. The aroma of strong coffee, the stinging scent of frying eggs, fresh fugasa bread, and early morning fish are Aldo's A.M. realities.

My favorite breakfast here is the two egg and Italian Sausage plate. The eggs are fried to order in plenty of butter and the Italian sausage is filled with fennel and rich pork butt. The combination of flavors will send strong invigorating signals to the sleepy grey matter hunkered up inside your skull.

Though breakfast is the favorite repast here, lunch is nothing to shove under the mat. On a clear day with a slight breeze and a strong ocean scent, Aldo's is ideal for sitting on the patio deck, watching the yachts drift silently against the sun. While you sit and soak up the day, have Walter, Aldo's son, pop open a bottle of champagne while you fork your way through a pile of French Fried Calamari. The calamari here are light and tender, served in a blond batter with crispy chips and dill pickle tart tartar sauce.

When fresh and available, the salmon and chips is also a good lunch buy. Often times it is bought directly from one of the local fishermen just in with a good catch. The salmon was a thick mid-section filet with a nice pink hue and a fresh flavor. A variety of sandwiches and salads are also available.

Aldo's is a local hang-out, but it's also a hang out for anybody who likes good food, good company, and beautiful Santa Cruz ambiance.

ANDY'S ★★★★   Price Range: Moderate
BBQ

---

700 E. Campbell Ave., Campbell	Cash Only
Phone: 378-2838	No Reservations
Hours: Lunch: 11:30–2, Mon.–Fri.	No Non-Smoking Section
Dinner: 5–10 pm, Daily	Clumsy Wheelchair Access
Full Bar	

As chilling as it may appear, Andy doesn't have to worry about scaring people away. The barbecue he serves is a classic. This is a soulful establishment, well rooted in South Bay soil, basing its name on tradition, good food and good drink.

Once through the tattered front entrance, you are swallowed in the dark, moody charm of a beer-and-bourbon cocktail lounge. A lonely piano bar is off in a corner just waiting for a Billy Joel to sing a few sad tunes. The dining room, located at the rear of the bar area, is more shadowy than dark with flashes from the oak fire dancing intermittently along the drab cinderblock walls. Functional tables and chairs outfit the room, all of which were occupied the night we ate here. Andy's has become quite the gathering place for those seeking a pile of ribs and down-home country comfort.

All meat is prepared on flaming oak in a brick oven, ablaze in a corner for all to see. Ribs and chicken are hung in the barbecue chimney for hours of smoke cooking. The beef and pork here are choice, quality cuts; however, the meat is not delicate and requires a strong set of choppers to tear into its firm, grainy texture.

Portions run big here, so prepare yourself for a lot of eating. The prize of the house remains the Ribs ($8.25). They are served as a large, cut rack. The ribs run in size from long and meaty to tough, charred end pieces. I like to work my teeth on the end pieces, though I realize that some will prefer not to. Otherwise, the ribs were layered with deeply smoked pork meat. The oak smoke gives the meat a tingling, earthy flavor that is not like hickory at all. The oak at Andy's has been seasoned especially for his operation.

All dinners are served with a bottle of mildly tart barbeque sauce without that biting barbeque sweetness. It had a unique peppery aftertaste. Also served with the dinners is another Andy original. The baked potato here is different, not so much in the large size of the potato but in the sauce poured over the top. The sauce is a hot, milky cheese concoction that adds a creamy consistency to the spud. Personally, I enjoyed the taste of the sauce, but my guests did not.

Chicken is also a notable dinner item here. A whole half chicken is cut into large quarters, each piece laden with moist, smoky meat. A spread of that special barbeque sauce brought out the best from the chicken. We found ourselves nibbling the last morsels of meat from the bones. Andy figures his patrons are going to use their hands so he offers packets of Wash 'n Dry for post-dinner grooming.

Service at Andy's was attentive and fast, but due to the dinner rush, was not as friendly as it has been in the past. Drinks from the bar are separate from the dinners and when your drinks arrive, the cocktail waitress will request that you pay then. With fingers stained with sauce and your mouth full of chicken or steak, it can be difficult and embarrassing to pay on the spot. But that's the policy here.

Andy's is the type of restaurant that people will always tell their friends about. Though it is popular now, it still remains a "find." Some places are blessed with success.

ANGELO'S ★★
Pizza

Price Range: Bargain

436 Blossom Hill Rd., San Jose
Phone: 227-5502
Hours: 11 am–10 pm, Mon.–Thurs.
11 am–11 pm, Friday
Noon–11 pm, Sat.
4 pm–10 pm, Sunday
Beer and Wine

Checks and Cash Only
No Reservations
No Non-Smoking Section
Limited Wheelchair Access

Angelo's pizzaria was a part of Downer Square at the corner of Snell and Blossom Hill way back before the developers had a chance to strip the land of its last cherry tree.

Like most restaurants in South San Jose, Angelo's is wedged into a fashionless shopping center where the exterior walkways are forever tattooed with spilled ice cream and cigarette ash. Its interior is a long rectangle, festooned with booths and red-checked dressed tables.

The main focus of those enamored with Angelo's is its pizza. The pizza here is made from homemade bread dough which has felt the knead of human fingers. With such continual care, one can be sure an Angelo's pizza will possess a certain teeth-sinkable quality reminiscent of those fine New York pies.

The pizza sauce always has been a clean, tomato-tart blend, unspoiled by overseasoning or meat adjuncts. As a rule, fresh mozzarella cheese is generously applied and baked to a soft, liquid consistency. Occasional complaints have ranged from not enough cheese to an overcooked undercrust. I attribute this to quirks of inattentiveness by one of the rotating pizza-makers.

In addition to pizza, Angelo's puts out a decent plate of spaghetti and meatballs. The chef uses Costa pasta, the brand boasting a "fine quality." When attended correctly, it boils to a firm, starch-clean tenderness easily twirled onto a fork. The spaghetti sauce, like the pizza sauce, is a healthy Sunday-dinner concoction which relies on natural ingredients for flavor.

Meatballs here are moist and not too lightly packed. The ground beef is seasoned carefully with the garlic announcing itself subtly.

Service at Angelo's has always been coffee shop efficient. The waitresses are usually friendly and love to talk about the happenings around Downer Square. For a direct line on the current flap, find a stool at the counter and hoist a few tap-drawn brews.

ANTHONY'S PIER 9 ★★★★
Seafood / Continental

Price Range: Expensive

10745 N. DeAnza Blvd., Cupertino	A.E. – M.C. – Visa
Phone: 255-4711	Reservations Required
Hours: 11 am–11 pm, Mon.-Sat.	Non-Smoking Section
From 3:30, Sunday	Full Wheelchair Access
Sunday Brunch: 10–2:30 pm	
Full Bar	

As a diner looking back after a meal at Anthony's Pier 9, the total picture is positive. Produce, seafood, and meats have always been consistently top quality. However, as a critic analyzing each dish as separate components of the dinner, there have been flaws, chef oversights, little annoyances that have convinced me Anthony's has yet to reach its apex.

The menu is an Italian composition, highlighting fresh fish, shellfish, veal and homemade-style pasta. On all of my visits I have ordered a pasta entree, splitting it among my guests as an appetizer. Pasta is not to be missed here. It is made at the Florentine Pasta Factory and has the tender consistency of fine, homemade noodles.

The Linguini Alla Vongole is always a gratifying pasta dish. The noodles and clam sauce made with natural clam broth, garlic and butter form a perfect marriage. On a recent visit, I sampled the Fettuccine Al Pesto. The butter rich, creamy pesto sauce, springing with the bracing zest of sweet basil and garlic, is the triumph here. The sauce was so good, it overshadowed the fact that the fettuccine noodles were slightly overdone.

Following our pasta, we shared a portion of Insalata Mista. All of the ingredients, comprising slices of avocado, shredded crab meat, bay shrimp, tomato, mushrooms, raw spinach, and romaine lettuce, were fresh and attractively displayed. Unfortunately, the creamy Italian dressing used on this salad weighed heavy on the greens and fish. It wasn't a crisp salad. This is one of those little annoyances that made the Insalata Mista a fair offering instead of a total success.

Veal and Scampi All'Agro could have been a perfect dish had it not been undermined by a chef oversight on two separate occasions. It consists of three scallops of quality milk fed veal, some of the best I have eaten in a long time, and four jumbo, juicy scampi. Even the silken lemon, butter and garlic sauce was a masterful creation. But, the chef has gotten careless and drowned the veal, the scampi, even the vegetables in this tasty sauce. On two samplings now, this dish has been oversauced.

A total success was the broiled Swordfish. Anthony's buys only the freshest fish and the chefs here know how to prepare it to perfection.

A thick, slab of right-off-the-boat swordfish was simply broiled without masking additives or sauces. The flesh broke from the boneless mid-section in juice trickling chunks. A masterpiece! Likewise, the Salmon filet was a beautifully fresh piece of fish, correctly broiled so that the natural juices were fully retained.

When considering the service at Anthony's, again I am puzzled. Brigades of waiters, tuxedo clad renzos, busboys, and hostesses zig-zag through the dining rooms creating a weave of professional movement. The scene inspires confidence, yet little things always seem to go wrong. Two times we have called in for reservations. When we arrived, the hostess said she didn't have our names down and even got testy when we tried to explain we had called in. Busboys are inconsistent when it comes to replacing silverware after each course. Several times, we had to ask for a fork. This may sound picky, but in a restaurant of this caliber, things like silverware should never be forgotten. Our waiter this visit was humorous but exceedingly spaced out. He had to ask us many times what we were going to have and still forgot. I do commend him on the discreet pacing of our wine. He never overpoured and made sure everybody had an equal amount.

In terms of decor, Anthony's is a winner. It's chic nautical theme creates an ideal dining milieu. A custom made aquarium, aswim with exotic tropical fish, forms a stunning center piece in the main dining room. Wrap around booths and linen covered tables and chairs are comfortably situated around this refreshing visual attraction. Anthony's is a dress-up restaurant where you can rest easy, linger, and converse at length over long, well paced dinners.

THE ARMENIAN GOURMET ★★★★   Price Range: Moderate
Armenian

921 E. Duane, Sunnyvale	Master Card — Visa
Phone: (408) 732-3910	No Reservations
Hours: Lunch: 11:30–1:30 pm, M-Fri.	No Non-Smoking Area
Dinner: 5–8:15 pm, Wed.-Sat.	Limited Wheelchair Access
Beer and Wine	

When I think of Armenian food, I can't help think of the first girlfriend I ever went steady with. Her name was Sue Atamian and her mother, despite her strange desire to house 25 poodles in the back bedroom of their house, was an excellent Armenian cook, well versed in the preparation of her native dishes. Mrs. Atamian was the first person to introduce me to the deliciousness of this unique Middle Eastern food. The first and last time I ever had dinner there, she put out a spread of stuffed grape leaves, cheese turnovers, and a variety of shish kebabs that made me forget about the beauty of her only daughter.

With this vivid memory in mind, I went to the Armenian Gourmet in Sunnyvale, perhaps the only Armenian restaurant of its kind in the South Bay. It has survived for more than 8 years in a tiny little storefront in the Fair Oaks Plaza, hardly an auspicious location. My first visit was a noon-time stop off. My first step through the door was a rude awakening of how popular this place had grown through the years. All the tables were taken with gabbing technocrats. My olfactory was immediately stimulated by spicy scents mixed with the aroma of burning charcoal. I was intrigued, though slightly taken back by the noise, the crowded conditions, the total lack of decor, save for a few Armenian knick-knacks that were fully lost in the starkness of the scene.

After my first mouthful of food, I realized why The Armenian Gourmet has become so popular. The food was excellent. It was truly inspiring, well made, and authentic. Not a single American concession was made on the menu. That day I feasted on a plate of Lamb and Beef sauteed with fresh, large cut pieces of deep red tomatoes, green pepper, mushrooms, and onions. The sauce was a natural cohesion of the ingredients with only a light touch of seasoning applied. It was served with a fluff of perfectly cooked rice pilaf. Each kernel was firm, tender, and separate.

I left fully satisfied and returned the following week for an evening meal. The menu remains the same throughout lunch and dinner, so you won't meet with surprises. This time I hunkered in for a long meal and started with appetizers. The first was a simple dish of Feta Cheese and Black Olives. The sharply flavored goat cheese was exceptionally moist and full bodied, forming a harmonious balance with the marinated olives. A very light, palate awakening course. The Feta and olives were followed by a plate of Armenian style Hummos. This is a smooth, creamy dip made from chick peas.

Because the charcoal scents are so strong and alluring at The Armenian Gourmet, I found it necessary to eat the very item that met the fire of the charcoal grill. Of course, the kebab offerings are broiled in this fashion. Two styles of kebab are offered. The most commonly found Shish Kebab, which traditionally includes chunks of tender lamb, is broiled to perfection by the cooks here. The lamb was not dry or chewy. The chunks were very moist and easy to cut with the edge of a fork. Herbs and spices were sparingly applied to enhance the rich flavor of the lamb.

The shish kebab I enjoyed the most was the special Luleh Kebab. Quality ground beef is blended with scallions and herbs, formed into fat, generous sausages, charbroiled, and served on a bed of rice pilaf. The sausages were rich with flavor and exuded natural juice. Simply delicious.

If you want to sample a threesome of Armenian specialties, the John Michel Special provides the perfect opportunity to explore this Middle Eastern cuisine. It includes a shish kebab, sauteed lamb and beef, and luleh kebab with rice pilaf and pita bread. It can only be ordered in servings for two persons only, though it makes a great dinner when dining with a friend.

The Armenian Gourmet is a surprising little restaurant in that it serves excellent Armenian cuisine at reasonable prices. The portions are big and the flavors are deep and long lasting. I believe you will embrace this one.

AU BON VIVANT ★★★
French / Belgian

Price Range: Moderate

14510 Big Basin Way, Saratoga	All Major Credit Cards
Phone: 867-1455	Reservations Taken
Hours: 7:30 am–10 pm, Tues.-Sat.	No Non-Smoking Section
Sunday Brunch: 9 am–2 pm	Limited Wheelchair Access
Beer and Wine	

The glittering star of Au Bon Vivant is the bakery where racks of fresh croissants, petite Baguettes, and brioche are pulled from the ovens daily. Just having a Croissant Nature with jam and butter and a cup of strong, dark espresso is a fine way to begin or end a leisurely stroll along Big Basin Way in sleepy Saratoga Village.

But Au Bon Vivant's menu does not end with specialty breads. Both its lunch and dinner ledgers are relatively complete. Lunch entrees include several styles of crepes, salads, homemade pates, and fresh soups.

For an afternoon meal one day, I enjoyed Croquettes Ostendaises, a recipe from the Belgian Coast. Imported Gruyere cheese is formed into a cylinder, coated with egg and bread crumbs, then deep fried until golden crisp. The cheese melts down to a silken texture in the fry heat, yet retains its form. The flavors were rich and creamy, but very simple.

Dinners are heartier than the lunches, but still smaller in portion than what you are accustomed to having in other restaurants. Evening fare lists a few interesting pates made by the chef himself, plus croquettes, melon and Bayonne ham, and escargots. These hors d'oeuvres make a perfect pre-entree taste that will give a good sampling of Au Bon Vivant's purpose in serving authentic European items.

For entrees, you have seven menu items from which to choose and a possible special or two. Made in the style of Nouveau Cuisine is the headliner entree, Coquilles St-Jacques. Prepare for a departure from the creamy sauce versions of this seafood item. Fresh scallops are simmered in a stark, vegetable bouillon. No cream is used. I found it to be more like a scallop soup with flavors relying almost entirely on the scallops and bouillon without outside seasonings. It was natural and peasanty in its presentation.

A special from the South East of Belgium is the Saute de Por l'Ardennaise. Two, tender pork filets are broiled in pan with a flash of white wine. A sauce made from shallots, tomato, bacon cubes, and real cream is applied topside. The inherent richness of the pork was highly complimented by the woodsy, bacon-accented cream sauce.

Desserts include a rotating selection of homemade pastries, sorbets, chocolate mousse, seasonal berries, and an etheral carmel custard. You can also have a croissant for dessert. The two sugared varieties are the Croissant Chocolat and the Croissant Amandes.

Service at Au Bon Vivant has always been extremely efficient. The waitresses have little space to cover and, as a result, make sure your food is brought to the table kitchen hot and fresh. The owner is an astute manager who keeps a constant eye on the progress of his patrons and on his kitchen.

AU CHAMBERTIN ★★★
French

Price Range: Expensive

170 State Street, Los Altos	Master Charge — Visa
Phone: (408) 948-8721	Reservations Required
Hours: Lunch: Noon–2:30, Tues.-Fri.	Non-Smoking Section
Dinner: 5:30–10 pm, Tues.-Sun.	Limited Wheelchair Access
Full Cocktail Service	

The location in which Au Chambertin now resides has had so many proprietors I truly don't know what to expect from visit to visit. When I first started reviewing, it housed a continental restaurant called Mediterranee. We couldn't include it in Forkful because it went out of business just before press time. It then became The Pickwick, a British restaurant of sorts. It bought the farm within a short while and gave way to Au Chambertin under the proprietorship of Chef Lap and H. Tan, superb restaurant managers. Unfortunately, they were struck with wanderlust and took flight after only eleven months, according to one of the managers of Au Chambertin. They now own a restaurant in Santa Monica.

What then remains of Au Chambertin?

As of this printing, it is a quality French dinner house with a fine young chef at the helm. Chef Craig Emerson has rebuilt a new menu, reflecting his own culinary style that is at once innovative and yet classical in the strict French manner. He applies a light touch to his sauces and exhibits a keen sense of culinary heat physics.

On one recent visit, we commenced dinner with a homemade pate of fish. Puree of sole, salmon, and scallops formed layers in a firm slice of pate. The texture was foamy and light. It was served with a fresh, homemade mayonnaise with a backbite of fresh lemon.

That visit, we also had our palates assaulted by a horribly made Spinach Flambe. I blame this mess on our inept waiter, who bumbled around throughout our meal. He over-wilted the spinach, added an enormous amount of sugar to the dressing, and served it in such a rush the greens slid partially to the side of the plate. The service seemed to undermine the Chef's wonderul intentions.

Our entrees were excellent illustrations of Chef Emerson's culinary prowess. Our first was entitled Cote de Veau Californienne. A long, boned veal chop was crowned with a smooth avocado souffle, and finished with a hearty red wine sauce.

We also had an entree composed of thinly sliced beef tenderloin sauteed and flamed in brandy and finished in a sauce made with dijon mustard, worcestershire sauce, and sweetbreads. The beef was juicy and evenly marbled and the sauce was a light reduction, yet cohesive enough to form a glistening cape over the meat. The addition of sweetbreads cast a nutty dimension to the flavor.

Desserts comprise fresh berries, cakes, and other sinful confections that will be announced tableside. The most memorable is the Chocolate Three Layer Cake. Ultra rich layers of chocolate will send spasms of pleasure through your body. Don't miss it when available.

Au Chambertin remains a good restaurant, despite its shaky beginnings. My only hope is that the current proprietors, including Chef Emerson can hang on long enough to establish a reputation.

AUSTRALIAN RESTAURANT ★★   Price Range: Bargain
Australian

---

898 Lincoln Ave., San Jose   Cash Only
Phone: 293-1112   No Reservations
Hours: 10:30 am—9 pm, Tues.–Sun.   No Non-Smoking Section
Food To Go   Clumsy Wheelchair Access
Extensive Australian Beer List

Well, mates, how about a little spot of sustenance down under? And that's precisely where you're going when you visit The Australian Restaurant, probably the only one of its kind in California. This ramshackle little hut with its outrageous sign, EAT HERE BEFORE WE BOTH STARVE, is just a taste of what lies inside.

First of all, nobody's going to starve here. Even if you don't like the food, you won't leave hungry. The irascible Aussie proprietor and his lackluster crew will make certain of that. By mid-morning, they have their grill cranked up to full throttle. At any one of the tables, you can hear the abrasive sizzling and heart-stopping clatter of plates, cups, and huge Australian beer cans dinking against iced mugs.

The menu here is dominated by authentic Australian edibles like the tasty Snag'll Do. This is a dish of braised bangers (sausages) in a saucy brew stocked with barely cooked tomato wheels and fresh onions. The meat of the sausage was soft, like that in a bratwurst, but a little spicier. With the two fat, juicy sausages, you receive a large helping of french fries, a spot of frozen-style veggies, and a bowl of salad. I recommend the bangers first of all.

If the snags don't get to you, the Aussie Meat Pie will surely warm you up to this restaurant. A square pie of flaky, golden-baked crust is packed with a ground beef and onion mixture that tasted a little like a sloppy Joe, only not as sweet. It was the crust that moved me. It was very light and rang clean and crispy against the fork.

Similar to the meat pie is the Pastie, another Aussie favorite. This is a turn-over-style pie made from the same flaky crust. Filling the light crunchy folds was again the sloppy Joe style hamburger mixture. This meat conglomeration is indeed tasty and filling, but not complex in flavor or consistency. Having been to Australia, I know that the food there is very basic, though always hearty and nutritious.

A dish I recommend you avoid by all means is the Cottage Pie. Whatever it was meant to be, the results were dismal. A ketchupy ground beef formed a soggy bed for a topping of watery, tasteless mashed potatoes. It was edible, but hardly worth the money. Don't bother.

The interior of the Australian Restaurant is small, smoky, and cluttered with kangaroo skins, posters of Koala bears and of the infamous Australian outlaw, Ned Kelley. Half the ambiance is created by Claude Anthony, the proprietor. He gets mad easily, but is a warm-hearted soul down under. If nothing else, the place is perfect to quaff some of the finest Australian lagers, stouts, and pilsners assembled under one roof in the entire South Bay.

The Australian Restaurant is an interesting place to grab a hearty bite. The food may not be cuisine, but it's certainly wholesome and reasonably priced.

AZUMA ★★★★　　　　　　　　　　　　Price Range: Moderate
Japanese

19654 Stevens Creek Blvd, Cupertino	A.E. — M.C. — Visa
Phone:　(408) 257-4057	Reser. Recommended
Hours:　Lunch: 11:30–2 pm, Tues.-Fri.	Non-Smoking Section
Dinner: 5–10 pm, Tues.-Sat.	Wheelchair Access
5–9 pm, Sunday	
Beer – Wine – Saki	

Azuma is perhaps the only Japanese restaurant in the South Bay where traditional Japanese service is executed with exquisite savor. Beautiful Japanese women, dressed in kimono and cotton sandals, perform their table duties with charm, sincerity, and utmost concern for the patron. You will feel so very special here. Azuma has transported my senses on many occasions. The sweet, resounding "hai," uttered immediately following the service of each course, still rings in my ears.

Not only is the service worth it, but the food is reputed to be some of the best Japanese fare in town. I used to think it was the best, until such places as Kikyo, Hamasushi, Gifu, and even Komatsu came onto the scene. Now I consider Azuma one of the better Japanese restaurants in town. Many of the traditional dishes are performed by chefs who know the secret to delivering quality sushi, expertly fried tempura, and finely crafted bowls of sukiyaki and yose nabe.

On a few of my visits here, I was accompanied by a vegetarian friend of mine who reveled in Azuma's all-vegetable soup dishes. He loved the clean, fresh broths, unhindred by spices or flavoring adjuncts. Many of these soups, are made on the spot by the chef, whose sole purpose is to serve his patrons. If he can make something for you, just ask. He will do all he can to satisfy you.

Along with Azuma's raw fish specialties, like sashimi and Nigiri Sushi, you can order the common dishes like chicken teriyaki and tempura. I have been less impressed with these dishes. The tempura was greasy and leaden on one past visit, the chicken teriyaki, cold. There was little improvement on a subsequent sampling.

Azuma remains a contender, a strong contender. It no longer rests at the top, but must share space with other quality Japanese restaurants.

BENIHANA OF TOKYO ★★★
Teppan Steakhouse

Price Range: Expensive

2074 Vallco Fashion Park, Cupertino
Phone: (408) 253-1221
Hours: Lunch: 11:30–2 pm, Mon.-Sat.
         Dinner: 5–10 pm, Sun.-Thurs.
         5–11 pm, Fri. & Sat.
Full Bar

All Major Credit Cards
Reservations Recomm.
No Non-Smoking Section
Full Wheelchair Access

Benihana was the first teppan steakhouse to hit our shores from Japan. Not too long ago, this prodigious chain added another link in Cupertino, attached to the fashionable Vallco Shopping complex.

The layout is purely designed for the escapist. Tramping across the arched wooden slatted bridge to the foyer of the restaurant unfolds the provencial charm of a true Japanese interior. It certainly is refreshing and comfortable, but I have never been thoroughly convinced I had escaped the confines of the South Bay.

The Teppan procedure isn't inviting to all. You must sit at a table built around a long, teppan grill, sharing space with strangers. This communal situation is perfect for the gregarious members in your group, but could be hell for the introverts. This seating arrangement becomes extremely annoying when someone at your table is an insulting sort when intoxicated.

As already stated, your chairs are seated around this grill where Benihana's teppan chefs perform their culinary acrobatics. Most of what they do with their knives and salt shakers is purely theatrical. Most of them are jokers who quip continually with the customers, mumbling jokes under their breath as they slice meats and prawns with lightning dexterity. Occasionally, they miss. I recall a prawn fragment hitting the lense of a man's glasses. Another incident, I saw a piece of filet mignon splash down in a martini. All and all, however, these chefs know their stuff and perform with aptitude. The final results have always been mouth-watering.

The most desirable dinner here is the steak. The quality at Benihana is top and is always seared to the correct degree of doneness. All dinners include soup, salad, griddle fried vegetables, prawns, rice and tea. Prices are steep, but the steak is worth a sampling.

Other Teppan steakhouses in the South Bay are House of Genji, Fujiya, and Shogun in Los Altos.

THE BIG YELLOW HOUSE ★★★
Country Cooking / All You Can Eat

1181 E. Calaveras Blvd., Milpitas
Phone: (408) 263-3454
Hours: Dinner: 5–9 pm, Mon.–Thurs.
      5–10 pm, Friday
      4–10 pm, Sat.; 3–9 pm, Sun.
      Sunday Brunch: 10–2 pm
Full Bar

A.E. – M.C. – Visa
No Reservations
Non-Smoking Section –
  [Upstairs]
Full Wheelchair Access

As a rule, I avoid chain restaurants. The robotic methodology of most, put me, my tastebuds, and my desire to have fun under the covers for a night of unintruded sleep. Occasionally, a chain restaurant comes along that breaks from the computerized tedium and puts on a worthwhile performance. The Big Yellow House is one of those chain establishments that brings a ray of hope to a sadly abused Milpitian landscape.

The Big Yellow House is exactly that, a big, yellow house. A Mid western Gothic farmhouse replication juts from the earth, defying some mythic twister to tear it from its foundation and trundle it far, far away.

The House offers two amenities that cannot be overlooked. First, you can eat all your bucket will hold for a reasonable set price. And, when I say all you can eat, I mean all you can eat. I have seen patrons the size of Fatty Arbuckle down platters of food until the legs on their chairs began to creak under the heavy bulk. Not everybody who comes here are professional trenchers, however, the all-you-can-eat program is inspiring in a day and age when prices are soaring and portions are diminishing.

The second amenity of The House is quality of food. It's not gourmet, but it certainly upholds good old American standards. Two entrees are offered nightly. One is always chicken with the second rotating from items like baked Virginia ham, to pork chops, to meaty beef ribs. Served with the entrees is all the mashed potatoes, applesauce, vegetables du jour, corn muffins with honey butter, soup, and salad you can fill your cheeks with. Food is served in bowls, tureens, and platters for family-style service.

The Big Yellow House is also a great place to bring the kids. There's a lot of food, a lot of memorabilia to look at, and the prices are cheap.

BIRDCAGE WOK ★★
Chinese Food / All You Can Eat

Price Range: Bargain

2980 Stevens Creek Blvd., Town and
    Country, San Jose
Phone: 246-4080
Hours: Lunch: 11:30–3:30, Mon.-Sat.
          From Noon on Sunday
          Dinner: 4:30–9 pm, Mon.-Sat.
          12–8:30 pm, Sunday
Beer and Wine

Master Card — Visa
No Reservations
No Non-Smoking Section
Limited Wheelchair Access

The Birdcage Wok Chinese Smorgy is a good friend to the pocketbook and to the belly. For a low fixed price you can eat all the Chinese food you desire. And don't think the food is going to be bad for such a price. It was very good, very fresh, and abundantly displayed.

There are two serving tables loaded up with a variety of foods. The first table offers rows of smorgy style salads, plus a crock of hot soup from which you serve yourself. The salads were exceptionally fresh in flavor and in texture. None of them were over-burdened with dressings. I sampled a colorful garbanzo bean salad with kidney beans in a light vinaigrette. In addition, I spooned a creamy ambrosia, heavy with peach halves and coconut.

Remember not to fill up on salads. Your next stop will be the Chinese food table. It is important to note that the Chinese food here is not what I would call Chinese cuisine. The dishes are basic, Cantonese style recipes which offer many items you can find on a fast food ledger. Although the dishes are take-out familiar, they are well done and filled with flavor.

The Chinese food table is comprised of steaming trays of chow yukes, fried rice, egg foo young, sweet and sour dishes, vegetable dishes, chow mein, fried chicken, egg rolls, won tons, plus many more. I went back for seconds for the fresh broccoli saute. The sprigs were deep green and crunchy to the bite. They were sauteed in a light sauce that glazed the vegetables in a transparent sheen.

I also went back for the fried chicken. What I liked most about this chicken dish was its fresh taste and its greaseless, crispy batter. I didn't detect an over-sprinkling of salt either.

The chow mein was noodle heavy, yet the bean sprouts were crisp and not limp or overcooked. If you like fried rice, you will find the rendition here to be very light and fluffy with barbecued pork bits that did little to change the flavor. Chow yukes presented wide assortments of fresh vegetables in a distinctive sauce defined with soy and spices. My one disappointment was the sweet and sour pork. The sauce was more sweet than sour and there were more bones than pork meat.

The Birdcage Wok presents a comfortable setting in which to have lunch or dinner. The lighting is low and the ventilation keeps the room cool and refreshing. There are plenty of booths, some of which are private, and conducive to quiet conversations.

A BIT OF WYOMING ★★
Hearty Breakfast / Lunch

Price Range: Bargain

2227 Alum Rock Ave., San Jose	Cash Only
Phone: (408) 295-4819	No Reservations
Hours: 6 am–4 pm, Mon.–Fri.	No Non-Smoking Section
7 am–4 pm, Sat.	Limited Wheelchair Access
8 am–2 pm, Sunday	

If you're the type that hungers for a Western style breakfast or an authentic buffalo meat burger, A Bite of Wyoming is your cup of tea. This place is a crankhouse of sizzling griddles and perking coffee pots from opening until closing. The title of this restaurant alone conjures visions of big portions that a cowboy just off the range would yee-haw to.

Big Valley bric-a-brac festoon the walls while bleached longhorn steer skulls stare down at you wth vacant eye sockets. It's western all the way. For breakfast, you can eat well on a plate of buffalo steak and eggs, served with a mound of hash browns, and biscuits. Lunch is highlighted by none other than Bill Cody's Buffalo Burger. For a change of pace, the Okie Sausage Burger is much spicier than the regular beef pattie.

For the most part, I have found the food here to be typical griddle fry quality. The buffalo meat is guaranteed real and fresh, and the portions big. You won't leave hungry or penniless.

THE BLACK FOREST INN ★★★　German

Price Range: Moderate

---

376 First Street, Los Altos
Phone:　948-5031
Hours:　11:30 am–8:30 pm, Tues.–Sat.

Beer and Wine

Master Card　—　Visa
Reservations taken for
　parties of five or more
No Non-Smoking Section
Clumsy Wheelchair Access

The Black Forest Inn is a 26-year-old family-style German restaurant, continuing to charm a faithful clientele with strudels of magnetic appeal. On most nights be prepared for a 10 to 15 minute wait.

The tables here are tightly clustered. Coupled with narrow aisles, the Inn poses a chore for a big person with expansive hips. A wheelchair would have an ordeal maneuvering the narrow straits here. Nonetheless, the close quarters spawn an inherent coziness that Joe Mangelli said reminded him of a back porch in a Catskill Mountain lodge. A rich, seasoned wood interior is enhnaced with Alpine murals and Bavarian bric-a-brac. In addition to the two dining rooms, there's available counter space and a honeycomb of tables situated close to the entrance.

Dinner dishes come with soup or salad. We spooned a thick, smooth split pea and had a crisp plate of greens dressed with a creamy vinaigrette. With these warm-up dishes, we had several slices of fresh German breads.

For those who enjoy Kassler Rippchen, you'll have to come on Saturdays. Saturday is the only day this deeply flavorful, toothy-smoked loin of pork can be ordered. We came on Friday and were denied this traditional German treat, but explored the other menu specialties with enthusiasm. The Sauerbraten with red cabbage and potato pancakes was appropriately puckering. Several slices of pickled roast beef infused the mouth with that awakening piquancy that only quality sauerbraten can impart. The red cabbage was equally sour and was cooked tender.

Potato pancakes are a specialty at The Black Forest Inn and can be ordered on the side. They were sturdy patties of creamy mashed potatoes fried to a golden-crisp exterior. Applesauce is served on the side.

Pork lovers should not miss The Black Forest's Pig Knuckles, served with sauerkraut and mashed potatoes. The knuckles come in different sizes, so if you want a big one request it when ordering. The bone of the large knuckle was heavily packed with smoky, moist, tender pork meat that fell from the shank without prompting. Encasing the meat was an edible wrap of pork skin and fat. Although doctors say "no" to fat, this is one case where skin and fat is an integral part of the total pleasure of eating pig knuckles. Indulge.

Sauerkraut, served with the majority of dishes here, was well attended. Each shred of pickled cabbage was tender and fresh tasting. The mashed potatoes were creamy and smooth and well buttered. Both side dishes were generously applied.

We also enjoyed two of the traditional German veal specialties: Wiener Schnitzel and Veal Cutlet, Holstein Garni, both served in big portions. The schnitzel presented three large pieces of domestic veal in a sizzling crisp egg and bread crumb jacket, the surface of which was drizzled with fresh lemon. Although the veal was not milk-fed tender, it was hearty with a deep, prominent flavor. Resting below each cutlet was a thin sheet of brown sauce, adding interest to the overall savor.

The veal cutlet Holstein Garni basically displayed the same style of breaded veal in the schnitzel, only the top of the cutlet was covered with a fried egg, the traditional trademark of this dish. The presence of the egg contributed a distinctive moistness to the veal not present in the Schnitzel.

As is the custom of almost every German restaurant, The Black Forest Inn pours vast quantities of beer for their patrons. Ice-cold beer is served by the pitcher or the half-liter stein. Also, a moderate selection of imported malt beverages is offered, including Bass Ale, Kronenbourg, and that light, bubbly lager from Germany, Dinkelacker.

The Black Forest Inn represents German cuisine with distinction. For 26 years now it has upheld the standards of good eating with a hearty Bavarian involvement. I look forward to returning here soon.

THE BOLD KNIGHT ★★★   Price Range: Moderate to Expensive
Steak

1600 Monterey Road, San Jose	A.E. − M.C. − Carte
Phone: 293-7700	Blanche − Visa
Hours: Lunch: 11 am−3 pm, Mon.−Fri.	Reservations Recomm.
Dinner: 5 pm-Mid., Mon.−Sat.	Poor Non-Smoking Sect.
1−10 pm, Sunday	Wheelchair Access
Full Bar	

What brought me to The Bold Knight was a continuous prompting by friends who think it is the best steakhouse in the South Bay. I know people who eat here once a week and have never gotten tired of the place or have said a bad word about it. This restaurant is doing something right. Part of its appeal lies in the fact that there are no pretentions. It does what it's supposed to do, nothing more, nothing less. And you even get a complimentary cheese fondue when you arrive.

For an appetizer, we shared the Captain's Seafood Plate which is really an entree item. Arranged around a dish of creamy tartar and cocktail sauce was the typical gathering of scallops, prawns, filet of sole, and oysters, all of which were breaded and deep fried. The scallops remained moist and juicy beneath the batter, an unusually light and crispy coating for an item of this nature. The prawns and the oysters, likewise, held up well, their natural consistency and sea flavor untainted by the frying process. The filet of sole, on the other hand, turned out dry.

After the Captain's plate, we were served typically pedestrian steakhouse salads. At the Bold Knight, you have a choice between spinach or tossed green. The spinach leaves were obviously fresh and carefully attended. Mushrooms and minced egg were added for flavor. What killed this salad was the startling vinegar dressing. It tasted as though the cook forgot to add even a dash of oil.

What the Bold Knight tables best is red meat, primarily steak. Probably the best steak on the menu is the Pride of the Cattleman. This piece of meat was so large it resembled the fist of a Kodiak bear I once saw. The waitress even smiled and commented upon serving the plates, "Looks like a little roast, doesn't it?" Yes, it did. And for a person hankering for red meat, this cut will fit the bill. Not only was the portion large, the meat was cooked to a delectable juiciness.

Other fine steak selections include the London Broil and the Cattleman's Porterhouse Steak.

Served with all the steaks and roasts is a whopper of a baked potato that will make you 10 pounds heavier just by looking at it. Of course, the potato is filled with the optional condiments like sour cream, butter and chives.

Service at the Bold Knight was exceptional. The floor staff is comprised of mostly waitresses with busboys serving bread and filling water glasses. Our waitress appeared to really enjoy her job.

The Bold Knight is a fine restaurant for what it does. Steak is its specialty and steak is what you should order when you come here.

BUY THE BUCKET ★★★   Price Range: Moderate
Italian / Seafood

4565 Stevens Creek Blvd., Santa Clara   No Credit Cards – No
Phone: 248-6244   Checks
Hours: 11 am–1 pm, Mon.–Sat.   No Reservations
           11 am–11 pm, Sunday   No Non-Smoking Section
Full Bar   Limited Wheelchair Access

Buy The Bucket is where beer drinkers come to bust their belts on suds and good grub. Hunkering along Stevens Creek, its impenetrable, green cinderblock walls give it the appearance of an above-ground bomb shelter. The stern angles of the exterior are softened by weathered placards: "Fresh Catfish," "The Home of the Steamed Clam," "Fried Chicken."

At first glance, anybody in their right mind would peg the Bucket as a place where bar overshadows food. Not true. The majority of the menu offerings at Buy The Bucket are performed by veteran cooks who give their all to the dishes they serve.

Most have Italian leanings. I was pleased with the tomato sauce that covered the pasta dishes here. A true Neapolitan brew, simmered long in the manner of the big pot, had a deep red color and a mellow tomato tartness.

A dish of spaghetti with meatballs or sausage is reasonably priced. With this order, we received a large mound of firm, correctly boiled pasta splashed amply with the aromatic red sauce. I prefer the sausage accompaniment over the hard-packed meatball, because it was more flavorful.

For you Italian diehards who remember way back when, the Bucket serves a fine rendition of the Easter Sunday riccota cheese-filled ravioli. Five, large, plump squares of pasta stuffed with a soft creamy cheese were boiled until tender. They held together perfectly under the fork.

The Bucket's claim to fame is its bucket of steamed clams Bordelaise style. Fat mollusks were steamed with bravura in a medicinal garlic, butter, lemon and clam broth. Included is a basket of well-buttered garlic bread.

Fried Calamari, although fresh frozen, is an item served up with tender loving care by the cooks. A large heap of both smooth outer body and tentacles are battered, quick fried, then placed atop a garnish of lettuce. The squid ringlets were tender and sweet, holding up well in the hot oil. This item is served with salad and a side of cocktail sauce.

If you're still not satisfied, The Bucket bakes a jewel of a pizza. The crust is a thin yeast-fragrant wheel fired to a golden brown. Several pizza combos are offered which may combine sausage, pepperoni and mushroom or Canadian ham, beef and onion, peppers and olives.

I can't comment on everything presented on the menu, but what I have had has been well made, seasoned with commitment, and always hot on arrival from the self-serve tray. You won't go away hungry, that's for sure.

CATHAY ★★★   Price Range: Moderate
Chinese

1339 North First St., San Jose	A.E. — M.C. — Visa
Phone: (408) 275-8348	Reservations Required
Hours: Lunch: 11:30–2 pm, Mon.-Fri.	Non-Smoking Section
Dinner: 5–10 pm, Daily	Limited Wheelchair Access
Full Bar	

Years before San Jose began to expand gastronomically, Cathay was doing business. And doing a good business. It's been many years now and Cathay continues to do a healthy trade. There are those who think Cathay when they think of Chinese cuisine. I accept this mode of thinking, however, there is so much competition, especially in the Chinese food business, Cathay is usually very low on my priority list. The food is good, but not the best by a long shot.

One of the dishes I have recently sampled does compare to some of the best I have eaten, Parchment Wrapped Chicken. Morsels of chicken breast are folded and cooked inside foil. Getting the marinated chicken out of the wrapping takes some fancy handywork. Be careful. You may stain your nice new suit. Once freed from its tinfoil encasement, the chicken will provide a delicious little tidbit that will enliven the appetite. This dish brings a mountain of these foil-wrapped goodies, so pace yourself.

What I have discovered of late is that Cathay is not what I always thought it was, a Cantonese restaurant. Though the menu lists many Cantonese specialties, there are also many hot and spicy dishes worth chop-sticking through. One of those is Kung Pao Chicken. This recipe was followed very closely by Cathay's chefs. A dice of boned, chicken breast, vegetables, hot peppers, and peanuts was wok fried in a very hot wok. The flavors were seared and bonded in a flash. The chicken meat was fully infused with the spiciness of the peppers which were tingly and hot, but not blistering. Peanuts were plentifully added. I found myself picking the peanuts from the plate one by one. A weird habit that no one should incur.

Another dish that I fell head over heels for was the Lemon Duck. Thoroughly boned duckling was chopped, pressed into squares and golden fried. Before serving, the crispy squares were hacked into chop stickable pieces. The sauce was not sweet and sour sticky. It was more of a light glaze with a lemon tangy essence.

Cathay Beef is worth a taste or two. Beef tenderloin is sliced into wide pieces, then seared over a grill. They are quick fried with a sweet marinade springing with the aromatics of 5 spices. The final presentation brings the beef over a bed of crispy vermicelli. Another intriguing presentation is the Chicken salad. Shreds of cooked chicken are tossed with crispy noodles with vegetables in a sesame oil flavored dressing.

Cathay is the type of restaurant that will not disappoint you. It delivers consistently. Though not my favorite, I like to come here every so often to see what's going on.

THE CATS ★★   **Price Range: Moderate**
Oakwood BBQ

Highway 17, just So. of Los Gatos   Master Card — Visa
Phone: 354-4020   Reservations taken for
Hours: 6–11 pm, Tues.–Sun.   parties of 5 or more
Entertainment   No Non-Smoking Section
Full Bar   Limited Wheelchair Access

The Cats Tavern and Restaurant is a classic roadhouse etched against the craggy landscape of Highway 17's first stretch out of Los Gatos. It is an innsy, very popular place that keeps its tables filled and its oakwood BBQ stoked up for the continued service of steaks, chicken, and ribs.

I have been to The Cats on four occasions and have had ample visits to analyze its good points and its flaws. As a restaurant, my opinion of the food tends to vary from visit to visit. Quality has fluctuated from excellent to barely mediocre. The cooks who operate the oakwood grill have been inconsistent in their preparation of the meats. Food items have come to the table overcooked, undercooked, perfectly grilled, and charred like a charcoal briquette.

On the other hand, The Cats remains extremely popular. Why? Ask most of the regular customers and they will tell you that the prices are reasonable and the portions are large.

But reasonable prices and big portions are not all The Cats has to offer. The Cats is perhaps one of the best places to relax, sip a cocktail, and listen to live music. There is a lay back, adult feeling about this place where you can hide out with your betrothed, your friend, your joy, or your sorrow and drift away on the notes of gentle samba.

The decor is funky and cluttered. You can trip if you don't watch your step. Both lounge and dining room are equipped with many wobbly tables haphazardly arranged. There is a fancy long bar in the cocktail area and a glowing sizzling brick BBQ chimney in the dining room. Prints of cats and various antique-looking odds and ends round out the basic decor.

The food on my latest two visits was by far the most disappointing. I won't deny that the portions are generous. If you want to fill your bucket and perhaps bring a few substantial scraps home for the hound, The Cats delivers gloriously. One of my guests ordered the Chicken and received a complete half of a very large bird bulky with meat. The skin was glazed with honey. Unfortunately, the meat was dry and, in places, stringy. It was so dry, the meat was difficult to chew and swallow. Not only was the meat dry, but the chicken had a strong, gamey taste that the oakwood fire could not disguise. In fact, in all the meat selections we had that night. we did not taste that alluring BBQ flavor or the wood. On past visits, I have had much better luck.

One of the most popular items on the menu is the Rib dinner. I recall having had an excellent plate of ribs here on one past occasion. There was plenty of meat on the bones and it was cooked to perfection. This time around, the pork meat on the ribs had the consistency of paper. It was almost mealy. The meat broke apart in the mouth to the flush of saliva, offering no resistance to bite at all. I was surprised. The BBQ sauce on the side had a diluted, sugary aspect with accents of nutmeg and other Thanksgiving spices.

The best item for the evening was the Culotte Steak. Delivered to the table direct from the crackling wood glaze was a solid hunk of beef trimmed completely of fat. It was so thick, it took a sharp knife several strokes to cut from surface to base. Each incision with the knife brought juice from the steak. The meat was rich with beef texture and taste and was very filling. The steaks are good buys here.

With our dinners, we received a salad with choice of dressing. The greens were fresh and crunchy, but the dressings were over-applied. With entrees, we received large baked potatoes, opened at the center and filled with a generous pat of butter. Also, our dinners came with a small serving of a sauce that tasted and looked like a Mexican-style salsa and a basket of garlic bread. For an additional side dish, we ordered Fresh Mushrooms sauteed in butter and wine. They were nothing to write home about. The mushrooms were small and overcooked. The sauce was a soupy mixture with a slick of butter on the surface and little wine flavor.

The service at The Cats has always been friendly and warm. The people really go out of their way to please you here. The proprietors are on station and perform their dining room duties with a smile and a good word for their patrons.

The inconsistency in food quality at The Cats doesn't seem to stop people from coming here. This place is always crowded and the customers seem very happy to be here. I heard plenty of laughter and even a few comments on how good the food was. Reasonable prices and large portions doesn't always determine quality food. But, at The Cat, these two amenities has kept them going strong

C. B. HANNEGAN'S ★★★
Ribs / Pub

Price Range: Bargain to Moderate

208 Bachman Ave., Los Gatos	Master Card — Visa
Phone: (408) 395-1233	No Reservations
Hours: 11:30 am–Midnight, Daily	No Non-Smoking Section
Full Bar and Pub	Limited Wheelchair Access

When you're looking to get down with an "ice cold pint of John Courage Ale and a pile of sauce ribs," C.B. Hannegan's is your dinner spot. Since it opened a few years back, it has become legendary for the montage of antics that transpire during business hours. C.B.'s is creating an image of true grit, good food, good brew, good company.

The place does grow crowded during dinner time and stays busy until it closes in the early A.M. For the most part, people come to drink at the bar, gawk at each other, socialize, and talk about life in Los Gatos. You can't be alone here, so if you are meek and shy, find a table in another restaurant.

Though the food has had its ups and downs, I find, for the most part, it serves the patron well. Of course, ribs are very popular here. And they are perhaps some of the biggest I have gnawed in a long time. I can't say the bone shafts are packed with a lot of tender meat. It's chewy and, sometimes, there is much fat to contend with. They are cooked over seasoned oakwood which infuses the meat with a woodsy flavor that harmonizes well with the pork.

Another favorite of the house is pizza. The pizzas here are very well made with a thick, tender crust and a generous topping of cheese and meats, if you so prefer. One of the best pizza makers here is a man named Fred Handsfield. When he's twirling the dough in the back, the pizzas are usually exquisite pies, baked to a juicy, teeth sinkable quality. I believe there is a special talent to pizza baking which Handsfield has a gift for. Unfortunately, his working hours are brief, the days during which he works are few.

Hannegan's offers other food items like hot links and a host of sandwiches. The links are hot and peppery, the meat cooked tender. The portions, however, have been decreasing of late. This is a disappointment. There was a time a half order would suffice as a meal in itself.

C.B. Hannegan's is the place to go for a lift of spirit when life has dealt you a punch in the nose. You can eat hearty and drink a barrel of ale with the fashionable Los Gatans.

CENTRAL CHINA ★★
Szechwan/Hunan

Price Range: Bargain

1362 S. Winchester Blvd., San Jose	Master Card — Visa
Phone: 374-3840; 374-3842	Reservations Taken
Hours: 11:30 am–9 pm, Tues.-Fri.	No Non-Smoking Section
12:30–10 pm, Saturday	Limited Banquet Facilities
12:30–9:30 pm, Sunday	Clumsy Wheelchair Access
Closed Monday	
Beer and Wine	

Central China is closer than you think. In fact, it's geographically situated on Winchester Blvd. in a refurbished free-standing building that once housed Mike's Hero Sandwiches. In its short existence, this Chinese restaurant has established a motley clientele, seeking to burn their lips on fiery Szechwan/Hunan dishes, wokked up by energetic cooks. Central China is not a dress-up kind of place, though you won't feel silly walking in wearing a three-piece suit or a Parisian sundress.

The inside looks like a hut heavily decorated with Chinese wall pieces that add color but no taste. Red plastic tablecloths smack the eyes mercilessly and the constant beat of country/western music twangs in the background. There's nothing like listening to Dolly Parton sing her lungs out while you chopstick your way through a plate of meat and hot peppers.

The food at Central China can best be described as homestyle, rib-stickin' spicy Chinese food. I can't call it cuisine, because it lacked the inherent delicateness and finesse that I attribute to cuisine. It was basic, highly spiced, and pepper powered. Of course, not all the dishes are hot and spicy. You can go the mild route with an adequate plate of Oyster Sauce Beef or a nutsome rendition of Almond Chicken. But, on wintry days, there's nothing like a little hot red pepper to thaw the chill from the bones and recharge your sensibilities.

My companion and I had a plate of Twice Cooked Pork. It was a large portion of water chestnuts, green peppers, and bamboo shoots. The portion of pork, however, was inadequate. All ingredients were tossed fried in a glazy, semi-sweet hot sauce. Dried, hot red peppers were plentifully added. I strongly recommend that you be careful with these blistering dynamos. Eating too many can cause severe gastronomic responses. With the spicier dishes, ask for a bowl of steamed rice. The glutinous consistency provides a balance to the extreme degrees of pepper heat.

Another special is Garlic Chicken. The portion of chicken meat was more plentiful in this dish than the pork in the former item. The thoroughly boned pieces of chicken were cut into chop stickable cubes, then sauteed in a sauce heavy with the pungency of roasted garlic. For a unique taste of poultry, I recommend ordering Smoked Tea Duck. Presented is a platter lined with hacked squares of roast duckling, the skin cooked to a crackling crispness. The bird is served with a dish of thick, hoison sauce and several sweet Chinese buns. With this one, discard the sticks and use your fingers. It is the only way to get at the tender strips of meat hidden under the tiny, curving bones.

A dish I did not like at all was Prawns with Lobster Sauce. After having my palate geared up by the peppers and garlic, the blandness of this dish was immensely striking. There were plenty of prawns, but the sauce was starchy thick and flavorless.

The waitresses at Central China were happy ladies, performing their table duties in perpetual motion. Their understanding of English was limited, yet orders were not fouled up. Our waitress suggested a fine, white wine called Wan Fu which proved to be an exceptional compliment to the spiciness of the food.

CHEF CHU'S ★★★   Price Range: Moderate
Chinese / Mandarin

1067 N. San Antonio Rd., Los Altos   **Master Card — Visa**
Phone: (415) 948-2696   **No Reservations**
Hours: 11:30 am—9 pm, Daily   **No Non-Smoking Section**
Full Bar   **Limited Wheelchair Access**

Aside from being one of the most photogenic Chinese chefs on the Peninsula, Chef Chu is one of the most popular. His restaurant is known far and wide and has continued throughout its many years in business to hold the edge on the popular vote. I have gotten involved in heated debates with Chef Chu faithfuls who swear that his cuisine is the best around. I don't agree. I do agree, however, that Chef Chu's Mandarin specialties deserve attention and are quality preparations. But, as far as being the very best, I will not submit to this persuasion. I have had better and I have had worse.

Of the dishes I most admire here, the Mu Shu Pork remains one of the better renditions I have eaten. The presentation has always been carefully prepared. Shredded pork, mushrooms, bamboo shoots, egg, and other color balancing ingredients form a flavorful combination. I find the pancakes at Chef Chu's to be most unusual. They are very strong, pastry skins that form sturdy wraps for the pork mixture. With a swab of hoison, this Mu Shu recipe comes together well.

Chef Chu's dry braised dishes deserve a serious taste, especially the Dry Braised Prawns. Large, succulent gulf prawns are simmered long in a spicy tomato-based sauce that penetrates the meat of the prawn thoroughly. Hot and spicy dishes are also done well here, the Kung Pao dishes being the most inspiring. Kung Pao chicken or Kung Pao prawns are two of my favorites, and always include the Kung Pao additions of hot red peppers and peanuts.

For a long time, I had been told that Chef Chu's special banquets were worth the money if you can get a large enough group to partake. On one evening, I was invited to a Chef Chu banquet served upstairs and at a large circular table. In all honesty, I found the banquet to be mundane, the dishes haphazardly prepared and without the strong, vibrant flavors I had found in dishes sampled on singular occasions. Even the guests who had spent time organizing the banquet personally with Chef Chu were disappointed.

CHE PANISSE ★★★★
French / Italian Cafe

Price Range: Expensive

1517 Shattuck Ave., Berkeley	No Credit Cards
Phone: (415) 548-5525	Reservations Required
Hours: Downstairs: 6–9:15 pm, Tu.-Sat.	No Non-Smoking Section
Cafe: 11:30 am–10:30 pm, M-Sat.	Limited Wheelchair Access
Beer and Wine	

To earn my wings as a true restaurant critic, a trip to Che Panisse was mandatory. Actually, a few trips were in order to come to a full understanding of this highly notable restaurant. Alice Water's culinary movement has become the toast of the State. Some critics have even deemed her restaurant, the best in the State. This reviewer won't go that far, but I will admit Che Panisse's unequalled superiority among North and South Bay restaurants. The food I have sampled here has exhibited a highly innovative and exciting style of cookery. Menu development alone sets many French restaurants on their proverbial bottoms. Since its opening over ten years ago, Che Panisse has presented a totally different menu each evening in its existence. That's quite an accomplishment.

Che Panisse is divided into two separate restaurants. The cafe occupies the upper quarters where a brick, wood-burning pizza and bread over resides as the focal point. From the earthen hearth of this famous oven, superb pizza and calzone (pocket pizza filled with goat cheese, mozzarella, herbs, and prosciutto) are drawn forth in repetitive splendor.

The chefs upstairs do wonderful things with pasta, breads, sauces, fresh fruit, cheeeses, and wholesome, locally grown produce. Seafood is also locally caught. One of the highlights is Oysters from Pigeon Pt. The flavor and texture of these specially cultivated mollusks inspire the appetite to open its vast reserve.

There are no reservations taken upstairs, so expect at least one hour wait during peak hours in shoulder to shoulder waiting conditions.

Reservations, however, are taken downstairs and you must plan on a 2 to 3 week advance notice. Che Panisse is incredibly popular due to endless publicity, so you'll just have to wait a little longer to enjoy it.

All dinners downstairs are pre-fixed. I found the set price to be somewhat expensive when compared to restaurants of like caliber. Nonetheless, the experience will not disappoint. Each evening offers only one set menu, so you have no choice in the matter. All the better.

One of our dinners began with Radicchio salad with tender, sweet pigeon breasts, duck livers, and thin sheets of prosciutto topside. Radicchio is a reddish, leafy vegetable that is crisp and delicate. A very clean, refreshing walnut vinaigrette textured with the natural juice of the pigeon breast was applied very lightly. Flavors did not strike the palate,, they assuaged it.

Following our salad, we spooned an incredibly delicate leek and potato soup. The balance achieved in this famous French recipe was inordinate. The flavors were mild, yet rich and deep. Not one ingredient was salient or over-applied.

Our entree was a filet of salmon baked in rock salt, with a side of spinach, and a large serving of allumettes (match stick French fries). The succulent salmon was drizzled with a light lemon/butter sauce flavored with fresh tarragon, basil and thyme. Each spice became an integral part of the sauce, blending into the flavor in whispering tones.

We concluded with a cheese course, followed by a dessert of boysenberry ice cream and sherbet in almond cups. Included were several vine-ripened blackberries.

What strikes me most about Alice Waters and her brand of cuisine is its simplicity, though I realize to achieve such exacting and meticulous results takes a great deal of thought, preparation, and painstaking commitment to serving the finest cuisine possible. Even the decor achieves utter elegance through straight angles, stark white linen, and a remarkable cleanliness that nearly squeaks underfoot as your walk from entrance to table.

CHEZ YVONNE ★★★
French

Price Range: Moderate to Expensive

1854 El Camino Real, Mountain View	A.E. – M.C. – Diners – Visa
Phone: (415) 967-6742	Reservations Recomm.
Hours: Lunch: 11:30–3 pm, Mon.-Sat.	Non-Smoking Section
Dinner: 5–10:30 pm, Mon.-Sat.	Limited Wheelchair Access
Full Bar	Entertainment

Tradition doesn't go away like a little ball of fuzz in a stiff breeze. When a restaurant, like Chez Yvonne, establishes tradition it'll take Armageddon to shake it from its foundation. Chez Yvonne has been a Mountain View staple for over 33 years, one of those old-time French restaurants that stays and stays, never faltering, rarely changing.

The food here isn't the greatest cuisine I have sampled. I have had much better and have paid much, much more. The offerings are primarily of a provencial nature, somewhat hearty, throwing no curves in delivery. What you see is what you get. One thing Chez Yvonne excels in is reasonable prices. You can breathe easy with this, especially if you are used to shelling out top dollars for an entree at other upper crust French and continental establishments.

The interior of Chez Yvonne evokes visions of a bawdy Paris at night. Let your imagination go, become part of the atmosphere. The Chez Yvonne fantasy unfolds the moment you enter through the bright red doors, catch glimpses of red-checked tablecloths set against the dark, sultry, night simulation. Striking dioramas of French street scenes and French axioms intensify the decorations. We slid into a large, slick red leather booth and were swallowed by the setting, by the dim romantic lighting, by the ambiance of fine French wine chilling in moisture-beaded wine buckets.

One aspect of the show I didn't like was the strolling guitarist, his eyes hidden behind the mask of Zorro. He sang with a loud, operatic voice that sent spasms up and down my spine. From a distance, he was okay. But when nearby, watch out.

Chez Yvonne offers an interesting menu, listing primarily French dishes with a moderate line-up of American favorites. For many years this place has been known for its special 16 oz. steaks, which include the specialty Club Roast.

We began our meal with an order from the daily special announcement, mussels, steamed Bordelaise-style (seasonal). A tureen of large, sweet mussels crowded together in clouds of fragrant steam wafting from their shells. They sat in a tangy sauce of garlic, butter, natural broth and lemon.

Many of the menu items are listed as favorites of certain entertainers. My selection was a toss-up between Coquille St. Jacques, Raquel

Welch's favorite, or Chicken Jerusalem, Joey Heatherton's favorite. I went with the Chicken simply because I haven't seen Joey perform in a while and thought that a taste of her favorite might help me to remember her fancy dance steps. It didn't.

Nonetheless, the Chicken Jerusalem, a dish I have yet to understand, presented a large portion of meaty chicken pieces. After being browned, the chicken was covered with a thick, milky white gravy, chunked with the traditional ingredients of artichoke hearts and sherry mushrooms. You'll have to like cream sauces to appreciate this one. In fact, you'll have to like the color white to appreciate the plate. From the cauliflower, covered with a white sauce, to the white rice, everything was a field of white. Green beans or carrots would have broken this glacial scene.

Our second entree is listed as Robert Goulet's favorite, Veal Piccante. Robert Goulet? Whatever happened to him? Anyway, this dish was quite good. It consisted of three medallions of milk-fed veal sauteed in a sauce of fresh lemon juice, garlic, capers and demi-glaze. The consistency of the demi-glaze, or mother sauce, was a smooth even reduction in which the tangy complements of capers and lemon juice blended well. The garlic was strongly defined, but not overbearing.

The service here was efficient. Our waitress never rushed us or delayed the delivery of our entrees from the kitchen. All dishes were brought to us fresh and hot.

Chez Yvonne is not going away. It's a warm, friendly tradition that all of you must try at least once in your life. The food was basic, the prices were appetizing, and the ambiance will sweep you away somewhere in time.

CHINA DELIGHT ★★   Price Range: Bargain
Hunan / Szechwan

2037 Woodard Road, San Jose	Master Card — Visa
Phone: (408) 377-3562	Reservations Optional
Hours: 11 am–9 pm, Tues.–Fri.	No Non-Smoking Section
Noon–9 pm, Sat.	Limited Wheelchair Access
4–9 pm, Sunday	
Beer and Wine	

I have been dazzled by the food at China Delight. And I have left, shrugging my shoulders with a mediocre bellyful. I have a friend who swears by it. I have another friend who won't go anywhere else. I have another friend who won't come here at all. Though China Delight has been in business for some time now, it still can be considered one of those little finds that keeps getting discovered over and over again. Its location is non-descript and lodged in a remote corner in back of Cambrian's Race Street Fish and Poultry.

In general, the cuisine at China Delight is well made. The dishes are very hot and peppery, though balanced in color and texture. One change I don't like at all is the reduction of portions. Portions were small to begin with, but now they are even smaller. Well, that's the breaks I guess.

One dish I always like here is Twice Cooked Pork. This is one dish that seems to be getting better each time I come here. Juicy pork slices are toss-fried in a braise of green pepper segments and cabbage. A tawny, cohesive hot pepper sauce coats all ingredients evenly. The flavors are very direct.

Mongolian Beef will set your mouth ablaze, even more than the Twice Cooked Pork. The pepper fire in this dish is merciless, leaving the flavor of the beef slices in a whimpering, submissive state. Ask for a lot of steamed rice with this one. Other dishes of note are the Kung Pao Chicken and the Hunan Chicken. For a taste of the chef's aptitude, the Hunan Chicken will display his abilities better than the Kung Pao variation. Beef and Broccoli and Pot Stickers are perfect for that complete dinner fandango. Both are spicy, but not lip blistering.

Unlike two of my friends, China Delight is not my favorite Chinese restaurant. I like the restaurant it spawned, Jasmine, a little better. But, China Delight isn't a fluke, either. The chefs here know what they are doing and do it with a basic blast of pepper and spice.

CHUCK E. CHEESE PIZZA TIME THEATER ★★★
Pizza / Video Games   Price Range: Moderate

2445 Fontaine Road, San Jose	Cash Only
Phone: (408) 238-0755	No Reservations
Hours: 11 am–11 pm, Sun.-Thurs.	No Non-Smoking Section
Till Midnight, Fri. & Sat.	Limited Wheelchair Access
Beer and Wine	

I once said I'd never go back to Chuck E. Cheese Pizza Time Theater. My experiences at the big granddaddy off of Tully Road had driven me to the point of near mental exhaustion. It was bad enough that Chuck the rat trapped inside that massive wall of glass overlooking Highway 101 nearly led me to my death on several occasions. But, he kept leering at me on my way home from work. Leering and smiling with those huge buck teeth until I was forced to enter.

As my first review stated, the video madness was totally out of control. When this particular Pizza Time Theater grows crowded, human beings become pinballs jettisoned from point to point. There were babies crawling on the floors, there was trash everywhere, there was a discordance of screams, guffaws, and horrible chortles. The lines were slow and disorganized. And most of all, the pizza wasn't worth the trouble. It was okay, but just not worth the trouble. And it was overpriced.

Well, I broke my promise to myself. Nearly a month after I said I wouldn't go back, I found myself inside this bedlam once again. This time I had a purpose. I wanted to play a video game. This visit, the crowds were less and as a result the madness was lessened only by degrees. Quickly, I ate through a small cheese and pepperoni pizza which wasn't bad. The crust was semi-thick with a cracker crispness and a sweet tomato sauce covering. Cheese was applied generously, though I suspect the computer had something to do with the amount of cheese used on the pizza.

After I ate, I sampled a few of the games until I was hooked on a game called GORF. Before I saw my insipid face reflected in the radar shield and realized I was on the brink of total madness, I had spent over five dollars in quarters. Five dollars! Wow. Think of the profit. Think of all the quarters the kids are feeding into the slots of all these games. Millions.

Finally, I left with another promise to myself that I'd never return again. I had my fill of Chuck's brand of pizza making and I certainly had my fill of video games.

If you are planning on visiting a Chuck E. Cheese, I recommend you visit one of the smaller places. They are less frenetic and more enjoyable. But, then again, I'm totally sour about this video pizza craze that has infested our hearts and minds. Maybe, I'm wrong about Chuck. Maybe, he's the only one who really knows.

COL. LEE'S MONGOLIAN BARBECUE ★★   Price Range: Bargain
Mongolian BBQ [All You Can Eat]

304 Castro St., Mountain View	Master Charge — Visa
Phone: 968-0381	Reservations Taken
Hours: Lunch: 11–2 pm, Tues.–Sat.	No Non-Smoking Section
Dinner: 4:30–9 pm, Tues.–Sun.	No Wheelchair Access
Beer and Wine	

Unlike all the rest, when the hungry hordes hit the Castro Street original, Col. Lee's takes on the distinct appearance of a Mad Magazine spoof. People are everywhere, standing, sitting, leaning against walls, talking and chortling. Babies scream out unsavory lullabies while the manager, who knows little English, tries to seat people in the teeming dining area. During peak hours, count on a 20-minute wait.

Why do people continue to engage in this foray of dining activity? Simple. Col. Lee's offers a unique all-you-can-eat Mongolian barbecue. For a set price, you receive a plate of spring rolls, generously packed and tasty (but greasy), soup, a basket of soft-dough sesame bisquits, rice, tea and fortune cookie – and as many bowls of barbecue as your bucket will hold.

The process at Col. Lee's is simple. Just follow the people and you can't be misled. The first step is to grab a bowl and begin your slow movement along the food line toward the grillmaster stationed at the end. The line is loaded with assorted vegetables, including fresh bean sprouts, carrot chips and onions, plus bowls laden with thinly sliced lamb, beef, pork and turkey. From experience here, I suggest you fill your bowl generously. What you have may look like a lot, but remember it cooks down substantially. After packing your bowl, a proper dousing of special sauces and marinades will insure that characteristic spiciness on which Col. Lee has built his reputation.

When, and if, you reach the end, you will be greeted by two grillmasters. When I visited there, these guys looked as though they had been put through the wringer. Their smocks were stained and limp from the constant billowing steam rising in thick sheets from the black gridiron. Each grillmaster wore a deep expression of utter exhaustion. Anyway, once you have handed your bowl over, they unload its contents onto the grill and begin to sizzle your food. Around the grill they go, slapping and prodding the ingredients in a circle around the outer edge of the iron. At the finish of a complete revolution, the meat and sprouts are done. The bowl is handed back.

The final result was a very tasty mix, marinated through and through with spiciness. I enjoyed 2½ bowls before throwing in the towel. Some people, however, went back three and four or five times before they had had their fill. I saw little waste.

Col. Lee's Mongolian barbecue offers a good food value. The ingredients were certainly wholesome, the all-you-can-eat idea a pleasant attraction. If you don't like torrential crowds, maybe one of the newer locations will suit your fancy.

THE CREPE SHOPPE ★★
Normandy Crepe

Price Range: Bargain

---

71 North San Pedro St., San Jose
Phone: 998-2883
Hours: 7 am–3:30 pm, Mon.–Thurs.
        7 am–9 pm, Friday
        Closed Sat. & Sun.
Beer and Wine

Cash Only
No Reservations
No Non-Smoking Section
Limited Wheelchair Access

The Crepe Shoppe bases its entire operation on one, single food item: The Normandy crepe.

Unlike other crepe renditions that usually leave you hungry, The Normandy recipe as served at The Crepe Shoppe is no feather weight. It provides a substantial bellyful that is quite hearty and always filling. When you depart this quaint little shop tucked along San Pedro Square, you will feel well fed.

The pulse of The Crepe Shoppe's kitchen centers around the four imported Normandy griddles where the crepes are made. These griddles are circular and totally specialized for the making of these famous French pancakes.

Other than beverages, The Crepe Shoppe's menu lists only crepes. On my most recent visit, I sampled the headliner crepe, Ole. Filling this large, semi-thick skinned pancake was a layer of mashed avocado, tomato, melted cheese, black olives, and diced bits of hot chili pepper. Covering this plump, rectangular crepe was a tomato tart, green chili salsa. Though this salsa was an adequate complement for the guacamole insides, I found it to be lacking the complexity of the more authentic Mexican style salsas.

We also sampled a Mushroom and Cheese Crepe. For my own particular tastes, I enjoyed this crepe much better than the former. Filling the center was a thick layer of strong white cheese that had melted down to a smooth creamy texture. Woven into the cheese were many slices of fresh mushrooms. Ladled onto the crepe was a thick, mushroom style gravy in which I detected a whisper of sherry. The appearance of this sauce was not as pleasant as its flavor.

On an earlier visit, I forked my way through The Crepe Shoppe's perennial daily special, The Americana. This crepe is more filling than the rest and consists of hamburger, cheese, lettuce, tomato, and just about everything else you would expect to find in a cheeseburger. The flavors are quite simple with little spice to tantalize the palate.

The Crepe Shoppe also offers several fine dessert crepes. When strawberries are in season, the strawberry crepe is not to be missed. The berries were sweet and ripe and generously packed into the butter swathed pancake. Whipped cream crowns this decadent enticement.

All crepes are made fresh before your eyes and no preservatives are used. In my opinion, prices were slightly inflated, though I couldn't complain about leaving hungry.

THE CROW'S NEST ★★★   Price Range: Moderate
Steak and Lobster

Santa Cruz Yacht Harbor, Santa Cruz	A.E. − M.C. − Visa
Phone: 476-4560	No Reservations
Hours: Lunch: 11:30−2:30 pm, Daily	Non-Smoking Section
Dinner: 5:30−10:30 pm, M–Sat.	Wheelchair Access
Full Bar	

On a crystal clear day in Santa Cruz, one of the best places to observe the scenic tranquility of the ocean and the sky is the Crow's Nest in the yacht harbor. The Nest has been in business for a long time and has established itself as the local hot spot for spirits and food.

When the weather permits, the patio at the Nest allows patrons to dine and sip cocktails under the unblemished skyscape.

Our table afforded us a view of the yacht harbor itself. Over a glass of wine and a well prepared lunch, we were entertained by the reeling gulls overhead and by the colorful sailboats drifting past the jetties to open water. When the winter chill descends on the Cruz, the Nest turns on the outdoor heaters, maintaining the warm comfort of its patio. The interior quarters are equally comfortable, enriched with wood, glass, carpet and plants.

The luncheon menu (Saturdays and Sundays included) is not extravagant. Fish, chicken and steaks are prepared without fanfare. In addition to the entree, the bill of fare demands a trip to the well stocked salad bar and a carafe of wine.

I found the entrees to be simple presentations carefully attended to by the kitchen staff. We ordered the Catch of the Day which was a fresh slice of swordfish. The portion was ample, while the firm, moist texture of the fish had been maintained over a gentle fire. It was served with seasoned rice and chunky tartar sauce.

Our second entree was a plate of London Broil. I was surprised by the tender quality of the beef slices, bedded down on a cushion of rice. Each slice was cut semi-thick. The meat was correctly charbroiled, exhibiting the proper crispness at the edges while the center was red and juicy. Served along side for dipping was a sweet, processed-tasting barbecue sauce.

The other entree we ordered enjoys popularity with the diners who visit the Nest on a regular basis. The Chicken Teriyaki is a light offering, featuring two sweetly marinated chicken breasts, grilled over a charcoal blaze. I found the flavor of the chicken and teriyaki to be commonplace.

For those wishing to forego lunch for a spirited beverage, the Nest has one of the most comfortable bars in Santa Cruz. Two serving stations are available, one inside and one ouside. On prime nights and on weekend afternoons, both are filled. After ten at night the Nest becomes a hotbed of singles activity, with live bands.

DARTANIAN'S ★★★★   Price Range: Expensive
Continental

1655 Saratoga-Sunnyvale Rd., Cupertino	A.E. – M.C. – Visa
Phone: (408) 257-1120	Reservations Required
Hours: Lunch: 11:30–2:30, Tues.-Fri.	Non-Smoking Section
Dinner: 5–10 pm, Tues.-Thurs.	Limited Wheelchair Access
Till 11 pm, Fri. & Sat.	
From 4 pm, Sunday	
Full Bar	Entertainment

In my first review, I mentioned that Dartanian's was aspiring to the goal of excellence. A second visit proved to me that this goal was being attained. The food, the service, the atmosphere were all much improved from the first visit. It appears that the management has gotten its feet firmly planted and is beginning to swing with the favorable attention it has been receiving from its increasing patronage.

Dartanian's Chef and Proprietor has worked with Emile Mooser at the Swiss Affair and displays the delicate handedness implicit in Emile's cuisine. I am particularly impressed with Dartanian's version of Noisettes of Lamb Parisienne. Three, thick medallions of lamb tenderloin (domestic spring lamb is available in spring) are glazed in a finely reduced brown stock and finished with pats of melting garlic butter. The first time I sampled this dish, the noisettes were ringed in a rine of spiced fat. The second time I sampled this dish, the fat was missing.

Only the milk fed best veal is served at Dartanian's. Saltimbocca is a savory recipe here. Veal scallops are sheathed with paper thin slices of prosciutto, then sauteed in butter and wine and topped with melted cheese before serving. This is a Roman specialty worth a sampling at Dartanian's.

I have eaten Soft Shelled Crab on two separate occasions. The first preparation was a fair offering. The bottom portion of these shell edible crabs was overcooked and slightly burned. The burned flavor invaded the otherwise delicate taste of these gelantinous crustaceans. My second sampling proved to be much better. The bottoms were perfectly cooked, the crabs sauteed in a light butter-based sauce and garnished with shaved almonds.

In addition to many commonly seen Continental items, Dartanian's offers several dishes that are personal specialties of the chef. Daily specials, like fresh fish, will be announced tableside. Pastas are all freshly made on the premises and can be ordered with a variety of sauce preparations.

Since my first encounter with a half conscious waiter at Dartanian's, the tableside attention has, like everything else here, greatly improved. In fact, the service has been exquisite on subsequent visits.

Red velvet and polished wood paneling cast a glimmer of ocean liner luxury to Dartanian's spacious lodge motif where crystalline chandeliers hang from the high A-frame ceiling. The interior is meticulously maintained and well ventilated. I found tables to be evenly spaced with ample room for leg extension and private discussion.

DAY AND NIGHT ★★★
BBQ

Price Range: Bargain

2118 University Ave., East Palo Alto	Cash Only
Phone: (415) 324-0281	No Reservations
Hours: 11 am–10:45 pm, Mon.-Wed.	No Non-Smoking Section
11 am–12:45 am, Thurs.	Limited Wheelchair Access
11 am–2:45 am, Fri. & Sat.	

Take Out

The main purpose for going to Day and Night is to eat some of the best BBQ ribs and links this side of Flint's BBQ in Oakland. Aptly named for its business hours that extend into the fog shrouded evenings, Day and Night has become the perennial take out haven for barbeque lovers. I remember on one occasion the front curbs were jammed with Jags, Rolls Royces and Cadillacs.

The cooks here employ in-house secrets for "queuing" ribs that put many I've sampled in second place category. Though spicy hot links and other soul food favorites are offered, pork ribs remain the specialty of the house. Ribs here can be ordered by the pound or by the small ends which are infinitely more meatier. Each rib is accurately cut so that each bone shaft is laden with moist, luscious pork. Meat literally pulls from the bones effortlessly.

The Day and Night rib is cooked free of sauce. The sauce is applied just before serving. This carmel colored brew is a piquant blend with specks of herbs and hot peppers. Though spicy, the sauce does not blister the lips.

Day and Night is not the type of place you can spend time. It is primarily take out. The building is dingy and old, but houses one hell of a kitchen. Just get your food and chow down in the comfort of your own car or home.

D & G BBQ ★★   Price Range: Moderate
Soul BBQ

1940-C University Ave., East Palo Alto   Cash Only
Phone: (415) 325-5129   No Reservations
Hours: 11 am–Mid., Tues.–Thurs.   No Non-Smoking Area
**   Till 2 am, Fri. & Sat.**   No Wheelchair Access
Take Out

Next to Day and Night BBQ, D & G is one of the best rib joints in the South Bay. The ribs here demand attention, full attention. Located in the reviving Whiskey Gulch area of East Palo Alto, this miniscule storefront pumps out true, soul food ribs that will put hair on a bald head.

The cooks here live their recipes. You can see it in their eyes. You can see the sauce stains in their hands. You can feel it in the hickory smoked environment of their kitchen. There is no eating on the premises. You pick your food at a counter and you get the hell out and go home. That's where you mess your face up and get down on D & G's ribs.

The ribs here are spicier than Day and Night's. The sauce is a deep rust red that leaves definite needle activity along the lips and mouth. The pork ribs are my favorite. The meat smokes out very tender, but not tender enough not to require some teeth tugging. But once you get into these ribs, you'll taste the sweet pork and the deep woodsy flavor of the hickory. Portions are demanding and the eating ordeal will be messy. If you plan on eating in your car, get enough napkins.

The beef ribs here are big, club-sized things, packed with hearty meat that challenges the teeth. Either the meat gives up and tears from the bone or you may be investing in a set of dentures. Yes, the beef ribs are tough, but the meat, once in the mouth, chews well and has a great hickory flavor.

With your rib dinner, D & G offers homemade potato salad and pretty decent sweet potato pie.

DI CICCO'S ★★★
Italian / Pizza

Price Range: Moderate

2509 So. Bascom Ave., Campbell
Phone: 377-5850
Hours: 11 am–Mid., Mon.-Sat.
     From Noon, Sunday
Beer and Wine

Diners Club – M.C. – Visa
Reservations Optional
No Non-Smoking Section
Limited Wheelchair Access
Seating Capacity: 100

When Charles Magonia gives me a tip on a restaurant, I usually follow it up quickly. But when he invited me for a plate of linguine and clams at Di Cicco's, I questioned his judgment.

Despite my doubts, Magonia wasn't wrong. Di Cicco's has established itself as a purveyor of basic Italian favorites, offering a few zesty departures for the seekers of cuisine.

The dish Magonia comes here for is the linguine with clams, red sauce. The sauce applied here is different from the big-pot brew ladled onto Di Cicco's pedestrian pasta dishes. The sauce for this dish is freshly made to order and possesses a deep, imported olive-oil foundation. Fresh pieces of garlic you can spear with a fork, slices of mushrooms, fresh tomato and an abundance of chewy, tasty clams combine to form the perfect complement for linguine. The other outstanding characteristic of this dish is the proper way the pasta is boiled. It is *al dente*, each strand firm, tender and separate.

The second dish we sampled is much heartier than the former, *rigatoni ricotta*. A fair warning to all: this dish is heavy and rich and will dispense your hunger for a long time. A large plate of *rigatoni* (pasta tubes), once again boiled correctly, is covered with a thick, smooth, evenly blended sauce made with sweet, creamy ricotta. Forming a center circle atop this pasta extravaganza is a tart marinara sauce. Just this little bit of tomato sauce provides the perfect balance to the dairy-rich ricotta.

For a side dish we ordered a plate of veal Milanese. A large slice of veal is dipped in beaten egg, coated in bread crumbs and sauteed in olive oil. It is served with lemon wedges, a tradition in Milan. Frankly, I was quite delighted to find this dish so simple and good. It reminds me a great deal of wienerschnitzel. Also served with the veal is a scattering of straw mushrooms that had the flavor of sauteed green peppers.

Service at Di Cicco's is friendly and efficient. The owners are always available for a comment or two and like to hang out near the entrance to the kitchen.

DINAH'S SHACK ★★★★   Price Range: Moderate
Smorgasbord

4269 El Camino Real, Palo Alto   **All Major Credit Cards**
Phone: 493-9510   **Reservations Recomm.**
Hours: Lunch: 11:30–2:30 pm, M–Fri.   **Non-Smoking Section**
        Dinner: 5–10 pm, Daily   **Limited Wheelchair Access**
Full Bar — Entertainment   **Seating Capacity: 200.**

Dinah's Shack has a rich character that one can almost touch. Its beginnings date way back to 1926 when it first opened its doors for business. Dinah's character begins to take form at the entrance where you're welcomed by two sculptured dogs, once the property of the famous Flood Estate.

The interior unfolds a rich and alluring ambiance of New Orlean's sophistication. John Rickey, the proprietor, has made Dinah's a show-case for some of his most prized art pieces. Paintings from Leland Stanford's personal collection and from the Winchester House bedeck the walls throughout the restaurant. Classical European sculptures of polished marble, tuliped gas-style lamps, and an endless luster of age-old comfort create the perfect place to dine.

Most notable is Dinah's bar and lounge where the classical touches are enriched by planking. Carved into this old wood is a striking profusion of initials that create fond memorabilia for the Stanford alumni who left their past engraved in these walls.

In addition to John Rickey's famous art collection, Dinah's Shack offers other artistic amenities that are both noteworthy and quite peculiar to Dinah's. The most mentionable is the nightly presence of harpist Phyllis Schlomoritz. Her music creates a tranquil setting for the many diners filling their plates at the smorgasbord table.

The great majority of Dinah's patrons come here for one thing: the smorgasbord. According to one of the regulars, it has achieved world renown and allures visitors from other countries to stop by for a hearty bite. What makes Dinah's smorgasbord so interesting is its consistently good, 40-item lineup that is constantly being replenished and cared for by three attendants.

The Smorgasbord offers both the often-seen salads and entrees plus an array of uncommon items, like fresh marinated pigs feet, delicate cinnamon sweet rice pudding, thinly sliced pastrami blended with fresh vegetables, black-eyed peas and many others. Dinah's is an all-you-can-eat affair, so pace yourself and you will be able to enjoy a great deal more.

I began with cold items and found myself savoring a creamy rich potato salad and a delightful pickled herring. Fresh fruit abounds, though I enjoyed the clove-spiced peaches most of all. There are usually four hot entrees. I sampled a goulash bulked with tender beef chunks in a wine-accented gravy, and a helping of Southern-style macaroni and cheese. Most unique.

To say that Dinah's ends at the smorgasbord is a gross understatement. Actually, this restaurant's stock in trade is its famous Southern Fried Chicken. The chicken here is prepared according to the original recipe. I received a whole half chicken, cut into four large, meaty sections. The notable aspect of this fried chicken recipe is the batter jacket that does well in retaining the natural juices of the bird. The batter is not at all heavy and fries out to a thin, delicate texture that crackles against the teeth. With each menu entree you can have either soup and salad or take one trip around the smorgasbord table for anything except a second hot entree.

Delving into Dinah's menu, we ordered a plate of Pacific Salmon Steak. Though the fish was a generous cut of deep-pink salmon, I was not impressed by its flavor. I was more taken by the creamy, butter-lemon sauce that covered the filet.

The service at Dinah's is, like many other landmark establishments, staffed by veterans who have been with the restaurant for many years. They know Dinah's Shack and seem to enjoy working there. Just ask a question about the restaurant's history, and they will answer without a moment's hesitation.

Dinah's is the type of place that withstands the movement of time. It's a chunk of history bolted into the Earth so securely that only doomsday will force it to change.

DOMENICO'S ★★★★
Italian / Seafood   Price Range: Expensive

50 Fisherman's Wharf, Monterey	All Major Credit Cards
Phone: 372-3655	Reservations Required
Hours: 11:30 am–10 pm, Daily	No Non-Smoking Section
Full Bar	Full Wheelchair Access

A thunder storm was threatening Monterey the evening we set out for a second visit to Domenico's on the wharf. Frankly, I was a little worried by the dark clouds, but the thought of fresh fish and steaming, homemade pasta was strong enough to push back the chilly elements. After all, good food hath charms to sooth the savage breeze.

Domenico's dining room features a windowside view of the wharf where rows of fishing boats rock slowly in the currents. The lighting inside is muted at night to enhance the dazzling scene of evening lights along the coast. While inside, the night storm exploded. Flashes of lightning lit the dark sea with a white phosphorescent glow.

As hinted to before, Domenico's prepares two things exceptionally well: seafood and pasta. On my two visits, the fish has always displayed a right-off-the-boat freshness. We started with a combination plate of freshly shucked oysters and clams. In a word, they are delicious. Both shellfish items have a crisp, though mild, sea flavor, with the natural ocean salt defining the gentle sweetness of the meat. The oysters, particularly, had a firm, seductive texture.

I have come to realize that Domenico's menu is almost unnecessary, except for the listed pasta dishes. Most of what is served here takes the form of a special, usually fish. The menu is limited to accommodate the fresh items that change daily in the marketplace. The proprietors want the best for their patrons and shop for it every day. Much of the fish comes from the local fishermen and is purchased right on the spot. At Domenico's it is important to trust your waiter's judgment. He will tell you what is the freshest special for that day.

After our clams and oysters, we pursued the shellfish further and ordered a batch of fresh mussels simmered in a very stout bouillabaise style sauce. Domenico's kitchen makes definite commitment to flavor. Strong garlic and sweet wine are most dominant in this bread-dipping brew.

This mussel dish put our taste buds on sensory alert. From there we proceeded to the pasta. Firstly, there is nothing better than home-made pasta. It has an Easter Sunday quality that is uncommonly tender and firm with an airy characteristic that enlivens the mouth with a rippling effect. Finally, we ordered from the menu and went with pasta Puttanesca.

The Puttanesca sauce is even more flavorful than the sauce that came with the mussels. It is a highly tangy, tomato-based blend with fresh tomato chunks, marinated olives and pieces of garlic you could spear with a tine on your fork. The deep, almost vinegar-piquant flavor gives this sauce a lip-smacking quality that goes well with the homemade noodles.

After an extended breather, we sampled a line-up of fresh fish specials. We went with the waiter's enthusiastic suggestions and ordered the sea bass and swordfish, both brought in from the water that day. The two fish selections are served in large portions, grilled over mesquite charcoal and drizzled lightly with melted butter. The swordfish displays a thick mid-section filet with a firm, meaty body that breaks off in succulent end-grain pieces. The sea bass is more delicate and flakier than the swordfish — soft and silky against the mouth. Both entrees are served with fresh vegetables.

Putting the kitchen to the test, we ordered a red meat dish, Filet Mignon, covered with what the waiter said was one of the chef's special sauces, a Marsala blend. Luckily, our cuts were obviously from the very heart of the tenderloin. Rich with a natural beef flavor, the meat was so tender it cut with a fork. What disturbs me is the Marsala sauce which, in my opinion, was not even a sauce. It appeared that the chef merely drizzled the filet with a little Marsala and called it a sauce. Any complexity brought about from the blending of wine with demi-glaze and spices was amiss.

Domenico's is worth a trip to Monterey. It is a quality restaurant that is achieving what it set out to accomplish. The fresh fish and homemade pasta in themselves are worth at least one trip to Monterey's often-forgotten wharf.

DON THE BEACHCOMBER ★   Price Range: Moderate
Cantonese / Polynesian

5580 Stevens Creek Blvd., Cupertino   A.E. − M.C. − Visa
Phone: (408) 996-3547   Reservations Recomm.
Hours: Lunch: 11:30−2:30 pm, M–Fri.   Non-Smoking Section
        Dinner: 5−10 pm, Daily   Full Wheelchair Access
Full Bar − Brunch

To ponder what has become of Don The Beachcomber since I was a child, brings tears to my eyes. To me, the Beachcomber used to be a very special place where movie stars congregated in the tropical world created by the Don and his compatriots. The food, then, was very good. It wasn't Polynesian, but it was quality Cantonese.

Changes throughout the years have taken the charm from this Polynesian paradise. What remains is a novelty house, a place where you come for a very expensive rum drink served in big pineapples or large clam shells. The Polynesian trappings are all intact; the gently bubbling fountains, the glowing multi-colored lamps, the rain forest, the tiki gods, the thatched bamboo railings. For appetizers and a cocktail, the milieu can be enjoyable and refreshing. If you come for dinner, prepare for some disappointment.

Since those days long ago, the quality of the food has steadily declined. In recent years, I have watched the Beachcomber groping for business. Bargain buffets and economy gimmicks have become manifestations of the struggle. The buffet items are attractively laid-out, but have been basically overcooked and lifeless. The meats are lost in glutinous sauces, the vegetables limp, and the fruit tasteless. It reminded me of take-out Chinese food on a buffet line.

Most of the people who come here partake of the buffet. The price is usually reasonable and you can eat all you want. Outside of the buffet, the regular menu items can become costly unless you come on a night when there is some sort of bargain going. The menu continues to list the original items, like Beef Manu, Mandarin Duck, Lobster Chungking, and Chicken Almond. The Chicken Almond continues to be well prepared with a generous supply of diced chicken breast and whole almonds in a clean, natural sauce. Lobster Chungking has been awfully short on lobster of late and long on that rather tasty sauce, made from unbeaten egg, Chinese wine, and scallion. The other items I have sampled recently have come out flat – Beef Manu, especially.

Service at the Beachcomber has always been cordial and, lately, apologetic for the breakdown of quality. I sympathize with them and hope that someday the Beachcomber can get back in his little grass shack.

DURKEE'S SEAFOOD MAMA ★★★   Price Range: Moderate
Seafood

---

820 Bay Avenue, Capitola	**Master Card — Visa**
Phone: 476-5976	**No Reservations**
Hours: Lunch: 11:30–5 pm, Mon.-Fri.	**No Non-Smoking Section**
	Full Wheelchair Access —
Beer and Wine	**[Elevator Available]**

When fortune or friends draw you over the hill to the sea shore, Durkee's Seafood Mama will be there to satisfy your hunger. The specialty here is fresh fish and shellfish sizzled over searing hot mesquite charcoal and served in an ambiance of pure Santa Cruz-style tranquility.

Seafood Mama's hand-out menu is intentionally limited, leaving room for a crew of daily catches announced tableside. Common favorites, like King Salmon, swordfish, halibut, and red snapper, rear their scales intermittently throughout the year. All seafood is subject to season, weather and fishing luck.

Thresher Shark is a favorite among the locals in Capitola and is offered nearly all the time at Durkee's. It is a reasonably priced catch at $4.50. The entree delivers a juicy and evenly grained cut of Thresher with the smoke of the mesquite a gentle influence.

Meals include your choice of two side dishes. With our thresher shark, we opted for the fresh fruit. Included was a colorful display of crisp, sweet watermelon wedges and equally sweet orange slices. We also had a serving of Durkee's homestyle rice pilaf.

When Eastern Scallops are fresh, you'd be missing a delicious treat to avoid them. This entree includes a long skewer of large, plump scallops divided by squares of honey-cured bacon. The mesquite blaze does well trapping in the natural juice of the milky sweet scallops, keeping the texture firm and mouthwatering.

Durkee's Seafood Mama is a comfortable restaurant. Forest green upholstery and walnut stained tables and chairs created a color motif of quiet elegance. Decor is striking in its tasteful simplicity. Cleanliness is outstanding and parking is trouble free.

EL BURRO ★★   Price Range: Moderate
Mexican

1875 So. Bascom (The Pruneyard), Campbell	Master Card — Visa
Phone: 371-5800	Reservations Recomm.
Hours: 11:30–10 pm, Mon.-Thurs.	Non-Smoking Section
To 11 pm, Fri. & Sat.	Wheelchair Access
From Noon on Sunday	
Full Bar	

"Only a fool argues with success." My father's nettlesome quote echoed in my ears as I descended the tile steps into El Burro, one of the few original Prune Yard restaurants to survive.

On a Tuesday night the place was hopping. And although I have never been overwhelmed by any great stroke of Mexican chefery here, I must say I was impressed with the sheer numbers that occupied almost every table in the house.

El Burro offers several amenities that cannot be overlooked, even by a fool like me. It is comfortable, warm and attractively decorated with Mexican geedunkery.

On warm days, you can sit outside in El Burro's garden patio that overlooks the Prune Yard's central courtyard.

The chips are crunchy, the salsa homemade and moderately hot, the margaritas bountifully iced and tequila-tasty.

El Burro is conveniently located off Highway 17 and for the most part has eliminated hassles.

The fare here is pretty much what one would expect from a Mexican restaurant of this size. It is predictable and highly Americanized, which means you will receive watered down versions of favorite Mexican recipes. For many, this is just fine.

I have tried many items on El Burro's long and extensive menu and have yet to be surprised. Beef, chicken and pork dishes dominate.

I have sampled chili verde on several occasions. The presentation of this dish has varied little through the years; the in-house recipe followed like a precise formula. It consists of large, tender pork chunks trimmed close to eliminate unwanted fat. The meat is simmered in a gravy-thick green chili sauce that has a tendency to gel once it cools. It is an average offering with a modicum of spicy flavor to tantalize the palate.

Like many mega-Mexican restaurants, El Burro serves entrees on massive, oven-hot platters loaded down with Spanish rice and liquidy pinto beans covered by an excessive amount of melted cheese.

El Burro lists a long cavalcade of enchilada variations ranging from *montadas* (enchiladas topped with two eggs), to the enchilada Suiza, a special recipe of the house.

We sampled a chicken enchilada and found it fair. The corn tortilla is filled with an abundance of boned chicken, then covered with a strong chili-flavored red sauce and finished with melted cheese.

The service at El Burro is exactly what you would expect: mostly young, costumed waiters and waitresses of high school or college age.

El Burro won't dazzle you with titilating Mexican cuisine, but its atmosphere is festive.

THE ORIGINAL EL CHARRO NO. 1 ★★★   Price Range: Moderate
Mexican

799 So. First St., San Jose	Cash Only
Phone: 292-3710	No Reservations
Hours: 11 am—10 pm, Daily	No Non-Smoking Section
Mexican Beer	Limited Wheelchair Access

Lost and bewildered stragglers don't wander into El Charro #1 as much as they use to. Its hole-in-the-wall status has altered considerably through the years. Progress and healthy business has given El Charro a clean, neat appearance that is non-threatening to the weekender seeking good food and comfortable surroundings.

The salsa is unique to this restaurant. Some like it, others don't. It is a thick, tomato puree hot sauce without added ingredients like onion or cilantro. Its texture is such that it does not run from the surface of a chip, but clings in a thick spread. Flavors are one-dimensional, though direct and peppery hot. El Charro did disappoint me in its stingy policy for the allotment of tortilla chips. Only one complimentary basket is allowed. After that it becomes extra tariff, about 50 cents for each additional serving.

If you are interested in an appetizer, I recommend a plate of El Charro's specialty, Guacamole. This ever-popular dip is special not in its complexity, but in its simplicity. Ripened avocados are coarsely mashed to a point where chewable chunks are visible in the green puree. Little seasoning is added, which means you taste pure avocado.

El Charro's menu is a standardized ledger of certain Mexican dishes that have been on the menu since the beginning. For a real Mexican dinner, the Chile Verde is perhaps the single most popular dish on the Mexican table. El Charro's batch is a stew of diced pork tenderloin, all fat trimmed cleanly from its edges. The pork is simmered in a green chile gravy that is deeply imbued with the natural juice of the pork. The chile provides a green shade to the sauce as well as a smack of piquancy. This dinner was served with a portion of mashed refried beans, covered by a moderate coat of melted cheese. A serving of Spanish rice proved to be a pedestrian example. The kernels were dry and the flavor hollow.

If you like beef, the Chicano will provide a taste of the red meat in an El Charro-patented sauce. Squares of beef sirloin are simmered long in a tawny, red chile sauce that, in its final reduction, is more gravy-like than saucy. When the meat was finished, the sauce became a perfect sopping condiment for flour tortilla.

The spiciest entree is the Chile Colorado. Never before has this dish been so deeply pungent in flavor and aftertaste. Instead of beef, the commonly seen meat for this stew, El Charro uses pork which gets lost in the deep, rust-red sauce.

I ran into trouble when I ordered El Charro's Chicken Enchilada and a Beef Taco. The enchilada might have been homemade, but it tasted aged and flat. The sauce was soupy and bland, though the chicken was generously applied. The beef taco was less of a dissapointment than the enchilada, but still it couldn't be classified as one of El Charro's more inspiring items. The corn tortilla was pan-fried to a crunchy firmness, forming an uncrackable pocket for the beef. I had expected the taco to be filled with stringed beef. Instead, I discovered a ground beef mixture, devoid of spice and almost of flavor. It was topped with shredded lettuce, which helped to dilute the flavor even more.

The service at El Charro was probably the most efficient tableside management I have experienced in a restaurant of this size. Our waitress, dressed in a black and white uniform, never dallied in bringing the dishes straight from the kitchen.

EL FARO TACO BAR ★★★   Price Range: Bargain
Chile Verde

---

674 13th Street, San Jose   Cash Only
Phone: 297-7468   No Reservations
Hours: 10 am–6 pm, Mon.–Sat.   No Non-Smoking Section
Domestic and Mexican Beer   Limited Wheelchair Access
Take Out

El Faro Taco Bar serves one of the best plates of Chile Verde in the South Bay. Recently, El Faro's recipe for this celebrated Mexican pork stew took first prize in the San Jose Mercury's Chili Cook-Off.

The Chile Verde here is indeed special and made from scratch daily. The recipe is a family tradition laced with care and dedication by the proprietors who begin their culinary chores in the early A.M.

The basic foundation for Chile Verdi is pork. At El Faro, the pork is cut into large, mouthable chunks – then braised until fork tender in a natural gravy powered with fresh jalapeno peppers and onions. It is the green of the peppers that give this dish its color and its name, Verdi. The jalapenos contributed a spicy hot quality that stimulated the palate without burning the lips. Even the tenderfoot can handle the degree of spiciness in this rendition.

Most entree plates are served with morning-made pinto beans, fresh Spanish rice, and a large tortilla. For added fire, El Faro brews up a pepper explosive salsa that will send searing needles along your mouth and throat. Beware and spoon with caution.

When I come to El Faro, my first choice is always the Chile Verde. It makes for a hearty, rib sticking meal that will allay your hunger for many hours. Other items on the wall menu are less impressive. The Chile Colorado, for example, lacks the complexity of flavor and the sauce consistency so implicit in the Verde. The Colorado is also made with pork chunks that are simmered long in a rust red chili gravy that is actually mild in flavor. You can order the Chile Colorado and the Chile Verde as a burrito for a reduced price. Burritos here travel well if you find you must take out.

El Faro is considered a taco bar which means they specialize in tacos. A taco can mean almost anything wrapped up in a tortilla, but, for the gringo, it is almost always seen as meat folded up in a crispy corn tortilla shell. El Faro's basic taco was a mediocre construction of black pepper flavored hamburger layered into a crispy, pre-packaged tasting tortilla shell. It was garnished with shredded cheddar cheese and iceburg lettuce. The corn tortilla shell lacked the pan fried flavor I have come to expect from a hole in the wall taqueria. Nevertheless, I don't come here for tacos. I come here for the Chile Verde.

El Faro is located in an off beat section of 13th Street in the midst of constant blue collar activity. The dining quarters are clean and neatly maintained. For such a small place, there are several tables that handle the business flow quite adequately. For unintruded privacy, come as early as you can.

EL PARISO ★★
Mexican: Cocido-O-Caldo

Price Range: Bargain

---

43 Post Street, San Jose
Phone: (408) 294-2010
Hours: 10 am—8 pm, Daily
Beer

Cash Only
No Reservations
No Non-Smoking Section
Limited Wheelchair Access

Squeezed into a storefront slot on newly recobbled Post Street in San Jose's emerging downtown is one of those perennial hole-in-the-wall Mexican restaurants that plucks the heart strings with sentiment and pads the belly with good food. At any given time during the day, you can hear the festive tunes of Mexican music, pouring from the tattered doors of El Pariso. It's here where the diehard jalapeno eaters congregate with their friends over bowls of menudo and bottles of icy Mexican beer.

El Pariso specializes in a famous family dish called cocido-o-caldo. This Mexican-style beef soup is guaranteed to clear the cobwebs from the brain. Two, tender knuckles of boiled beef are served in a steaming hot bowl of vegetable broth. Unwieldy chunks of fresh carrot, potato, wheels of squash, and other veggie odds and ends abound in this loosely based stock. The caldo is presented with a side of rice and beans, flour tortillas, and, if you ask, a raw, whole jalapeno that will ignite an explosion of sensation in your mouth. Be prudent.

There are other Mexican items on the wall menu; however, if you come here, go for the best. The beef soup is considered by many to be the prize brew in all of San Jose.

EL TORITO'S: WHO-SONG & LARRY'S ★★
Mexican   Price Range: Moderate

---

49 Lakeside Drive, Santa Clara   A.E. — M.C. — Visa
Phone: 727-4426   No Reservations
Hours: 11 am–11 pm, Mon.–Thurs.   Non-Smoking Section
        To Mid. on Fri. & Sat.   Wheelchair Access
        From 10 am on Sunday
Full Bar   Happy Hour

Fashioned after the famous Hussong's Cantina in Ensenada, Baja, California, El Torito's Who-Song & Larry's presents a bedlam of pre-fabricated fun that assaulted my sensibilities at every turn.

The noise was deafening. In addition to an explosion of chatter, various thumpings, piercing chortles, guffaws and whirring blenders, concocting a myriad of fish-bowl margaritas, roving bands and guitar players competed with a blaring stereo system. The chaos thickened when a gorilla riding a bicycle rode through the restaurant hitting people on the head with a rubber bat. In spite of my prudish outlook on restaurants that force fun down your throats, the people I saw eating and drinking appeared to be having a wonderful time.

Surprisingly enough, the food wasn't bad. Before being seated, we munched an order of Nach-o-ritos at the appetizer bar called the Taco Cart. Four pastry hats were loaded with stringed beef, beans, melted cheese, guacamole and sour cream.

They were simultaneously juicy and creamy with a distinct beefy flavor. A jalapeno ring topped each nacho, providing a stinging shot of hotness. None of the chilis or salsas was diluted or tame, so often found in gringo Mexican restaurants.

The menu is a cartoony affair with several pages of choices, some fadish like Larry's potato skins, others unique like the Mexican pizza. For dinner, we sampled two of the Especialidades: Carne Adobada and Carnitas Simon. The adobada served up three slices of beef sirloin. Grilled into the charred face of the meat was a hot chili powder that gave this dish an authentic Mexican barbecue flavor. On the side was a spread of pinto beans topped with a sensible amount of melted cheese and a refreshing salad of tomato, onion and fresh cilantro. Raw onion rings and raw jalapenos garnished the top of the meat. The Carnitas Simon was a bountiful display of succulent roasted pork served with a variety of authentic dressings, including a spicy salsa salad.

When we turned our attention to the infamous numbered combinations that mix and match common Mexican offerings, our luck with the food took a sudden tailspin. We ordered a #4 that brought us an enchilada, tostada and a tamale.

An El Torito tostada is a dazzling head turner that, for me, was pointless to ingest. First of all, a large infant seat-shaped flour tortilla is gooped with beans, cheese, tomatoes and lettuce (more than a rabbit would want) and topped with guacamole. The ingredients created a creamy pap that provided little flavor. Even salsa did little to help. Likewise, the enchilada was weak. A corn tortilla was spread with cheese and onion, folded, then covered with a processing tasting enchilada gravy. I've had better luck at home with a can of El Pato sauce.

The tamale presented good beef shreds lost in a heavy encasement of *masa*. The *masa* was just too thick, appearing more like a corn meal bun than a quality tamale wrap. I tasted corn and little else.

The service was most efficient. The waiters and waitresses made our uncomfortable situation as nice as possible by being attentive, asking us if we wanted more beer, chips or salsa. Though certain aspects of our dinner were exceptional, the noise and incessant frenetic activity took me to the point where I wanted to stand up and start tearing my hair out. Force-fed fun isn't fun to me. However, apparently I'm in a select minority. Who-Song & Larry's has been packed from day one.

EMILE'S SWISS AFFAIR ★★★★   Price Range: Expensive
French / Swiss

545 So. 2nd Street, San Jose	All Major Credit Cards
Phone: 294-2558	Reservations Required
Hours: Dinner: 5:30–10 pm, Tues.-Sun.	No Non-Smoking Section
Full Cocktail Service	Limited Wheelchair Access

Emile Mooser is the most highly regarded chef in the South Bay. His restaurant, The Swiss Affair, has earned continued praise for excellence in dining. I visit the Swiss Affair when I yearn for consistent top notch cuisine served in the exquisite French/Swiss tradition. I have yet to be disappointed.

Like the master chefs who inhabit the greatest restaurants around the world, Emile's dishes are typified by a delicate style in the blending of sauces, the preparation of meats and seafood, the visual presentation of each food item. Only the finest meats and produce are used in Emile's kitchen. Emphasis is placed not only on flavor, texture, and visual harmony, but also on the service of foods that are nutritious and wholesome.

Emile's menu is a precise compilation of appetizers, soups, salads, entrees, and desserts; plus he offers daily specials that are announced tableside. Because I find myself strapped with indecision after realizing all the fine specialties, I often settle on the Les Grenadines des Frois

Rois. This translates into filet of beef, veal, and lamb, each presented in a complimentary sauce. Les Mignonettes de veau aux Crevettes combines tender milk-fed veal scallops with juicy prawns in a mild cream sauce.

Emile's prize dinner is the "Le Table Du Chef" which is meticulously planned and prepared by the chef himself. It is a presentation of several specialties, from appetizers to soups to entrees to desserts. These items are reduced in portion so you can taste several. Le Table is made for 4 or more and requires a week's advance notice.

On one visit when I experienced this special dinner, we sampled many items including a memorable appetizer of Scandinavian cured salmon with homemade mayonnaise blended with lemon, mustard, and fresh dill. It was followed by a strikingly attractive Salad Melee, an assembly of seasonal greens and celery root with a light vinaigrette. Soup included the famous Consomme Forestiere, a hearty broth stocked with several mushroom varieties then sealed with a pastry top. Entrees were four: a veal dish in a natural sauce made with cream, a lamb tenderloin with garlic butter, a breast of chicken, and a delicious roasted quail glazed with a vinegar based sauce. Capping off the Le Table was Emile's famous Grand Marnier Souffle, followed by a plate of brie with fresh fruit and a glass of port.

Though the dining quarters are not as private or as comfortable as I would like them, Emile has made efforts of late to widen his dining room and to space the tables at a more comfortable distance. When it comes to food, however, and, let's face it, food is the primary concern, Emile's Swiss Affair will not disappoint. The dining experience here is worth every dollar. I know people who save up each year just to come here on their anniversary. They have never been dissatisfied. And they've been married for 15 years. On last notice, they are still going strong.

ERNIE'S ★★★★★   Price Range: Expensive
French

847 Montgomery St., San Francisco	All Major Credit Cards
Phone: (415) 397-5969	Reservations Required
Hours: 6:30–11 pm, Nightly	Non-Smoking Section –
Full Bar	[Upon Request]
Dress Code Enforced	Limited Wheelchair Access

Ernie's astounds the senses with a sweeping panache of San Francisco luxury, exquisite cuisine, and unending, professional service that leaves you pampered beyond belief. You will feel special, even swept away by the entire experience at this sparkling San Francisco jewel. It's expensive, but worth the price. Coats and ties for men and dresses or dress slacks for the ladies is required dinner attire.

The chef in the kitchen is the renowned Jacky Roberts whose credits are unending and quite impressive. He was the culinary maestro at Reagan's inaugural dinner. All of the dishes I have sampled have been masterpieces of visual and palate appeal. His recipes are awesomely inspiring and form a divine marriage between the traditional and the nouvelle forms of French cuisine. Helping matters, he only uses the very best ingredients in his creations which account for the consistent depth of color, texture, and fulness of flavor in all components of his dishes.

On a recent visit, I sampled a half dozen, freshly shucked oysters that had been delicately poached. A sauce composed of the natural oyster juice, cream, and seasoned white pepper was lightly applied. They were finished with truffles and julienne of leek. The oyster literally melted in the mouth.

Also for appetizer we enjoyed a giant Ravioli Stuffed with Fresh Bay Shrimp. The pasta envelope was cooked tender with the ample center pouch filled with chopped, sea sweet Bay shrimp. Languishing across the ravioli was an incredibly smooth cream sauce, alive with garden fresh sweet basil.

On subsequent visits, I have sampled an excellent Lobster Pate with Tangerine Sauce and a warm Goat's Cheese on Limestone Lettuce Salad dressed with a walnut oil dressing.

An entree that could have made the cover of *Gourmet Magazine* was the Breast of Duckling sauteed with green onions and ginger sauce. The succulent breast was sliced into thin scallops that framed a fully boned leg of duckling. The meat of the bird was roasted rare, a degree of doneness that accentuated the fresh, game flavor. A sauce of duck stock and fresh ginger was poured topside.

On another visit, I sampled Filet of Veal, Mushroom Duxelle with pink peppercorn sauce. Thick, juicy medallions of provimi veal were gently seared to a pink midsection. The veal was crowned with mushroom duxelle and a sauce strongly flavored with the pink peppercorns.

Saddle of Lamb is also a unique entree selection at Ernie's. A quality cut of lamb tenderloin, which includes the kidneys, is stuffed with a fresh goose liver forcemeat and ringed in seasoned fat. It is then roasted to a turn and served with an expertly reduced brown sauce laced with Madeira. A *tour de force.*

Expect nothing but the best for dessert as well. Fresh cakes, rolled out to your table on a glittering cart, will captivate your attention. If you can't make up your mind with a pastry, fresh berries and a sundry assortment of fresh fruits are always available. Don't be shy.

Ernie's is an occasion restaurant worth saving up for. It is definitely one of the Bay Area greats, the likes of which are few and far between.

EULIPIA ★★★★　　　　　　Price Range: Moderate to Expensive
Continental

---

374 So. 1st Street, San Jose　　　　　A.E. − MC. − Visa
Phone: (408) 280-6161　　　　　　Reservations Recomm.
Hours: Lunch: 11:30 −2 pm, Mon.-Fri.　Non-Smoking Section
　　　　Dinner: 5:30−10 pm, M–Thurs.　Limited Wheelchair Access
　　　　Till 11 pm, Fri. & Sat.
Beer and Wine

Eulipia is the darling among the chic set who inhabit the beautiful new office buildings of Downtown San Jose. Eulipia has become one of those innsy lunch spots where local dignitaries gather for fine cuisine and sensitive business chatter. Deals are made, clients are entertained, and future employees are interviewed all within the confines of Eulipia's tasteful, New York cafe ambiance.

Since Eulipia altered its coffeehouse image several years ago, it has had the fine luck of having good chefs pilot its burners. There have been three, each possessing a propensity for concocting light, balanced sauces and presenting entrees with enormous visual appeal. The current chef trained at the Culinary Institute of New York.

Though the chefs have changed, many items on Eulipia's pleasantly limited menu have remained steadfast. The Mixed Grill is one of my favorites. It offers a medallion of beef and two dainty lamb chops, both fired to perfection, and surrounded by a visually beautiful display of greens and veggies. Glazing the meat is a tart, red wine sauce that compliments both the lamb and the beef.

Fresh fish follows the seasons on Eulipia's menu. I have had mouth-watering filet of sole simply prepared and accompanied by a light cream sauce, plus a seasonal cut of King salmon, also prepared without overly spiced sauces or condiments.

Chicken dishes are properly executed by Eulipia's kitchen staff. I have always admired the top quality of chicken used in such dishes as Normandy Chicken and Chicken Cordon Bleu. The meat of the bird has been juicy and tender with a fresh, ungamey flavor.

Service is efficient and, particularly quick in bringing dishes straight from the burners. Nothing waits under the lamps here. Sauces have never come to the table with a lukewarm cover skin.

Eulipia has blossomed. It is a nice addition to a reviving Downtown San Jose.

FALAFEL DRIVE-IN ★★

Middle Eastern

Price Range: Bargain

2301 Stevens Creek Blvd., San Jose
Phone: 294-7886
Hours: 10:30 am–7:30 pm, M–Thurs.
          10:30 am–8:30 pm, Fri. & Sat.
          11:30 am–6 pm, Sunday
Take Out

Cash Only
No Reservations
Limited Seating Space

Soft Drinks

The Falafel Drive-In has prevailed for 17 years. Lost in a muddle of sofa-clearance shops, leather stores and other tiny businesses, the battered sign barely peeks out over the street, making this spot almost impossible to find, unless you know exactly where it is. As ridiculous as it may sound, I've known people to walk past the Drive-In and swear they didn't see it.

Nonetheless, the Falafel Drive-In is there, still thriving in San Jose. The plant is nothing much to look at. It's a basic hamburger-stand operation with an order window and a small, smoky interior set with a few benches. In front of the place are five cream-yellow tables set along a walkway painted hot red-orange. There's nothing complicated about the menu, either. It hangs over the counter announcing a few hamburgers, tacos and other gratuitous items that I suggest you forget. Go for the Persian eats and you will not be disappointed.

By far the best item made at the Drive-In is the falafel. This tasty Persian-style sandwich makes concession to the vegetarian and the meat eater alike. The falafels come in two sizes here, small and large. For those who have never had a falafel, it is a slice of pita bread, its hollow center filled with tiny fried vegetable balls spiced with cumin. With the small greenish ball, the unleavened pita bread is crammed with other fresh veggies like cucumber slices, tomatoes and lettuce shreds. A creamy, yogurt-tart sauce is applied over the top and then finished with a spritz of a fiery-hot relish. The relish stimulates the palate immensely, so by all means ask for it. Eating one of the Drive-In's falafels is a messy ordeal. It never cooperates and always drips mercilessly. Grab plenty of napkins.

In addition to falafels, there is another Persian delight that provides a Middle Eastern alternative to guacamole. It is called hummus. Hummus is a creamy-smooth garbanzo-bean mash, blended for the sole purpose of dipping pita bread. The dip is dusted topside with hot cayenne pepper and comes with a side of that hot relish. The flavor was luscious and rich and made for a perfect meatless lunch. It is garnished with freshly cut vegetables that can be used as palate cleansers and is served with two pieces of pita bread.

Service is what you might expect at a hamburger stand. You give your order through a window to a counter girl who then goes to work fixing your eats. She is accompanied by one or two cooks who come out of the back every once and a while.

FAMOUS PACIFIC FISH CO. ★★★
Seafood   Price Range: Moderate to Expensive

---

177 West Santa Clara St., San Jose	American Express — Visa
Phone: (408) 298-7222	No Reservations
Hours: 11 am–10 pm, Daily	Non-Smoking Section
Full Bar	Wheelchair Access —
	[Downstairs]

The Famous Pacific Fish Co. is one of those restaurants that is giving San Jose's struggling downtown a boost of ego. It is a seafood restaurant that employs the popular mesquite wood charcoal that sears in the natural juices of the fish. The grill is located in the center of the dining room where woodsy fumes permeate the interior with gentle scents of sizzling fish and mesquite.

Fresh fish abounds and is listed on blackboards hanging in certain places throughout the restaurant. Unfortunately, the listings are hard to read and I am forever relying on my hawk-eyed guests to see what is offered. Whatever is seasonally fresh has a strong possibility of being listed on The Fish Company's blackboard. Such items as King Salmon, Thresher Shark, Petrale Sole, Schrod, Sturgeon, Bass, Halibut, Swordfish, and many others can be purchased at moderate prices. On Mondays, the Fish Co. offers a special on Alaskan King Crab Legs. The legs here are large, spiny and bludgeon heavy with sweet white meat. A shell cracker is provided which came in handy often during my foray with this leg. On more than one attempt to break into the hard shell, I nearly punctured my hand on one of the crab's nasty spines.

Fresh fish has always come from the grill moist and succulent, striped attractively with the charcoal symbols. I particularly like the Halibut when it is available and also the Scallops which are always available. The Scallops are skewered and grilled quickly so that the milky sweetness is fully retained and slightly infused with the mesquite flavor.

I have never been thoroughly impressed with the service here. The waiters and waitresses never seem to have a handle on what they are doing and disappear often. They know little about wine and only a little more about the quality of fresh fish. I put more faith in the buspeople who work the areas than I do in the waiters and waitresses.

THE FISH MARKET ★★★★   Price Range: Moderate
Seafood

3150 El Camino Real, Palo Alto	Full Bar (Santa Clara)
Phone: (415) 493-9188	A.E. − M.C. − Visa
3775 El Camino Real, Santa Clara	No Reservations
Phone: 246-FISH	Non-Smoking Section
Hours: 11 am−10 pm, Mon.-Sat.	Full Wheelchair Access
From Noon−9 pm, Sun.	

Seafood has swum its way into our culinary consciousness. Meat eaters by the groves are diving into the salient pool, turning from blood red steaks and chops to the fruits de mere. Several years ago, before the finfare phenomenon really began to sprint, a brave, highly progressive fish house opened in Palo Alto, called The Fish Market. Within days of opening, this place was a madhouse of business, the scents of fresh fish and the buzzing of electronic cash registers the ultimate realities here.

Since then, many seafood restaurants have opened, a great number of which have copied The Fish Market's delicious concept of sizzling fresh fish over 1000 degree hot mesquite charcoal. Though The Fish Market isn't the first to employ mesquite, it is certainly one of the first to use it in the Peninsula and the South Bay. Mesquite wood is a very hard material that burns extremely hot, very clean, and exceedingly long. This method sears in the natural juices of fish, leaving the flesh firm, moist, and naturally succulent with a slightly smoky accent.

Fish at The Market is handled with caution. The entrees I have sampled have yet to be overcooked, dry, or fishy tasting. A great majority of the seafood is brought in fresh daily. The freshest selections are chalked in on a blackboard located overhead. Such fish as rainbow trout, petrale sole, Pacific red snapper, Ling Cod, Dungeness Crab, Troll Chinook Salmon, and other seasonal catches are abundantly provided. The fresh items are usually those that go first. Don't be late, or you may have to find alternatives.

On many occasions I have sampled fresh King Salmon. It was a fully boned filet served unadorned, wearing only a neat series of slanting grill marks across its pale pink surface. The meat exuded juice when pulled apart with a fork. The fish was served with Romano style potatoes and cherry tomato garnish.

I have also sampled filet of Pacific Red Snapper. The snapper was smaller in size and not as succulent as the Salmon. Nonetheless, it was fresh tasting and strongly imbued with the flavor of the mesquite smoke.

For swallowers of raw mollusks, The Fish Market offers Bluepoint oysters or Cherrystone clams by the platters. They are shucked by the order and are delivered to the table with shells brimming with natural sea juice. When in season, you can have steamed mussels. This feast includes a bucket of these meaty mollusks simmering in a garlic potent natural broth. Order enough bread to sop the hot liquid.

Both locations of the Fish Market are almost always frenetic with business. It is fish house ambiance at its unstrung best. The floors are chowder tile, the ceilings are astir with rotary blade fans, and the tables are closely set for elbow rubbing harmony. The service is adequate, but the collegiates can get harried when the rush is on. Because there are no reservations you better plan ahead and come early, or settle on a fifteen minute wait in crowded conditions.

FLORENTINE ★★★
Italian

Price Range: Moderate

10275 S. De Anza Blvd., Cupertino	A.E. – M.C. – Visa
Phone: 253-6532	No Reservations
Hours: 11:30 am–10 pm, Mon.-Thurs.	Non-Smoking Section
Till 11 pm, Fri. & Sat.	Limited Wheelchair Access
From 4 pm, Sunday	
Beer and Wine	

After dining at the Florentine Italian restaurant, I could have faced a firing squad with a big smile on my face and a cigar between my lips.

The Florentine, now in its 18th year of business, is a hearty, robust Italian eatery that believes in making people happy with homespun Italiano basics. This is no continental or high-class gourmet restaurant and I'm sure the aristocrats from the northern end of Italy's illustrious boot would turn their noses at the Florentine's substantial Italian grub. The distinct, simple favors of Florentine's specialties and pasta are reminiscent of Southern Italian dishes served prevalently in Naples, Calabria and Sicily, cities where the poorer folk subsist on plenty of pasta, tomato, garlic and strong olive oil.

Leaving Florentine's without having twirled into a plate of pasta would be a mortal sin. For the basic standard dish, Spaghetti and Meatballs will adequately warm your cheeks with a healthy pasta glow. The semolina was boiled to a starch-clean firmness and heaped onto a large plate. As a rule, the tomato sauce is crucial for the success of a Sunday Italian dinner. Florentine's big-pot brew made a hit at our table. It was a rich tomato blend with a light meat flavor and an agreeably sweet tomato-paste cohesiveness.

Away from the red sauce, we ordered a plate of Linguine and White Clam Sauce. Again, the pasta was boiled to that al-dente tenderness which for me is the sign of a conscientious chef. The linguini was dished up into a large bowl and was presented to the table steaming in a light-flavored sauce of butter, garlic, clam broth, parsley and a dash of cream. Four clams still in the shell, plus a generous serving of minced clams gave this dish a delicious dimension.

Our last pasta item was a plate of Tortellini. These fun-to-eat pasta twists were much larger here than at other Italian restaurants. They were boiled accurately and long enough for the meat and cheese stuffing to be thoroughly heated. We opted for the red sauce with our tortellini which was identical to the spaghetti sauce.

For those of you who have been spoiled by exquisite varieties of milk-fed veal served at high-grade continental and French restaurants, you'll have to alter your expectations a notch at the Florentine. The veal here had the flavor and texture of heartier cuts of veal that require some teeth activity and a few passes with a sharp knife. I like this brand of veal. It has body and a distinctive flavor that harmonizes well with headier sauce blends. We sampled the Veal Scaloppini and received four thick medallions of veal in a bread-dipping sauce of wine, olive oil, garlic, a squeeze of lemon and an abundance of fresh mushrooms. Eat this dish with a full basket of sesame-topped Italian bread.

I have also sampled Chicken Saute Sec. A whole half chicken cut into four meaty pieces was sauteed in a toothsome sauce heavy with wine, garlic and onion. Fresh mushrooms filled every available space left by the chicken pieces. I was impressed by the size of this portion. There was enough chicken to share without denying yourself a goodly amount.

Eggplant Parmigians has been typically disappointing. The eggplant slices were overcooked, covered heavily in tomato sauce, and sealed in by a coat of melted cheese. I prefer my eggplant dishes to highlight the eggplant and its rich natural flavor, not to be masked by sauces and cheeses.

For our last bite that evening, we nibbled a small pizza. The crust was semi-thick with a fluffy, soft, bread dough quality that baked to a golden underside. It was matted with a pure tomato sauce and then covered with cheese. The cheese remained chewable through the cooling process. Upon finishing our pizza, we tipped back the last of our Chianti, then ordered cups of espresso-bitter Cappucino.

Service at the Florentine is executed by young waiters and waitresses who appeared to serve their guests with an exceptionally friendly attitude. Our waiter was always prompt and never kept us waiting long for requests for additional bread, more wine, extra plates and forks.

For a young restaurateur just starting out, the Florentine would be a good example to study. Failure in restaurant business is far more prevalent than success. When a restaurant like the Florentine is so successful with such a simple, tasty format, it should be — aside from being envied — used as a guideline for others.

THE FLYING LADY ★★   Price Range: Moderate to Expensive
Continental / American

15060 Foothill Road, Morgan Hill   Master Card — Visa
Phone: (408) 779-4136;   227-4607   Reservations Recomm.
Hours: Lunch: Noon–2:30 pm, W–Fri.   Non-Smoking Section
         Till 3 pm, Sat. & Sun.   Full Wheelchair Access
         Dinner: 5–8 pm, Wed.–Thurs.
         Till 9:30, Fri. & Sat.
Full Bar

I have to give Irv Perch and his family credit. The new Flying Lady is an astounding accomplishment. The behemoth construction alone will draw breath from your lungs. And to imagine, Mr. Perch even had huge life-sized airplanes anchored to his ceiling. It is a dream of conceptual grandeur that has materialized.

Unfortunately, the dream ends at the dinner table. After my first visit to Flying Lady II, I went back for a second evaluation. It took a third visit to convince me that the kitchen here needs some serious attention. What I have eaten here has been vapid, often flavorless, and, due to the long distance from kitchen to table, usually lukewarm.

All dinners are complete meals, including soup, bay shrimp salad, green salad, entree and dessert. On all my visits, the soup has been a thick, somewhat glutinous chicken stock flecked with shreds of chicken and overcooked bits of vegetables. The shrimp salad was a fine offering the first time around, a flaccid, fishy compilation the next. The salad was a real yawner. If it wasn't for the somewhat snappy dressing, a bleu cheese and Ranch style brew, I might have fallen asleep at the table.

One of the best entrees on the menu is the Smoked Pacific King Salmon. It has always been a thick, succulent midsection steak, correctly baked. The smoke flavor was distinctive and light and did not detract from the inherent flavor of the salmon.

A real eye roller was the Veal Cordon Bleu. I have had it twice and both times it was pathetic. The veal tasted to me as though it had been in a freezer for many moons. It had the texture of a tenderized veal pattie with very little discernible veal flavor. The cutlet was fried in oil and the bread crumb jacket gave away the fact by absorbing the oil flavor. The common additions of ham and cheese gave this dish thin upstrokes of integrity.

Another headshaker was Veal Roulades, billed as Irving's favorite. Again that tough cut of veal was used. The cutlet was breaded and fried and covered in a poor brown sauce. It appeared to me to have an artificially thickened consistency with a strong salty bite. Don't bother.

The safest dish on the menu is the Prime New York. A very ample slab of New York loin roast has been consistently pink and juicy. Save for a little gristle, the meat is fine quality with a fork tender texture.

The experience of the decor is a one-time affair. Yes, it is a spectator's delight with the unending aviation fixtures and the life sized maniclones. If you are an airplane buff, you will appreciate Perch's efforts. I am not and the whole show became rather tiresome after awhile.

It is hard for me to recommend a restaurant where the food hasn't been good. But, on the other hand, the new Flying Lady is the largest, or one of the largest restaurants in the world. That's something to see, even if you are a finicky restaurant critic.

FOO LOO SOO ★★★★   Price Range: Moderate
Gourmet Chinese

1731 Winchester Blvd., Campbell	Master Card — Visa
Phone: 374-9011	Reservations Taken
Hours: 11:30 am–9 pm, Closed Tues.	Non-Smoking Section
Beer and Wine	Limited Wheelchair Access

I have known about Foo Loo Soo for some time. I remember when it was just a tiny restaurant with a cluttered little market as its appendage. Flimsy tables and chairs, a slow-walking, pipe-smoking proprietor, and a few of culinary compatriots were and still are fixtures of this unique gourmet restaurant. When Foo Loo Soo discovered its few tables weren't enough to seat the diners flocking in for a bite, it moved to a new, larger location in a shopping center along Winchester Blvd.

The new site retains the market at which you can purchase any number of Chinese goods, from original-recipe almond cookies to canned lychee nuts to hot-pepper sauces and marinades. The dining room, to the left under a golden dragon archway, is a long rectangle with a continuous row of gold-linen-covered tables. The room is clean and starkly attired with only a few Chinese ornaments breaking the boxy angularity. As in the beginning, the savory aromas of sizzling spices and wok-frying meats delight the olfactory, promising a delicious Oriental repast.

Don't expect typical Chinese food at Foo Loo Soo. The menu draws from not one province but nearly all the provinces representing culinary Mainland China. The styles are unlimited, featuring dishes from Szechwan, Hunan, Peking, Mandarin, Taiwan, and Canton. The chef creates gourmet interest by utilizing spices uncommon to the Americanized understanding of Chinese food. Don't be surprised if you taste anise or the sweet lacing of white wine or the pickled tartness of mustard greens.

We started our meal with a plate of Mandarin-style Green Onion Pancakes. Though flour constitutes the base for these griddle cakes, they had the thick consistency of potato pancakes. The soft, creamy batter was flavored strongly with green onions. They are fried to a crispy outer layer, leaving the interior moist and mashed-potato soft.

After the pancakes, we indulged ourselves with a plate of eight Mandarin Pot Stickers. Foo Loo Soo's rendition of these authentic dumplings is once again unique. They are long, candy-bar shaped and tightly supplied with a mashy mixture of vegetables and spiced meat. A hot pepper-pod paste, vinegar, and soy sauce are ideal condiments for these exquisite dumplings.

After our appetizers were cleared away, our a la carte dishes were delivered en masse, transforming our table into a veritable display case. Occupying the far right corner was a Szechwan dish I have yet to have anywhere else, Szechwan Beef Stew. Clumped high on a platter was a mass of soft, stewed beef infused with tongue-tingling spices, including the licorice essence of anise. It doesn't look as good as it tastes. This stew is a peasanty, winter dish, very simple, very filling.

Crowding the plate of beef stew was another Szechwan-style dish, Pork with Szechwan Mustard Greens. Our waitress warned us that this was a dish only the Chinese patrons ordered. I don't know why. It wasn't hair-raising in any way. In fact, it was quite tame in both presentation and preparation. Pork tenderloin was cleavered into long strings and toss-fried with the pungent leaves of mustard green. The mustard came through as a tangy, pickle flavor, not anything a novice would turn the nose to.

Teetering on the brink of the table was a platter of Foo Loo Soo Roast Duck. Through Chinese friends of mine, I have come to appreciate the authenticity of eating duck with a Chinese dinner. Foo Loo Soo's special duck entree presents succulent Long Island duckling, the skin seasoned and brushed lightly with a sweet marinade, then roasted until golden and crisp. Before it was served it was hacked into handy segments perfect for manipulation with the sticks or the fingers. Use the fingers. You can get at the hidden swatches of meat that way.

Our last dish was an order of Mandarin Pan-Fried Shrimps. This was one of the first dishes to alert me to the gourmet aspect of Foo Loo Soo's brand of Chinese cookery. Fresh medium-sized shrimps are sauteed with herbs and white wine. They are cooked only for a short while to maintain the sleek, moist texture.

Foo Loo Soo is one of the top 10 Chinese restaurants in the South Bay. The dishes here are not ordinary. They are inspiring and demonstrate the versatility of the Chinese chef.

FRANKIE, JOHNNY, & LUIGI, TOO ★★★
Italian   Price Range: Moderate

939 El Camino Real, Mountain View	Master Card — Visa
Phone: (415) 967-5384	No Reservations
Hours: 11–1 am, Mon.–Thurs.	No Non-Smoking Section
Till 1:30 am, Fri. & Sat.	Clumsy Wheelchair Access
Till Midnight, Sunday	
Beer and Wine	

Spaghetti and meatballs is the ultimate hedge against the terrifying reality of doomsday. I bow to the likes of Frankie, Johnny, and Luigi, Too, Mountain View's vigilant little Italian restaurant that keeps its pasta pots fired up like an Olympic Torch. The cooks here are astute attendants of the stoves, always ready to pump out yet another dish for the hungry, the lonely, and those addicted to tomato sauce.

Frankie, Johnny, and Luigi, Too, has become a legendary purveyor of good pasta, rich, home-crafted sauces, and Eastern style pizza pies. No wonder it's the heartthrob of culinary Mountain View. No wonder people don't mind waiting to get a table. This place has a radiant charm that transmits vibrations all the way to Gilroy.

The food here follows home style recipes found predominantly in the South of Italy. It is hearty, immediate, and filling. The red sauce that accompanies many of the pasta dishes is a true big pot brew with a deep, savory tomato flavor and a clean, fresh red color. It ladles onto pasta in thick, even coats and is always applied in amounts that cover all the semolina strands.

You can't go wrong with a basic dish of spaghetti and meatballs. The pasta is usually boiled just right and I am surprised it is. Usually at places like this, they don't have time to care for the pasta the way it should be, and it may come out a little soft. The portion was very demanding. You'll need to use somebody else's stomach to finish it off. Lasagna is also a fine entree that will leave you belly up for a good part of the day. Frankie, Johnny, and Luigi's recipe calls for a lot of cheese, and thick lasagna noodles set in multi layers. It comes to the table like a sauce covered block, standing about five inches in the plate.

Higher up on the price ladder, you can fork an average dish of Veal Parmigiana. The veal wasn't the most pampered veal I have tasted. It was somewhat chewy, though full of aged veal flavor. The sauce covering the veal was exceptionally tart, providing a perfect counterbalance for the dairy rich melted cheese covering. Again, the portion is large and merciless.

If you just want to have a pizza, Frankie, Johnny, and Luigi will set you up in style. The pizza dough is pliable and tender with an olive oil moisture that gives the crust its unique texture when baked. Cheese is generously applied and a meatless sauce covers all, leaving nothing naked. Toppings are many, so you be the judge of this fateful decision. Prices vary.

Frankie, Johnny, and Luigi can get crowded. It is a small, table-cluttered place with a loud, friendly atmosphere. All types of workers are welcomed. I do suggest that you come early for lunch or dinner if possible. At off hours, parking is easy and tables are no sweat to find.

FUNG LUM ★★★★   Price Range: Expensive
Chinese

1815 Bascom Ave., Campbell   A.E. — M.C. — Visa
Phone: 377-6955   **Reservations Required**
Hours: Lunch: 11:30–2 pm, Mon.-Fri.   **No Non-Smoking Section-**
        Dinner: 5–10 pm, Mon.-Fri.   **though well ventilated**
        Till 10:30, Sat.   **Wheelchair Access**
        Noon–9 pm, Sunday
Full Bar

Since Fung Lum opened its doors several years ago, I have fielded a roll sheet of complaints centering around the restaurant's prices and service. Believe me, service can get whacky here. One complaint described a waiter who "had the attitude of a Bowry Boy." The waiters here have gotten sassy; on a few occasions even argumentative. It goes without saying that experiences with arrogant waiters can certainly chill an evening. I have also encountered busboys at Fung Lum's who appeared dizzy and soporific. During these occasions, plates were cleared at will, not by necessity.

In regards to the other point on criticism — prices — I will agree that they are high, just as prices at Emile's and Paolo's are high. What most people don't realize is that Fung Lum is not your typical storefront Chinese restaurant. Many of the dishes on the menu transcend what you would normally expect from Chinese food. Fung Lum serves Chinese haute cuisine, basically Cantonese in style, though there are dishes representing other Chinese provinces.

For me, food is my main objective for coming here, but I must admit, the palatial opulence of the interior can inspire great dining. The main dining room is a vast, imperial courtyard bounded by gilded cornices and imported inlaid teakwood. The rich surroundings are accented with Oriental murals, carved jade, plush carpeting and linen-covered tables. When Fung Lum gets crowded, an air of banquet festivity fills the room. It can be noisy.

Few complaints have centered on Fung Lum's cuisine. In the seven times or so I have dined here, I have yet to be dissatisfied with the food. This time around, we commenced with an appetizer of Skewered Beef Saday. Four generous portions of beef tenderloin were broiled on bamboo skewers, then served with a special saday sauce. This spicy condiment is made from krill (a very small, shrimplike crustacean), garlic, shallots, chili and salt. Though the spiciness was clearly tasted, there was no pepper sting.

Fung Lum serves a good example of quality Cantonese cuisine. Texture and visual appearance are high points while quick stir-frying is the preferred cooking method. The Cantonese chefs at Fung Lum never overspice their dishes, and have always maintained balance in flavor and sauce consistency. Following our appetizer course, we sampled one of the most valued specialties of the house, Minced Squab. A tender, sweet squab was finely minced with 10 ingredients, including bamboo shoots for moisture retention, then presented along with fresh, crisp lettuce leaves and hoison sauce. The procedure here is to fill the hollow of a lettuce leaf with the squab mixture, spread with hoison, wrap, then eat. The flavor was clean and fresh with the crispness of the lettuce balancing the soft texture of the squab. The portion was large enough to feed four very well.

For those who appreciate the complex flavor and texture of the mushroom, Fung Lum serves a plate of Black Mushrooms with Oyster Sauce guaranteed to give you a gastronomic sendoff. The deep, exotic, almost loamy, flavor of this mushroom lingers long in the mouth. A large selection of these sleek, ebony-colored mushrooms were sauteed in a rich, mildly salty oyster sauce.

The Cantonese chefs are famous for their finess and exactness in saucemaking. A dish that typifies this skill is Fung Lum's Beef with Walnuts. Thin scallops of beef tenderloin were sauteed with meaty chunks of walnuts and meticulously chopped celery and carrot in a brothy sauce spiked with minced ginger and garlic. The sweet pungency of the ginger was most notable as it coalesced with this distinctive walnut earthiness. Nothing was left of this dish when we were finished.

Highlighting their mastery of seafood, Fung Lum's chefs present a creation specialty called Salt Baked Prawns. The technique here is to slowly bake fresh prawns while still in their shells. A coating of salty is also baked into the prawns. This process seals in the natural juices while crisping the shells into a thin, crackling consistency that is edible. The portion was more than generous considering how expensive prawns have become at local fish markets. There were so many we couldn't finish them all.

Having Fung Lum with us is a compliment to the South Bay. Despite the complaints, I feel that overall this restaurant is a quality establishment that will continue to beckon the well dressed as well as the lovers of Chinese cuisine.

GALANO'S ★★★   Price Range: Moderate
Italian

1635 Hollenbeck Ave., Sunnyvale   Master Card — Visa
Phone: 738-1120   Reservations Taken
Hours: Lunch: 11–20:30 pm, Mon.-Fri.   No Non-Smoking Section
        Dinner: 5–10 pm, Mon.-Fri.   Limited Wheelchair Access
        from 4 pm, Sat.; from 2 pm, Sun.
Full Cocktail Service

Galano's finds middle ground between the commonplace spaghetti house and the continental restaurant. Despite the drawbacks, there is an undeniable charm working at the basic foundation of Galano's. The food is festive and it's different. The menu is very manageable and is not riddled with the all too common Italian favorites.

Galano's does indeed have a master chef piloting its burners. For over 10 years now, the chef/proprietor has cooked his way into being a very popular personage, his food a sought after commodity. Like the rest of the people who packed into this restaurant, I enjoy Galano's brand of Italian cookery, but have never left without realizing the flaws. There have been problems with certain dishes that have kept me from giving this restaurant a completely glowing report.

One dish I give my unmitigated recommendation to is the Prawns Fradiavolo. The chef displays his attention to detail in sauces in this dish. He didn't come off heavy handed and found tasteful balance with his ingredients. Six, fat, juicy gulf prawns were served in a freshly crafted tomato and garlic based sauce laced with a rich olive oil essence. The sauce exhibited an extraordinary depth of flavor with an afterflash of hot pepper that stimulated the palate, but did not burn it.

Following the prawns, we split an order of Linguini and Baby Clams with a white sauce. Though I enjoyed eating this dish, I found its presentation to be somewhat disappointing. The sauce was generously supplied with baby clams. Unfortunately, it had a glutinous texture that was too thick for this style of pasta dish. The pasta was an ample portion of tubular, unlinguini-like strands that were overboiled and slightly gummy. The high point to this dish was the freshly grated cheese, a mix of Parmesan and Romano.

The spaghetti sauce, on the other hand, was a superb tomato and spice composition. The flavor was a poetic blend, highlighting fresh garlic, tomato, and a quality olive oil that penetrated the nostrils with its rich bouquet. The pasta in the plain Spaghetti with Meat Sauce was firm and tender, boiled closer to al dente than the linguini.

In addition to specials of the day, there are a limited number of entree selections under fish, chicken, veal, and beef. We went for one of Galano's prize veal dishes, Veal Bocconcino a la Romana. This veal selection is Northern Italian in essence. It is comprised of milk fed veal scallops sauteed in a heavily wine accented sauce composed from a light stock. The veal is finished with a layer of prosciutto and a cover of melted cheese. The flavors were highly complimentary; however, the salt from the Italian ham strongly influenced the taste.

Both entrees were very filling. Portions were generous from beginning to end. All entrees are served with your choice of minestrone, clam chowder, or tossed green salad. Entree side dishes include either a small serving of spaghetti or ravioli. Surprisingly enough, the ravioli were not pasty and broken apart. The pasta envelopes remained whole and tender, keeping firm under a spread of Galano's excellent tomato sauce.

Overall, Galano's still remains an Italian restaurant worth a sampling. It is different from all the others. The chef transcends the ordinary with his dishes and shows his expertise in many of his selections. Of course there are flaws, but sometimes, flaws lose their strange hold when the wine is hearty and the atmosphere is warm and inviting. Buon Appetito!

GASTHAUS ADLER ★★★   Price Range: Moderate
German

1380 S. Main St., Milpitas	Master Card — Visa
Phone: 946-6144	Reservations Suggested on
Hours: Breakfast: 7–9 am, Mon.-Fri.	Weekends
Lunch: 11–2 pm, Mon.-Fri.	No Non-Smoking Section
Dinner: 5–10 pm, Tues.-Sat.	Wheelchair Access
Full Bar — Extensive German Beer List	

Located on Main Street in the shadow of the Ford Assembly Plant, Gasthaus Adler is where working-class heroes hunker down to hearty German repast.

Everything about this place is hearty. The food, the atmosphere, the people, the air. Ambiance is created more by the local patronage than by the colorful Bavarian banners, brightly painted planking, and wildlife trophies. On my visit, there was a diner who looked like Sean Connery playing a role in a 007 thriller and a butcher with tree-trunk arms who huddled at a rear table chowing down on plates of steaming ham hocks with his biker buddy.

If you want to eat well, then Gasthaus Goldenen Adler is worth the drive to Milpitas. The dishes here are cooked up at the hands of authentic German chefs. We started with a strong tomato-based vegetable soup that made our eyelids shutter momentarily. Salads made with crunchy iceberg lettuce followed immediately. Between soup and salad, we wet our whistles on brimming goblets of Dortmunder Kronen, the famous German lager drawn straight from the tap. It is served slightly chilled so that you can taste the deep malt flavor of this quality brew.

The house specialty is Ham Hocks, a large portion that requires a huge platter. Taking up most of the space is a big, hulking ham hock laden with a deliciously edible coat of pigskin. Beneath this tasty wrap of fat is deeply smoked ham that breaks from the bones in large moist segments. Forming a bumper stop for the hock is a helping of home-made sauerkraut that purveys the right amount of piquancy to enhance the ham's smoky flavor. Also accompanying the hock is a selection of vegetables, including fresh carrot slices, long, tender green beans and several crispy rounds of fried potatoes. Dig in.

Pork is a favorite meat on the menu here. For a delectable alternative to the ham hocks, you have the opportunity to enjoy the famous German dish, Kassler Rippchen. Two high-rise pork loin chops, edged with a tasty trim of fat, are smoked through and through and broiled to a turn. These chops are traditionally hearty and require some work with a sharp knife.

Adler also serves a pork alternative to the much admired wiener schnitzel (veal) called Schweine Schnitzel. Boneless pork loin slices are breaded and pan-fried until the outer coating is golden brown and crisp to the touch. Of course, veal lovers can go the traditional route with the Wiener Schnitzel. This dish presents slices of pounded baby veal, breaded and pan fried. What I like most about schnitzel is its simplicity. Both the pork and veal schnitzels are served only with wedges of lemon.

A German restaurant would lose its wings if it didn't serve Rouladen. There was some mixed discussion about Adler's rendition, but generally I found it to be a pleasant presentation. Slices of beef are rolled up around a stuffing of chopped meat flavored with a little bacon. The texture is very moist with the natural juices fully intact. The flavor is less tart than other Roulade versions. Adler seems to tone down that characteristic tartness that one would expect from a German restaurant. But, frankly, I prefer it this way.

Dessert here is nothing to write home about. Rum cake and cheese-cake are the major offerings and both are mediocre.

Service is conducted by friendly matrons who have had extensive practice handling diners with big appetites and a lot to say about every subject. They love to laugh along with the jokes and even frolic when the time is right.

Gasthaus Goldenen Adler is a basic German restaurant that stands tough on its theme of hearty food, hearty brew and hearty spirit.

GAYLORD INDIA RESTAURANT ★★★★★
India   Price Range: Expensive

---

317 Stanford Shopping Center, Palo Alto   All Major Credit Cards
Phone: (415) 326-8761   Reservations Recomm.
Hours: Lunch: 11:30–3 pm, M–Sat.   No Non-Smoking Section
     Dinner: 5–10 pm, Daily   Full Wheelchair Access
Full Bar — Sunday Brunch

To use a term coined by the famous surfer, Dewey Weber, describing the exhilaration of being locked inside a wave, I was "stoked," when I heard Gaylord Indian Restaurant had come to the Santa Clara Valley.

Gaylord's elegant interior befits the well-dressed clientele. Dark green velvet banquettes create demure counterpoint to the pale peach walls and clean white table linen. Authentic silk paintings bedeck the walls, the colors of which take on depth and interest in the gently flickering candlelight.

The chefs at Gaylord are well versed in the alluring complexities of their native India dishes. Fresh spices, brought in from all over India, are prepared daily and specially made for each individual dish. Curries were pungent and rich, drawing focus on the almost secretive elements that go into making these distinctive spice blends. Gaylord's brings food and spirit into delicious union.

Gaylord's menu lists a complete host of exquisite Northern Indian dishes. Tandoori is a specialty, which can be fully appreciated in the Mixed Tandoori Grill or the Baba Kabab. The latter brings three, extra large cut lamb chops, marinated, and roasted in the special firey clay ovens that defines the Tandoori process.

Curries are highlighted by the hot and spicy Gosht Vindaloo, braised lamb chunks, or the popular Rogan Josh, lamb in onion and tomato sauce. Savory rice dishes, like Prawn Biryani, Indian breads, like Poori or Aloo Paratha (whole wheat bread stuffed with potatoes and peas), plus other intriguing dishes, like Raita (yogurt with cucumbers), give Gaylord's menu a myriad of depth and color.

Service is top notch and waiters are well trained in the intricate dishes they serve. However, I was disappointed with the presentation of our dessert and tea course. The sweets were uninspiring and the tea no better than your common blend from Lipton's. Nonetheless, Gaylord's isn't a dessert shop. It is a serious Indian restaurant serving excellent native dishes in elegant surroundings.

GERMANIA ★★★★★
German

Price Range: Moderate

---

255 North 1st Street, San Jose
Phone: 292-0291; 279-9652
Hours: Lunch: 11–2 pm, Mon.–Fri.
　　　　Dinner: 5–10 pm, Tues.–Sat.
Full Bar

Cash Only
Reservations Recomm.
No Non-Smoking Section
Limited Wheelchair Access

The proprietors of the new Germania are true blooded Germans who have instilled their native spirit in every nook and cranny of the new site. The sharp aromas of freshly made sauerkraut and roasting pork permeate the air. There is a friendly feeling here, one that glows with the good cheer of clanking beer mugs, bellowing laughter, and nostrils sniffing the steam of homespun German foods.

All of our dishes exhibited a careful attention to detail and to preparation. Meats were moist and oozing with natural flavor, while asides like sauerkraut, red cabbage, and hot German potato salad were striking in flavor and piquancy.

All dinners include soup, salad, entree, bread, dessert and coffee. And don't think the desserts are gratuitous scoops of sherbet or ice cream. They comprise fresh cakes layered with rum cream, chocolate, fruit, and a varied assortment of luscious fillings. You won't go home hungry from Germania.

When I think of German cuisine, I think of highly piquant flavors that drive deep into the taste buds, bringing a definite expression to the face. The food at Germania is made to inspire facial expressions and an occasional ahhh released in the deep pocket of your throat. Germania's menu lists a wide variety of specialty dishes. With a day's advance notice you can indulge your appetite on Schweinshaxe or pig's knuckles with sauerkraut and hot potato salad. The knuckles here are very large and heavy with moist pork meat. Surrounding the meat is a thick layer of fat and pig skin that is delicious to eat. The knuckles are roasted until the skin is a deep brown and crackles slightly against the fork. This dish will take you to the very limit of your appetite.

On certain nights when Jaeger Steak is offered as a special, by all means don't miss it. The foundation of this recipe calls for a juicy, tender New York steak smothered with a bacon-accented saute of fresh mushrooms and tomatoes. It is served with a pan hot German-style potato salad. This salad brings large chunks of boiled potato together with bacon and onions in a pickled tart mixture.

My current sampling of Germania's Rouladen was by far the best I have had. A roll of thin slices of braised tender roast beef is stuffed with bacon and onions. The meat was very moist and broke from the main body of the roll in soft, detaching grains. Adding a piquant definition to the basic flavor was the inclusion of pickles.

Germania's menu is heavy with pork offerings, the most celebrated being the Kassler. A thick chop of smoked pork loin is served au natural. The meat requires a sharp knife. It offers a hearty resistance to the bite that will get your teeth involved in some extensive motor activity. The pork is fully imbued with the flavor of smoke that will strike the olfactory with strong impact. Though only one chop is offered, it is a big chop, large enough to satisfy a normal appetite. It is served with hot potato salad, and sauerkraut.

When you are finished with your dinner, it is often customary to down a glass or two of Jaegermeister. This is a clove strong after dinner drink taken in one gulp to aid in digestion and clear the head.

The service at Germania is geared up for the festivities. The waitresses know how to maintain balance at the dinner table, bringing dishes hot from the kitchen, guiding novices through the menu, pointing out the best desserts and entrees. They know their liquor and will suggest the correct beverage to compliment your dinner choice. The owners, too, are attentive to their customers, maintaining a warm and congenial ambiance in their restaurant.

GERVAIS ★★★★   Price Range: Expensive
French

1798 Park Avenue, San Jose   Master Card — Visa
Phone: (408) 275-8631   Reservations Required
Hours: Lunch: 11–2 pm, Tues.–Fri. Non-Smoking Section
    Dinner: 5:30–10 pm, Tues.–Sat. Full Wheelchair Access
Extensive Wine List

Not too long ago, Gervais came out with a new menu that sent many of his customers into a tizzy of comment. The new prices are much higher than before and most of the dishes are a la carte. Gervais used to be one of the only French restaurants where you could still enjoy quality French cuisine at fairly reasonable prices. Not anymore.

Though the prices have changed, the exquisite quality of Master Chef Gervais Henric's classic French dishes has been well retained. I rate him as one of the top chefs in the South Bay and Peninsula area. He is not a man who follows culinary fads. He is a chef who is consistent in his treatment of classic French cuisine. His sauces have always been precise blendings that utilize some of the most silken demi-glaces I have yet to encounter in a French restaurant.

I highly recommend you order a bowl of mussels as an appetizer. The mussels here are always fresh, large, and meaty. The most outstanding aspect is the luscious, Provencale-style sauce the mussels are delivered in. You can taste the zest of the garlic, the tang of the fresh tomato pieces, and the delicate flavor of the natural juice of the mussel. I have yet to leave even a drop in the bowl. Sopping bread is a mandatory maneuver with this dish.

Entrees are highlighted by lamb and veal. I particularly enjoy the lamb filets swabbed in Gervais's special garlic butter. It is a simple presentation where the rich flavor of lamb is greatly enhanced by the garlic butter. When ordering veal, the new addition, the FANTAISE, combines a juicy veal medallion with three gulf prawns. The light brown sauce brings the delicate flavor of milk fed veal and succulent prawn meat into complete harmony. The sauce was not heavily seasoned, but had overtones of wine and herbs.

For just a simple steak, the Entrecote Grille would suffice quite adequately. The quality of the beef is outstanding. It is a fork tender cut of New York, trimmed completely of fat, and charbroiled to a juice dripping degree. The meat is simply finished in that garlic butter which brings the deep red meat flavor into full blossom.

Service at Gervais is conducted with professional dispatch. Silverware is always reset after each course, water and wine are consistently refilled, and dishes arrive fresh and hot from the kitchen.

Gervais's prices are now competitive with other top notch French restaurants in his league. He held out in keeping his prices down, but probably realized it was no longer feasible when the cost of produce and meat kept rising.

GIFU ★★★   Price Range: Moderate
Japanese

20625 Alves Ave., Cupertino   A.E. — M.C. — Visa
Phone: 252-6460   Reservations Recomm.
Hours: Lunch: 11:30—2 pm, Tues.-Fri.   Non-Smoking Section
        Dinner: 5—10 pm, Tues.-Sat.
        Till 9 pm, Sun.
Full Bar   Entertainment

Gifu is one of the better Japanese restaurants to open locally in the last few years. Sushi, teriyaki, tempura, sukiyaki and many other Japanese specialties are prepared in a traditional manner, which greatly emphasizes natural flavor.

Gifu presents a spacious, comfortably arranged dining room. Angles are sharp and clean and Japanese decoration is scarce, but tastefully done. For the diner seeking a light, low-cal repast, there is a long sushi bar where a bandannaed chef creates an assortment of raw-fish delicacies. Beyond the dining quarters, there is a sequestered hallway of tatami rooms that can be reserved for the party or couple seeking a unique touch of shoeless privacy. Reservations must be made in advance.

To get the ball rolling, we put the sushi chef to work on an order of Nigiri Sushi. After only moments of dextrous slicing, we were served a variety of raw fish set atop molded rice, spiked with spicy Wasabi. Arranged artistically in a sunken tray were tuna (sashimi), abalone, squid, octopus and mackerel. The octopus and the squid required some strong chewing, but were sweet and tasted of the sea. I was most impressed with the raw tuna; Gifu's sashimi presentation was exceptionally fresh with a supple, velvety texture and a deep pink hue.

Following our raw-fish appetizer, we sampled a cooked-fish entree for a second predinner enticement, Butter-Yaki Scallops. The most noteworthy aspect of these scallops is the striking freshness, evidenced by a firm tenderness and a creamy-rich flavor. The scallops are cut into quarter-size wheels, quickly seared in a pan with butter, then served sizzling hot on an iron skillet.

Japanese chefs are masters at preparing wholesome broth dishes. Gifu offers a healthy bowl of shabu-shabu, a switch from the teriyaki-sweet sukiyaki. This steaming soup dish is stocked with simmered vegetables and wide, thin slices of beef. The flavor depends almost entirely on the natural assimilation of vegetables, beef and stock.

Gifu dedicates a page of its menu to its deluxe dinner combinations, some of which offer three reduced-entree items in one. We enjoyed an array of teriyaki-marinated steak, sashimi and tempura. The delivery of each item is staggered to allow enough time to fully enjoy the three dishes as a separate course. First comes the steak. The meat is adequately tender, with a deep broiled-beef flavor dominating the teriyaki sweetness.

Following a masterful course of that deliciously fresh raw tuna, we received a plate of tempura. Prawns and vegetables, coated in a crispy, gossamer batter, are deep fried and served crackling hot. The batter is not oily and the jumbo prawns hold their natural juice.

Service at Gifu is conducted by kimono-clad waitresses who amble about the dining room with quick mincing steps. Service at a Japanese restaurant is an integral part of the dinner. When it's excellent — like it was during my meals at Gifi — it has a tendency to unveil the traditions of Japanese hospitality in all its color.

Other than slightly inflated prices, Gifu remains one of the better Japanese restaurants in the area. The food is prepared with savor by fine chefs and it's evident that the ingredients are as fresh as they can be.

GIORGIO'S ★★★
Italian

Price Range: Moderate

1445 Foxworthy, San Jose
Phone: 264-5781
Hours: 4–9:30 pm, Sun.–Thurs.
      to 10 pm for Pizza orders only
      to 11 pm, Fri. & Sat., to 1 am for Pizza orders only
Beer and Wine

Master Card – Visa
No Reservations
Non-Smoking Section
Limited Wheelchair Access

During my collegiate years when I found myself with more than seven dollars in pocket money, I'd go to Giorgio's Italian restaurant for a little cerebral nourishment. At that time, I thought it was top of the line Italian dining. Portions were big, prices were reasonable, and the ambiance inspired laughter and scathing jokes about relentless professors.

Though no longer my idea of top of the line Italian dining, Giorgio's has remained basically unchanged in its operation for 23 years. The fake purple and red vegetation still hangs like rags from the ceiling. From the slick, well-worn booths, the kitchen can still be seen where young cooks, wearing floppy chef's hats, buzz across the floor slats, sizzling sausages, twirling pizza dough, stirring sauce, and other appetizing activities. Stout aromas of frying garlic, of tomato sauces, Parmesan cheese, and the yeasty scents of baking dough stimulate the olfactory just the way they used to.

Probably my favorite dinner entree here is the Italian Sausage and Bell Pepper dinner for two. Don't order it unless you are really hungry. The portion is demanding. A deep dish platter is piled with fat sausage pieces. The sausages are meaty and firm and laced with zesty fennel seeds. The sausages are served in a freshly concocted marinara sauce, thick with bell pepper wedges simmered to a tender consistency. The sauce was strong with olive oil and garlic.

With this dinner, you receive an eye opening minestrone, an average salad, and your choice of spaghetti or ravioli. Go with the spaghetti. The ravioli were overcooked and pasty.

If you like cream sauces, you will run the gauntlet with Fettuchini Giorgio. A huge ramekin filled with thick ribbon noodles was presented. The noodles were aswim in a sauce made from a foundation of fresh cream, olive oil and butter. Garlic, parsley, onions, mushrooms, and a whisper of Marsala wine add additional flavor and carnival color to this extremely rich dish. This dish is good and I suggest that you divide it among you. If you eat it all by yourself, you just might leave Giorgio's on a gurney.

For the best of Giorgio's pasta, stick to the basics, like Spaghetti and meat sauce. The pasta is boiled tender and served in a huge coil splattered with a family style tomato sauce. It had a fresh, tart flavor with enough meat to give it a bulky consistency.

When it comes to pizza, Giorgio's does indeed make an excellent pie. The crust is a little thicker than the New York style pizzas, though it remains supple and tender through the baking process. The pizza sauce is a meatless brew that settles well with the creamy, dairy fresh mozzarella.

The service at Giorgio's is conducted by perky, fun-loving waitresses who appear to have a good time working here. Their support crew, made up of busboys, dishwashers, and miscellaneous workers, perform their duties with a towel snapping frivolity that could make you nervous if you are easily frazzled.

Giorgio's is a San Jose tradition, now in its 23rd year of business. It's still a reasonably priced restaurant where the food will pad the belly copiously and send you home with wide-open eyes.

GOLDEN FLOWER ★★★★   Price Range: Moderate
Chinese / Cantonese & Mandarin

2650 El Camino Real, Mountain View	Master Card – Visa
Phone: (415) 941-7613	Reservations Taken
Hours: 11:30 am–9:30 pm, Daily	No Non-Smoking Section
Beer and Wine	Limited Wheelchair Access

The Golden Flower presents Cantonese and Mandarin cuisine that echoes the style of simplicity employed by those chefs who have mastered nouveau cuisine in France. There was great emphasis on fresh foods, light natural sauces unhampered by thickening agents and flavor adjuncts. Most of all, each dish was distinctively constructed, achieving balance in texture, color and flavor.

Decor here is totally overshadowed by the quality of the food. Though inherently comfortable, the interior becomes just a place to prop your body while indulging on the many Chinese specialties placed before your chop sticks.

The menu is complete and very inventive, listing dishes I rarely see in other Chinese restaurants. Fresh fish and shellfish are abundantly represented. Fresh squid, crabs in season, Maine lobster, rock cod, sand dabs, clams, oysters, prawns, and sea snails are seen throughout the menu. In addition to the regular ledger, there is a special Chinese insert written in the native language. Ask for the written translation.

A unique first course is fish tripe soup, ample enough to divide six ways. The major composition is glutinous, transparent fish stock with profusion of tripe cubes, black mushrooms, whole peas, and flecks of aromatic corriander. The visuals are striking. The tripe offers a slight resistance to the bite, contributing an aspect of heartiness to the soup.

Gin Kiang Spareribs are considered a specialty of the house. Multi-biteful chunks of broiled pork remained connected to short, finger handy bones. The meat is served sizzling hot and lightly glazed in a sauce that is singularly sweet.

Among the items from the Chinese menu, you can order Braised Sea Snail and Fresh Squid with salt and pepper. The brasied sea snail, more correctly the fish of the conch, render delicate filets of white fish with a texture not unlike clam or squid. The fish is braised together with onions, carrots and mushrooms forming a clear, natural sauce. On the side of the dish, a small portion of a spicy sauce preparation is presented.

The squid with salt and pepper has tremendous visual appeal. Large plugs of scalloped squid filets are lightly breaded then deep fried to a golden color. In the breading there is a lacing of salt, pepper and perhaps a hint of 5 spices. On one visit, the squids were fresh enough, though very chewy, almost rubbery. This was a major complaint around our table that night.

When available, a total triumph is the Beef with fresh asparagus in black bean sauce. A stunning alliance of very fresh, crescent cut asparagus spears and strips of quality beef tenderloin is formed. Each ingredient is seared in wok so that the pure natural flavors are totally retained. A dark, slightly pasty black bean sauce was sparingly applied so that it covered the asparagus and beef with a veneer of smoky flavor.

To fully embrace the essence of The Golden Flower's cheffery, it is mandatory to order a dish served in clay pot. I have sampled two: fresh oysters in clay pot and sizzling chicken in original gravy in pot. The fresh oyster dish is by far the most commendable. Served in a sizzling clay pot are large, juice plump oysters out of shell with ginger and green onion. The clay pot technique traps in the natural juices, keeping all ingredients succulent and firm. Just one bite of a ginger pungent oysters and my mouth filled with a gush of juice.

Service was well executed. Our host was very helpful in guiding us to the most authentic dishes, while our waiter made sure all dishes were served straight from the wok without delays. As a result, our food was always sizzling hot and steaming.

THE GOOD EARTH ★★
Natural

Price Range: Moderate

---

206 N. Santa Cruz, Los Gatos
Phone: 395-6868
Hours: 8 am–10 pm, Daily
Beer and Wine

No Credit Cards or Checks
No Reservations
Non-Smoking Section
Wheelchair Access

Many More Locations

Non-preservative, whole-grain goodness is displayed in all of the Good Earth's dishes, sometimes to the point of being boring. No offense Mother Nature, but some of the dishes here lacked imagination, especially in the flavor department.

But the number of patrons in attendance gives testament to the fact that Good Earth goers are sick and tired of the grease, the mucky meats and fries, the boiled-to-death veggies that some restaurants steal your money to serve. In this regard, The Good Earth offers a refreshing retreat from gastronomic holocaust and certainly deserves a halo for its effort.

Having followed The Good Earth from its inception many years ago in Palo Alto, I must say that all of the kinks have been ironed out in computer-like fashion. Recipes, decor, service and plug is put to the music of business, like a calculated squiggle on a schematic. At the Los Gatos branch, decor is glorified 20th-century coffeeshop, complete with untainted wood, plants and glass. Design is Denneysque but wholesome.

The casserole philosophy is embraced vigorously. Multiple veggies, nuts and cheeses swam lugubriously in creamy sauces baked until bubbling in ramekins. This concept worked well with the Country French Lasagne, however. Un-Italian in every aspect except title, the lasagne was made with spinach pasta, layered thick with three kinds of cheeses and covered richly with two kinds of mellow sauces, a red and a white. A mouthful tasted creamy and tart all at once, with additional interest contributed by fresh mushrooms, squash and spinach.

The Olive Branch Eggplant was a different story. Presentation was, at first sight, a dazzling picture of color. Eggplant slices, artichoke hearts, onions, tomato, olives and cheese were ramekinized with integrity. But as William Butler Yeats wrote, when "things fall apart, the center cannot hold." Ingredients and flavor got lost in a soupy, cheesy conglomeration.

Salads seemed to be high on the priority list with many of the diners. And for good reason: The Good Earth has mastered raw greens. In addition to the vegetable granddaddy of them all, the Garden Patch which combines a vast host of raw veggies, there are such favorites as the Fresh Fruit Salad Supreme with choice of frozen yogurt, cottage cheese or ice cream, and the Cashew Chicken Salad, plus several more.

Shakes and energy blends are performed with ice-cream parlor pizzaz. One of the favorites of the house is the Surfer. A rich, silky thick blend of fresh pineapple juice, banana, coconut milk, honey and fructose was served in a tall soda-fountain glass. The sweetness of this shake was mild with a nice coconut aftertaste.

Service was adequate the times we have eaten here. It wasn't exceptional, but the smiles were certainly wholesome and the food never suffered from lengthy waits.

Not only is The Good Earth a restaurant, it is one of the only eateries that can be called a happening, a health-food happening. The place is hopping almost all the time and waits in the entryway are customary.

GRAND CHINA ★★★★   Price Range: Moderate
Hunan / Szechwan

5100 El Camino Real, Los Altos   Master Card — Visa
Phone: 964-6464   Reservations Suggested
Hours: Lunch: 11:30–2 pm, Daily No Non-Smoking Section
   Dinner: 5–9:30 pm, Sun.-Thurs. Wheelchair Access
   Till 10 pm, Fri. & Sat.
Full Bar

In general, the dishes served at Grand China reflect the patient artistry of a seasoned Chinese chef. Most satisfying were the smoothly textured sauces, thickened naturally without overwhelming glutinous consistencies. Each sauce adhered like a glove to the geometrically cut vegetables and meats.

Grand China excels in the preparation of Hunan and Szechwan dishes. Hot spiciness is a salient characteristic of these Chinese provinces. Three of the most popular regional sauces are offered here: garlic, hot pepper and chili.

Shredded Pork with Garlic Sauce was a heap of fat-trimmed, angularly cut strings of pork tenderloin. The meat was toss-fried with strings of bamboo shoots and scallions in a savory light-brown sauce laced with a peppery sweetness. The garlic was not dominant but its alluring virtues were nonetheless apparent.

The Shredded Beef with Hot Pepper Sauce was similar to the pork in presentation. The beef was cleavered into neat strings and toss-fried with a racier brown sauce, flecked with hot red-pepper pods and peanuts. The hotness of the pepper stimulated the palate, allowing it to accommodate a larger number of tastes simultaneously.

Lobster with Chili Sauce departed slightly from the robust garlic and pepper sauces. It was sweeter and richer in consistency. Small chunks of lobster, green pepper and water chestnuts were quick-fried with a reddish, tamely spiced sauce. The word chili was misleading, because I really didn't detect the hotness that it implied.

Hunan Lamb is Grand China's representative Hunan specialty and is specifically captioned in red on the menu. It was excellent. Leg of lamb was thinly sliced and mixed with equally thin slices of leeks, bamboo shoots and chard. All ingredients were coated thoroughly in a nutty, hot spicy glaze, ringing with an application of wine. This dish exhibited the chef's tendency to haute preparations.

Traveling far from the heat of the pepper, the Velvet Crab offered a taste of the sea concocted with less volatile spices. This Shanghai favorite mixed fresh crab shreds together with mushrooms, green peas, water chestnuts and morsels of ham. A frothy egg marination gave this dish a creamy flavor. I was particularly taken by the purity of its white color.

Another mellow alternative was the Tsao Liu Chicken, a popular item with the aristocratic residents of Peking. This traditional banquet plate comprised segments of chicken breast sauteed with snow peas, water chestnuts, tree ear mushrooms and laced with a dry white wine. The sauce was a silky-textured blend with a light taste of soy sauce.

For dessert, we forced ourselves to go beyond the fortune cookie by ordering Honeyed Banana Fritters. Sizzling hot, battered banana chunks coated in honey were placed in iced water. The honey hardened into a crunchy candy coating. The sweetness was almost too much.

THE GREENHOUSE ON THE FARM ★★★
American / Continental   Price Range: Moderate

5555 Soquel Drive, Soquel	Master Card — Visa
Phone: 476-5613	No Reservations
Hours: Lunch: 11:30–4 pm, Mon.-Sat.	Non-Smoking Section
Dinner: 5–9:30 pm, Daily	Full Wheelchair Access
Sunday Brunch: 9 am–2 pm	
Beer and Wine	Espresso Bar

The Greenhouse Restaurant is located on The Farm in Soquel, a conglomerate comprised of a nursery, a gift shop, a wine and bake shop, scenic pathways, and, of course, a restaurant. The Farm is the ideal weekend spot. You can browse, buy flowers, sit on a step and eat a chunk of poppyseed, walnut bread, talk to friends, or have a meal. It's all here and it's all very attractive.

The luxurious, old Cunnison House in which the Greenhouse Restaurant exists is probably the prime reason for coming here. The interior is a vision of provencial splendor. The main dining quarters are actually a greenhouse where comfortably spaced tables cavort beneath flourishing greenery and walls of glass panes. Sunday Brunches are magnificent with the sunlight filtering through the glass, drenching the room with a bright, cheerful ambiance. Lunches are also quite enjoyable here. The grounds come to life during the day and can be fully appreciated from most tables in the restaurant.

Dinner time is less impressive. The darkness has a tendency to erase the sun fortified beauty. During the evening, attention is focused on the amenities of the refurbished house and its many antique fixtures.

As for the foodfare, it pales in contrast to the decor and atmosphere. I can't say it is poor, because, in all fairness, it is not. The dishes I have sampled have been sufficient, certain ones very creative and much better than average.

During one eating visit, we sampled one of the kitchen's specials as an appetizer, Fettuccine Primervera. This dish was an interesting recipe of spinach noodles tossed with a heavy butter, cheese, and herb sauce with the addition of mushrooms, green pepper, and cauliflower. Combining the vegetables and spinach noodles was a good idea that embraced the organic spirit alive in the Santa Cruz area.

Though hardly a county fair prize winner, The Greenhouse's plate of Pork Ribs was not disappointing. The quality of the meat was evident. Long rib bones were fully lined with tender, sweet pork, barbecued and presauced with a surprisingly spicy hot, tomato based blend. I liked the fact that the sauce was not cloying or glue thick.

Turning from the heavy meat to the sea, we ordered the special Catch of the Day which turned out to be Pacific Red Snapper. It was a very fresh piece of fish that broke from the fork in solid, flaky chunks. The flesh of the snapper had a typically hearty texture and its flavor lightly accented with the surf. An evenly crafted lemon-butter sauce glazed the fish while a finish of shaved almonds formed an appealing garnish.

All dinners and lunches include unlimited amounts of delicious poppyseed walnut bread, a special bakery item of The Farm, plus rice and vegetable with your entree, and a trip to the salad bar.

The service is conducted by some of the most beautiful waitresses I have seen in a restaurant. They are very efficient in their tableside chores, making sure all of our needs were fully met. The dining rooms are well maintained and kept flowing harmoniously by the proprietor who made his presence known on several occasions. He seems to take a keen interest in his restaurant. You can feel his sincerity.

GUADALAJARA BAKERY AND MARKET #3 ★★
Mexican – Pan Dulces   Price Range: Bargain

---

45 Post Street, San Jose   Cash Only
Phone: 292-7352
Hours: 9 am–7 pm, Daily   Take-Out Only

The Guadalajara Market and Bakery #3 permeates the morning air with the sweet aromas of baking Mexican sweet breads, or pan dulce. Pan dulce comes in all shapes and sizes and in varying colors, some of which are so bright you'll need sunglasses to peruse. The bakers at Guadalajara make their breads every day in back of the store. All the pastries are guaranteed fresh and, unlike some markets where the pan dulce becomes landing pads for flies, the breads here are kept in clean, glass display cases. From the newly cobbled walkways of Post Street, you can peek through Guadalajara's front window and see these pastries lined up in delectable rows.

One of the most popular pan dulces is the cuernito or butter roll. This long, inflated crescent shaped roll is baked to a thin, sticky outer shell. When fresh and still warm, the bread inside is soft and airy with a light buttery color. One bite and your mouth is entertained by a delicately sweet, yeasty flavor, that is not at all cloying.

Another favorite of mine is the empanadita, or fruit-filled turnover. These pastries are large and fit neatly in a splayed palm. They are exceptionally sweet and are filled with either apple or pineapple. I prefer the apple. The spicy flavor went well with the sweet bread.

But Guadalajara does not end with its bakery goods. In front of the store is a long steam table where daily made Mexican dishes are kept hot during business hours. For a fresh, right off the burner sampling of Guadalajara's cookery, come early. The food arrives from the kitchen and is put out by 9 a.m. The trays are replenished throughout the day; however, the food grows progressively tired in appearance as the hours pass.

Menu items are strictly take-out, so you'll find that the burritos and tacos travel the best in a paper bag. The best burritos are those filled with either Carnitas or chile Colorado. I particularly like the chile Colorado recipe. Beef is cut into meaty chunks and simmered in a dark red chile gravy. It was spicier than the carnitas, or roasted pork. Also available in a burrito is barbacoa, or Mexican style barbecued beef.

In addition to being a bakery and a take-out eatery, Guadalajara is also a grocery store where locals come to buy imported Mexican goods. The store site is old and cluttered and can become cramped and confusing during busy hours. Just go with the flow and you will meet with little difficulty getting your eats and making it outside.

GUIDO'S ★★★   Price Range: Moderate
Pizza

1327 S. Bascom Ave., San Jose   Cash Only
Phone: 293-6969   No Reservations
Hours: 11:30 am–10 pm, Mon.–Thurs.   No Non-Smoking Section
       Till Midnight, Fri. & Sat.   Limited Wheelchair Access
       From 4–10 pm, Sunday
Take Out

Despite the nice, new, colorful sign, over-hanging the boulevard next to Zorba's aging monolith, Guido's interior remains dismal. The improvements that were made in recent months once again look tattered. The chairs, walls and ceiling wear the scars of continued abuse. More natural light is needed to filter out some of the dinginess brought on by a heavy feeling of smoky gloom. But, gloomy or not, it's always this type of ambiance that spawns the best-made pizzas. And this, Guido's does, hands down.

A Guido's pizza brings one to the primary foundation of quality pizza making, the crust. If the crust is poorly made, the pizza will be a disaster. Guido presents a crust that is made from a well-kneaded dough, fragrant with the yeast aroma. When baked, the dough rises fluffy with a crispy golden underside and a moist interior. Just one bite and the initial crackling, crisp sound bespeaks its fine consistency.

Guido's offers a variety of toppings, but I prefer pizza plain with just cheese and sauce. When plain, you can concentrate on the tenderness of the crust, taste the full, sweet, milky freshness of the mozzarella and savor the slight tartness of the tomato sauce.

If you like your pizza spread with meats, Guido's applies a wide variety generously. Pepperoni comes in expansive rounds. When baked, the oil of the pepperoni spreads over the bubbling elastic cheese, adding a spicy dimension to the basic flavors. Salami and sausage are also offered as meat toppings, but are not nearly as penetrating as the pepperoni.

For the works, you can order a combination that includes just about every ingredient possibility, except anchovies. I find the combination a bit too bulky and heavy to fully enjoy. The many toppings detract from the pure taste of the pizza and fill the belly much too quickly.

There is no table service at Guido's. You order at the counter and wait for your number to be called. You fetch your own plates, silverware and napkins. This low-maintenance mode of operation is OK, but I wish the people who work behind the counter were more affable. The tables in the dining room are not always bused as promptly as they should be. More than once, I have eaten my entire meal with the unsavory view of dirty plates and trays piled up on the next table.

The bottom line to Guido's is great pizza. I have learned to suffer the gloom and the beer-hall attitude because the pizza pies can't be beat.

HAKONE SUKIYAKI ★★★   Price Range: Moderate
Japanese

---

185 Castro Street, Mountain View   Cash Only
Phone: 968-8198   No Reservations
Hours: 11 am–9 pm, Mon.–Sat.   No Non-Smoking Section
Beer and Saki   Limited Wheelchair Access

In the final analysis, the reason for liking a restaurant should be based on good food, not the ambient frills. The quality of the food is the true source of satisfaction, and the food is why I like Hakone Sukiyaki. The Japanese food served here is down-to-earth, unpretentious, direct, filling and reasonably priced. What more could you want?

The specialty of the house is sukiyaki. Hakone's version is one of the best I've spooned in a long while. The broth of the sukiyaki was not at all bland, but very tasty with a gentle teriyaki sweetness and a steamy vegetable essence. It is served in an iron pan bulked high with the broth-cooked vegetables and meat. There was a bountiful provision of cabbage, snow peas, mushrooms, onions and cubes of tofu, and many curling strips of chewy beef, forming a massive tangle in the steaming liquid. After a bowl of this brew, you will feel revitalized.

If you are a combination-plate lover, you will find the ultimate appeasement in the Sukiyaki and Gyoza combo. In addition to a massive dinner tray, you receive a complete meal, including a clear fish broth for starters, a flask of hot saki and a scoop of creamy, green-tea ice cream for dessert. The combo tray is laden with food – the sukiyaki, a plate of six pan-fried gyoza, salad, rice, cabbage and condiment. The gyoza were particularly interesting. These airy envelopes of won-ton dough were stuffed with a pungent chopped meat and fried in a light oil until semi-crisp. A piquant dipping marinade, especially made for gyoza, is provided on the side.

We also sampled sashimi, a plate of freshly sliced raw tuna served on a bed of chopped iceberg lettuce. I haven't before seen iceberg lettuce used as a bed for the sashimi, but at Hakone, coffee-shop techniques are often employed. The tuna was a very light pink, almost translucent, with a fresh, clean taste and a firm texture.

The most accurate note to make about the service at Hakone is that you will be served consistently. Food comes from kitchen to table wafting tails of steam. Our waitress was friendly and conducted her tableside chores with the efficiency of a coffee-shop veteran.

The interior is a tired cinder-block affair with a large ceiling heater overlooking the assemblage of dejected-looking dinettes set up uniformly throughout. Don't be surprised to see a large number of single diners chowing down, or sitting at the counter or at a corner table smoking a cigarette over a flask of hot saki. You may even hear the wail of an infant erupting from somehwere inside the kitchen. Hakone is a family place with a low-key character that sets you at ease immediately.

HAMASUSHI ★★★ Price Range: Moderate to Expensive
Japanese

20030 Stevens Creek Blvd., Cupertino	A.E. − M.C. − Visa
Phone: (408) 446-4262	**Reservations Required**
Hours: Lunch: 11:30–2 pm, Mon.-Fri.	**Non-Smoking Section**
Dinner: 5–10 pm, Mon.-Sat.	**Limited Wheelchair Access**
Until 9 pm, Sunday	
Beer and Wine	**Sushi Bar**

Hamasushi has an extensive sushi bar and plenty of tatami seating for diners seeking to hide out in pure Japanese comfort. Since its opening a few years back, Hamasushi has catapulted to the top ten category, and has become a worthy competitor with Azuma, Gifu, and Kikyo.

Hamasushi's strong point lies in the service of fresh fish specialties, mostly raw, molded onto rice spiked with wasabi (green horseradish paste). From the simple sashimi to the assorted plate called Nigiri sushi, the chefs here work with seafood in a masterful fashion. Our sushi plates have always been neatly garnished, with each piece of fish expertly trimmed and very fresh.

Outside of fish, I have met with some disappointment at Hamasushi. Tempura has had its ups and downs. On my most recent visit, the crispy batter jacket was a little too greasy, leaving a visible residue on the plate. The prawns beneath the batter were, however, plump and juicy. I have always liked the Kaki Fried Oysters. The oysters have been large and fresh and the batter thick, but crispy and light. Teriyaki dishes have been prepared up to par, the pork teriyaki being the most impressive.

Service has been inconsistent, but more on the up side, than the down, on recent visits. The tableside attention has been very courteous and sharp without the aloofness I encountered on my earlier trips here.

Hamasushi is a good Japanese restaurant, one that is certainly worth a visit even if you repast on just a la carte raw fish delectables.

HARRY'S HOFBRAU ★★★   Price Range: Bargain
Steamtable Specialties

---

390 Saratoga Ave., San Jose   Cash Only
Phone: 243-0434   No Reservations
Hours: 11 am–11 pm, Sun. & Mon.   No Non-Smoking Section
         To Midnight, Tues.-Thurs.   Full Wheelchair Access
         To 1 am, Fri. & Sat.
Full Bar

Harry's Hofbrau is a gift to humanity, to those of us down on dough, cold, alone, or in need of gastronomic fuel that will propel us into the dark, lonely night.

Harry's lights burn amber bright from early lunch to the wee hours. Its steamtables are always stocked with fresh piping hot foods that won't summon forth the last greenback curled up with the threads in your pocket. The food isn't award winning cuisine; don't expect it to be. The chow is simple, hofbrau style preparations dished up hot from the steamers.

Finding a place to sit at Harry's has never been a problem. Even when it's crowded during peak feeding hours, you can still locate a table to plop your tray and tired bones. Harry's is a large, Bavarian meade hall with high Tudor ceilings and vast open aisles where those in wheelchairs can navigate. There is a long, straight, mug sliding bar where the jabberwockies in the bunch can sit, munch, and run the jaws as long as their beer holds out. And speaking of beer, Harry's pours a large assortment of imports, plus domestic brews and unusual spirits.

What I like most about Harry's Hofbrau is the grub and the affordable prices which have remained stable through our encroaching economic collapse. The foods are displayed in various trays set along a sectioned steamtable. At least two attendants are always on station to serve you entrees. Daily specials, hot plates, and sandwiches abound. With any entree you usually receive a vegetable, potatoes, or stuffing, and a salad. Extras like macaroni salad, potato salad, or any number of cold veggie concoctions, will cost you a little more. Most of them are freshly made and typical in flavor and portion.

For those who like turkey, I recommend Baked Turkey Leg. The turkey leg is a hulking, medieval club that can be eaten or used as a means of defense. I prefer to eat it. The meat is endless and cooked to a bone detaching tenderness. It is covered with a thick, tawny gravy that made the eating process a little sticky. Ask for the gravy on the side. I have sampled Cornish Game Hens on two occasions and was most pleased with the preparation. The hen was baked to a crispy exterior and served with rice and gravy. It was very meaty, especially for such a tiny bird.

After you pay, you move your food-laden tray off the line. From there you must fend for yourself. Don't be intimidated in your pursuit of a table. If it's still dirty, you may have to clean it yourself. The clean-up crew has been known to be a little harried at times and, as a result, a little forgetful. Don't fret. Remember, you didn't come here to linger. You came to eat and get back on the road.

HARVEST TIME ★★★★   Price Range: Moderate
Continental

7397 Monterey Street, Gilroy	A.E. – M.C. – Visa
Phone: 842-7575	Reservations Not Required
Hours: Lunch: 11:30–2:30 pm, M–Fri.	No Non-Smoking Section
Dinner: 5–9 pm, Mon.-Thurs.	Limited Wheelchair Access
Till 10 pm, Fri. & Sat.	
From 4 pm, Sunday	
Full Bar	

When I thought of Gilroy, I smelled garlic, I thought of K–FAT, Moose Turd Pie and Cousin Al, the professor of Blue Grass. I thought of The Garlic Festival. When I was actually in Gilroy, I thought of the quickest route out of town. I never for the life of me thought of fine cuisine. Not until now. Not until I had dinner at the Harvest Time Restaurant.

The Harvest Time has tremendous style that will pick you up and cradle you in its arms. The building itself has been around for nearly 100 years and reeks with historic charm. The interior is seasoned and elbowed smooth with tall ceilings, and one of the best beer drinking bars this side of the fault line. The decor is cowboy elegant, highlighted by two crystal chandeliers that hang in stark repose at the ceiling. Of course, vestiges of the steakhouse remain, but the people who now come here no longer hanker after bloody cuts of red meat. They are taking to the chef's fine cuisine and are glad they did. The Harvest Time is a source of pride for Gilroy and bespeaks a new culinary era moving into this stubborn South Bay appendage.

One of the most savory attractions of the Harvest Time is reasonable prices for top notch continental cuisine. Friendly price tags couple harmoniously with generous portions and fully complete dinners. A meal here includes soup du jour, tossed green salad, and ice cream or sherbet.

For those who admire top line milk fed veal, your desire will be sated by any one of Harvest Time's veal specialties. One of the best and one of the simplest veal preparations here is the traditional Wiener Schnitzel. The chef creates a masterpiece of utter simplicity in both flavor and texture, the focal point being the milky, tender veal. Two cutlets were delivered to the table still sizzling from the pan with a garnish of fresh lemon wedges and parsley.

The other veal dish we sampled was the Veal Escalope "Mascotte". It displayed several veal scallops delicately sauteed to preserve the milk fed consistency. They were finished with a demi-glace with wine and herbs for additional flavor. Mushrooms and Artichokes were also applied topside, casting yet another dimension to this veal specialty.

One of the chef's prize deliveries is Rack of Lamb "Persillade". Like this veal, the lamb meat was of top quality. The flavor was rich and deep and laced the mouth with juice. At Harvest Time, the rack is pre-cut into chops, served decoratively one on top of the other. The meat was roasted to order and came out precisely to our specifications. Flavoring the lamb was a mixture of mustard, garlic and parsley. The pungency of the garlic was most pervasive, permeating every pore of the lamb down to the last, tender morsel clinging to the dainty finger handy bones.

Forego the sherbet or ice cream for dessert and ask for the chef's unlisted specialty, Salzburger Nockerl. This is an Austrian souffle served without heavy sauces. It comes only with a thin dusting of powdered sugar which is the appropriate amount of sweetness for the fluffy eggs that embody this delightful souffle.

Service at the Harvest Time was truly memorable. Our waitress knew the food she was serving and knew it well. She answered all our questions with complete detailed descriptions. Not only did she answer questions, but she guided us to the best items on the menu, explaining the sauces and the cuts of meat all the way. In addition to knowledge-able waitresses, the chef is known to come around and greet his guests and may even sit down for a brief chat. The bartenders, too, are characters straight from the pages of a Steinbeck Novel. Some have been around for many decades.

HENRY'S ★★
Chinese

Price Range: Bargain

1865 West San Carlos St., San Jose
Phone: 295-2540
Hours: 4:30 pm–11:30 pm, Tues.-
        Thurs. & Sun.
        4:30 pm–1 am, Fri. & Sat.
Beer

Cash Only
No Reservations
No Non-Smoking Section
No Wheelchair Access

The first time I tasted Henry's Chinese food, I was at a birthday party at which a guest had brought a batch of fried shrimp with a special hot mustard – the kind Ralph Cramden wooed Alice with at the corner Chinese restaurant.

"Did you make these?" I asked. "No. I got them at Henry's on San Carlos." I couldn't believe it. My only lasting recollection of Henry's was of an old, worn-out storefront with a broken red neon sign, spelling out CHOP SUEY in big letters.

What I didn't know about Henry's is that it has been in operation for 34 years. Since 1948, Henry's has remained continually open. But from the outside it looks closed. I never went there – until I tasted those fried shrimp that night.

The first rule of thumb I learned at Henry's was not to expect gourmet Chinese food. This place is strictly food-to-go. It's a 1950s-style Chinese restaurant, a throwback to the time when Cantonese food was the only chow mein in town. What I like about Henry's is its unpretentious dedication to preserving the way it was. No tricks, no creative departures, just basic, eat-and-run Chinese food.

For starters, we ordered those delicious, batter-fried shrimp and a plate of egg roll. What I like most about the shrimp is the soft, puffy consistency of the fried batter. The shrimps remain moist through the deep-fry process.

The egg roll is very large. Each egg-dough wrap is stuffed with a crunchy bean-sprout mixture that falls out the sides after the first bite. Both the egg roll and the shrimp are greatly enhanced when dipped in Henry's special hot mustard and ketchup.

The unanimous favorite of the dinner table was the pork fried rice. The cooked texture of the wok-fried rice is firm yet gelatinous, with a steamy, pork flavor. Long strings of fried egg yolk and green onion fortify the flavor and add an appetizing splash of color.

Henry's sweet and sour pork is considered a specialty of the house. It is a true take-home variety. Fried pork nuggets are blended with a distilled sweet and sour sauce neither corn starch-thick nor bright cherry red.

For chow mein, we went with the hostess' suggestion, Henry's Special. A mound of starch-glazed bean sprouts are toss-fried with mushrooms and sundry bits of meat and shrimp. Eaten hot from the wok, this dish was adequate. But when it cooled, the special quickly congealed into a gooey mass of sprouts and veggies.

To earn your wings as a true San Josean, it should be necessary to dine at Henry's at least once. This place is thriving in South Bay history. The food may not be the best, but it will fill you with a bellyful of nostalgia.

HENRY'S HI-LIFE ★★★★　　　　　　　Price Range: Moderate
Steak / BBQ

---

301 West St. John St., San Jose	Visa
Phone: 295-5414	No Reservations
Hours: 5–10 pm, Daily	No Non-Smoking Section
Full Bar	Clumsy Wheelchair Access

Anchored near the fringe of San Jose's downtown renaissance, there stands a stubborn steakery and bar that clings to a rich and illustrious past. From the port-side windows of the ultra-modern bank towers, besuited businessmen can still glimpse the tantalizing trails of smoke puffing from good ol' Henry's Hi-Life.

This time worn, clapboarded chunk of history belongs to a rare species of restaurant which have become legendary in many cities throughout the United States. For more than 40 years, Henry's has been San Jose's special little joint where locals can tip back a few at the bar and grab a great steak at a reasonable tariff.

Henry's charm certainly transcends its quality steaks. The building itself is an endangered original; at one time, way back, it was a hotel. Today, easy access to Henry's has been cut off by the Julian downtown connector, leaving only a few side streets from which to reach it. This type of back street accessibility has only enriched Henry's endearing mystique.

The highlight of the Hi-Life is unequivocally steak, primarily the New York and the Top Sirloin. The sirloin is doubtless the larger of the two cuts; however, it lacks the tenderness of the New Yorker. If you've never been to Henry's, by all means go with the New York. This quality cut is served at an almost unreasonable thickness here. It took several passes with a sharp knife to cut clean through this cowboy-sized steak. My guest and I were amazed at the large, juice-dripping slabs of red meat speared on our forks after each cutting. Each mouthful delivered a rush of pure beef and smoke flavor that left us chewing longer than normal.

All orders are served with a common dinner green with your choice of dressing. Neither the lettuce nor the dressing was particularly memorable. Also included are an amply buttered baked potato and endless baskets of butter-soaked garlic toast. Breaking from the carbohydrate parade, we ordered a side of sauteed mushrooms. What a mistake! Sorry, Henry, these mushrooms were horrible. What looked like lawn variety mushrooms were swimming in a dark, brackish juice that was too tasteless and watery to assist the mushrooms back to life.

We also tasted an order of ribs, and I'd say ribs would be my second choice here. Each bone was packed with pleasantly tough pork meat sizzled to a smoky flavor. On a few of the ribs, I did detect a bit too much fat, but the fat did not detract from the taste.

Service at Henry's seems hand-picked to fit into the ambiance of the restaurant. Our waitresses were efficient and full of peppy discussion about life at Henry's and its unusual clientele. We were very entertained.

Henry's Hi-Life is a unique operation and shouldn't be missed by any of San Jose's residents. It is one of those good food classics alive with local history.

THE HUNGRY TIGER ★★★   Price Range: Expensive
Seafood: Lobster

1010 Saratoga-Sunnyvale Rd., Sunnyvale	A.E. − M.C. − Visa
Phone: 733-6000	Reservations Recomm.
Hours: Lunch: 11:30−2 pm, Mon.-Fri.	No Non-Smoking Section
Dinner: 4−10 pm, Sun.-Thurs.	Wheelchair Access
Till 11 pm, Fri. & Sat.	
Full Bar	Entertainment − Dancing

Against my better judgment, I was tempted into trying The Hungry Tiger by an aviation buff who eats here because the creators were fliers for the Allied Forces during World War II. But patriotism is not one of the factors that draws me to a restaurant. In this case, however, patriotism and dining proved deliciously compatible.

The exterior of this particular Hungry Tiger, startingly unique when first built, remains an intriguing design today. Massive tiers of barnwood jutt from the Earth like waves of wood. Once inside, you are swallowed by an interior of subterranean elegance. Wood prevails. Flickering lamps provided minimal lighting, though enough to navigate the pathways and steps.

For those hankering for red meat, don't come here. The Hungry Tiger built its name on seafood, primarily shellfish, and if you want fish, you won't be disappointed. Before taking a table in the main dining room, we stopped off at the Tiger's famous oyster bar. Here, we enjoyed three appetizers. First was an icy plate of freshly shucked littleneck clams on the half shell. The mollusks were indeed fresh, indicated by a firm but tender texture and a sweet, sea flavor. For those not up to slurping raw clams, the cooked Clams Casino proved to be an appetizing alternative. Prepared in front of you by the oyster-bar chef, the clams' freshness is sealed in by a seductive mixture of breadcrumbs, garlic, lemon and bacon, then baked until bubbling hot.

Probably the most celebrated entree at The Hungry Tiger is the highly regarded Live Whole Main Lobster. As you pass from oyster bar to dining room, you can see them skipping along the bottom of a large aquarium. When the music in the lounge started, these creatures fell motionless as though tranquilized by the lively tunes. Nevertheless, not even James Beard could argue that the lobsters here are not fresh. They are taken straight from the tank to the cauldron. We received a large, deep-red, shelled crustacean and a plate of cracking tools. Our first task was to break into the claws, digging out the moist inner meat. The real treat to eating whole lobster awaits in the curled tail section. When fresh like this, the meat of the tail is unforgettably moist and supple and rich with creamy sweetness that frozen or even fresh-frozen lobster cannot purvey. Drawn butter is provided, but don't be afraid to ask for more.

The next shellfish specialty at The Hungry Tiger is the Alaskan King Crab legs. On certain nights, the price for crab legs may dip. Economy nights are worth watching for. The Hungry Tiger doesn't fool around when serving up their crab legs. A virtual chorus line of legs were stacked like red logs on a large platter, claws and all. Unfortunately, the meat in the claws was somewhat dry. The meat connected to the ribbed interior of the long legs, however, were far from being dry. The leg meat was succulent and smooth.

As stated earlier, red meat is not worth ordering here. Though they can grill a steak, their main thrust is fish. We learned the hard way by ordering one of the daily specials, Scallops and Beef Brochette Combination. The scallops were tender plugs of fish wrapped in bacon and topped with a light cream sauce that enhanced the flavor of the scallop and the smokiness of the bacon. This side of the combination was enjoyable. The red meat side was pitiful. The beef had an old flavor and a vinegary aftertaste. Though red in the middle, the segments of meat chewed tough and juiceless.

The Hungry Tiger is a quality restaurant for shellfish and other oyster-bar specialties. You can't go wrong if you stick to the sea here.

IDA'S FIRESIDE INN ★   Price Range: Moderate
Continental / Seafood

2152 South First St., San Jose   A.E. — M.C. — Visa
Phone: 297-4831   Reservations Accepted
Hours: Lunch: 11–4 pm, Mon.–Fri.   No Non-Smoking Section
         Dinner: 5–11 pm, Sun.–Thurs.   Limited Wheelchair Access
         Till Midnight, Fri. & Sat.
Full Bar   Entertainment

Ida's Fireside Inn used to be one of San Jose's most beloved restaurants, a pioneer on Monterey Road with tremendous local color and tradition. Not long ago, however, a change occurred that white-washed the charm from this grand ol' restaurant, reducing it to just another mediocre establishment.

My first visit here since the renovation was a total disappointment. We sampled five dinners that night and only the prime rib was halfway decent. Realizing that it could have been an off night, I made a return visit — which was equally disappointing.

For those who remember Ida's way back when, dispel all of those memories. Though Ida's is in the same location, the interior is completely changed, except for a few antique odds and ends, like a beautiful old buffet that clashes with the ersatz appearance of the dining room. For non-smokers, Ida's is to be avoided at all costs. Atrocious ventilation.

To give credit where credit is due, Ida's is not without merit. The management bills itself as "The showplace of the lobster." You can see these monstrous crustaceans skipping along the bottom of a tank located in the dining room. The owners here buy only the best and the biggest whole Maine lobsters. They are boiled alive and served au natural. The lobster is sweet, succulent and plentiful, especially in their huge claws where the meat is a rare delicacy.

Outside of the lobster, you are looking for trouble at Ida's. The menu is expansive and long-winded, listing dishes from both a gourmet and continental ledger as well as many red-meat broiler items. Ida's deceiving plum is the service of huge portions at so-called reasonable prices. It is my staunch opinion that reasonable prices and big portions are never compensation for inferior food.

On this latest visit we ordered four entrees, beginning with the Scallops Saute Bonne Femme. I must say, the scallops in this dish were large, succulent and sweet. Ordered alone, it would have been an excellent dish. Unfortunately, the chef adhered to the philosophy of big portions and buried the scallops from view under a sticky, fondue-glutinous mixture. The style "bonne femme" calls for a sauce thickened with a paste of butter and flour. This sauce was burdened with a heavy application of butter and was so pasty it hung off the fork and was difficult to swallow.

For a second time, we ordered the double French lamb chops. The first visit, the chops were over-cooked and much too fatty. This visit, the chops were charbroiled accurately, but again, much too fatty. Just to get to the meat, we first had to cut away a thick rind of blackened fat that left a reduced portion of lamb. The remaining meat was overly marbled with more fat.

Ida's does prepare steaks with some aptitude. I was pleased to find a giant broiled porterhouse and a generous rib-eye steak to be quality cuts of beef.

It's too bad the good news runs short at Ida's. We met with another gastronomic holocaust when we ordered the Veal Oscar. The massive portion was heavily breaded and covered with chunks of crabmeat and spears of over-cooked, mushy asparagus. Obliterating this hill of food was a pasty-thick, tasteless white sauce that congealed much too quickly.

Service was hit-and-miss: slow and apathetic on my first visit, but well executed on my second. Our waiter was extremely attentive and went out of his way to assist us.

Like any restaurant, Ida's is not without potential. I happen to believe, however, that the kitchen is geared for the lobster and has forgotten to learn the basic recipes for certain continental dishes.

INAKA ★★   Price Range: Moderate
Japanese

5487 Snell Road, San Jose   M.C. − Visa − No Checks
Phone: 227-6863   Reservations Taken
Hours: 11 am−9 pm, Tues.−Fri.   No Non-Smoking Section
        From 4 pm, Sat. & Sun.   Wheelchair Accessible
Beer and Saki

Inaka offers fairly decent Japanese food at fairly decent prices. If you want a light meal with depth and flavor and you don't want to burn the petrol to drive into town from South San Jose, this storefront eatery will suffice. You can find a reduced selection of *sushi* (a boon for this area), adequate teriyaki and equally adequate tempura with a few creative flairs and interesting wrinkles for the adventurous.

On my latest visit, we started with a serving of Teka Maki. Molded rice and strips of raw tuna were wrapped tightly in seaweed, the color and texture of black snake skin. The seaweed wrap was tough to penetrate with a sharp incisor, though once through it and into the soft rice and fish, the taste proved pure and clean. Hot mustard and soy sauce accompany for added excitement.

For tuna purists, plain *sashimi* has run the measure stick from being sea-fresh, firm-bodied and rich-tasting, to mushy, pink and flavorless. Quality here depends greatly on season, catch and time of delivery. Ask the waitress for the lowdown. Depending on her mood, she will let you know when to order it and when to avoid it.

All complete dinners include miso, a small dish of *tsukemono,* marinated cabbage with a flash of pepper hotness, and a crisp green salad streaked with a piquant Japanese-style dressing.

Our first entree was *kushiyaki.* Served on a platter were three long skewers of beef chunks, layers of onion and bell pepper and zucchini. The charbroiled beef was rich with charcoal flavor, though chewy and tough to swallow. What killed this dish was the gluey teriyaki sauce that covered the skewers. It was too sweet and too thick. *Kushiyaki* also advertises shrimp along with the beef. Present were only two small shrimp curled into navels at the top of the skewers.

But don't despair. The *tonkatsu* was pretty good. Strips of pork meat were breaded and deep-fried until crisp. The breading adhered into a light, crumbly jacket with little grease residue. On the side was a provocative *katsu* sauce for dipping. It is a thickish blend of soy and ginger.

I sometimes like to order *gyoza* as an appetizer. Thin pastry envelopes are stuffed with a spicy ground pork then steam-fried. The flavor is garlic spicy and has a tendency to erupt later in the evening; the taste sensation, however, is worth the intestinal hoopla.

Service at Inaka is usually slow and aloof, the result of poor timing. The waitresses have yet to learn when to bring the check at the end of the dinner, when to take away plates, when to check at mid-meal. Despite their failings, their attitude remains amiable, innocent and sweet.

INDIA JOZE ★★★
Far Eastern Cuisine

Price Range: Moderate

1001 Center, Santa Cruz
Phone: (408) 427-3554
Hours: Lunch: 11–2:30 pm, Tu.–Sun.
       Dinner: 5:30–10 pm, Tu.–Sun.
Beer and Wine

Master Card – Visa
No Reservations
No Non-Smoking Section
Limited Wheelchair Access

India Joze has recently remodeled its location on Center Street. The new decor sports a nice paint job, original art, maintaining a Santa Cruz casual atmosphere. There are accents of elegance now, a far cry from India Joze's beginnings on Seabright Avenue.

Yes, things have changed at India Joze. The atmosphere is nice now and the Far Eastern exotic cuisine maintains its alluring quality. Unfortunately, the service has also changed. The waiters seem totally uninvolved with the patron and have, on two separate occasions, ignored their guests completely. There is a new dining room to the rear of the restaurant where serious diners are seated. This was seemingly included to filter out the moneyless crowd who come in to sip tea and eat nothing. Once in this room, it has been the experience of many that you are forgotten, swallowed up in a vacuum. Totally unacceptable. Even when I called India Joze to get some information, the host on two occasions was testy, obnoxious, and, in my opinion, flatulent with his own self worth.

When it comes to the cuisine at India Joze, it continues to dazzle my palate and send me off into orbits of culinary pleasure. I term the cuisine Far Eastern exotica because it involves several cuisines, including Indonesian, and East Indian. One of my favorite dishes is Sate Daging. Tender beef is marinated with fresh ginger and caraway and charcoal broiled to perfection. The meat is skewered and covered with a thick, mildly sweet peanut and coconut milk sauce.

India Joze is well known for his fiery curries and his unique wok frying procedures. On one visit, I had fresh crab meat in a coconut curry pungent with aromatic spices. The curry was spicy hot, though did not sear away the flavor of the crab. I have also sampled chicken curry; one sampling was extremely hot, so hot I nearly gagged. A second time, the fire was pleasantly tempered.

India Joze is a master at what he does. I classify his culinary work as pure innovation. His purpose is to stimulate the tastebuds, to help the average diner transcend the normal boundaries of the dining experience. I recall John Askins' (columnist for the San Jose Mercury News) article on India Joze. He made his dining experience here seem like a fantasy, an adventure into the realms of exotic cuisine. Maybe, you could soar, too. As long as you get a waiter to take your order.

JALISCO'S ★★★   Price Range: Bargain
Mexican

1536 West San Carlos St., San Jose   Cash Only
Phone: 295-3740   No Reservations
Hours: 11–10 pm, Mon.–Thurs.   No Non-Smoking Section
        Till 11 pm, Fri. & Sat.   Limited Wheelchair Access
        Till 9 pm, Sunday

Jalisco's is the perennial hole-in-the-wall Mexican eatery. To many, it is the only place to really chow down on home-style Mexican favorites. My general opinion of the food remains pretty much the same. It is consistently good, but not excellent. Prices, though, are very reasonable and business hours run throughout the day and night.

The restaurant is still a damp, dingy scene after all these years. From the outside, it appears abandoned. The anti-glare coating on the windows gives the exterior a weird, uninhabited aura. The inside is unkempt and eroding. When it rains, the ceiling may leak. Watch your step. If you want to be comfortable here, think comfortable and be sure to nestle your posterior at one of the many black booths.

Jalisco's is famous for its generous chip-and-salsa policy. You can have as many chips as you want. As for the salsa, you fetch your own from large containers set up on the kitchen counter. There are two salsas: verde and the basic red chili. Both will burn your lips and bring beads of moisture to your brow.

The main thrust of Jalisco's is to serve quick, tortilla-wrapped tasties. Though burritos, tacos and tamales are the main focus, you can still order full-fledged dinners that include large helpings of rice and melted, cheese-matted beans.

For something different, the taco or *burrito asado,* provide some interest. The main ingredient is grilled beef strips, chopped and rolled in a tortilla. I suggest the *taco asado.* The steak was wrapped into a corn tortilla, then pan-fried until the exterior was crisp. It is served with a coarse guacamole lumped with pure chunks of fresh avocado.

Jalisco's simmers up a spicy-hot batch of Chile Colorado. Tender beef chunks are stewed in a deep, rust-red chile sauce. Each bite gives the mouth a pepper hot afterflash that stimulates the palate immensely.

I was less impressed with the Chile Verde. There was plenty of pork, but the flavor of the sauce did not adequately reflect the alluring flavor of green chile. It was a loose pork-flavored gravy that was smooth and cohesive but not very tasty. Nonetheless, a generous splash of green salsa infused this dish with a spicy lift.

One of Jalisco's specialties is the tamale. They are homemade and always large and filling. I was particularly impressed with the texture and deep corn flavor of the masa. This cornmeal mash surrounds a large center of stringed meat in a spicy red sauce. A liquidy, enchilada style gravy is applied topside before serving.

There is no table service at Jalisco's. You order at the counter and wait for your number to be called. When busy, there can be some congestion at the counter. Be patient, it doesn't take long to get your food.

Jalisco's new restaurant is located at 4485 Stevens Creek Boulevard, Santa Clara, telephone 249-7278.

JASMINE ★★★   Price Range: Moderate
Chinese

---

20 South Plaza, Suite 204, Los Gatos	**Master Card — Visa**
Phone: (408) 395-2373	**Reservations for**
Hours: 11 am–9 pm, Mon.–Fri.	**Large Parties**
From Noon, Saturday	**Non-Smoking Section**
	Limited Wheelchair Access

The hearts and palates of Chinese food-loving Los Gatans are being wooed by the Lyndon Plaza insert, Jasmine. Though the title conjures visions of tranqil repose, the food served here is fiery and quite combustible. The order of the wok is Hunan-Szechwan cuisine.

In general, the dishes I have sampled displayed a precise, methodic culinary workmanship. Vegetables were cut to exact proportions. Meats were sliced, scalloped, and shredded to traditional size standards. Sauces were evenly crafted and did not rely on cornstarch for consistency. They were natural and glazy. Though the dishes were slightly oily, their distinct and direct flavors bespoke a chef well versed in the dishes emanating from the pepper producing regions of Mainland China. One recent problem I have noticed, however, is a much too liberal hand with onions. They came in practically every dish we ordered.

A consistent favorite of mine is the Pon Pon Chicken Salad. Julienne of boned chicken covered a bed of shredded iceburg lettuce. The temperature of this dish is cool, forming an interesting juxtaposition to the peppery sauce dressing the top.

Yu Shiang Pork is a smooth, spicy dish of shredded pork tenderloin and long, strings of fresh zucchini. The spicy temperature of the brown sauce was slightly blazing, yet it did not burn the buds.

Kung Pao Shrimp was a unique version of this ever popular dish. Juicy. oversized shrimp were quick fried in a pasty sauce that bonded to the shrimp and did not form a residue at the bottom of the plate. The flavor was pepper spicy and well defined by a deep charcoal smokiness. Peanuts and roasted peppers were sparingly added.

If Jasmine can hang in there, I believe it will compete with the heavy weight Szechwan/Hunan restaurants in the area. It is in the process of being discovered.

JERSEY'S ★★
Cheesesteaks

Price Range: Bargain

1781 Winchester Blvd., Campbell	Cash Only
Phone: (408) 374-1415	No Reservations
Hours: 11:30 am–Mid., Mon.-Sat.	No Non-Smoking Section
Noon–8 pm, Sunday	Limited Wheelchair Access
Pub	

Jersey's is a rousing, beer swilling tavern where darts fly, where burly discussion continues endlessly, where the authentic Jersey cheesesteak is griddled up in coarse, steamy fashion.

The atmosphere is well defined by the veteran rugby players who shoulder into this shopping center slot to nourish their racked bodies on cheesesteaks and limber their arms bending elbows with mugs of ice cold brew. One of the owners actually plays ball with the South Bay's premiere rugby team, The Seahawks. He has been known to assist his teammates financially to take them over to Australia, New Zealand, and other rugby countries where they compete annually.

The Jersey cheesesteak is a large, hefty sandwich composed of thin slices of griddle-fried steak, packed with sauteed onions, and cheese that melts down to a creamy liquid. The taste is just what you'd want, with a cold beer along side. The beef and cheese harmonize on all levels with the onion casting a slight spicy interest. Many variations exist, including the popular pizza steak. This is an Italian version of the cheesesteak with tomato sauce and lots of cheese.

JOSE'S ★★★★
Cuban

Price Range: Moderate

2275 El Camino Real, Palo Alto	Master Card – Visa
Phone: 326-6522	Reservations for 5 or more
Hours: Lunch: 11–2 pm, Mon.-Fri.	No Non-Smoking Section
Dinner: 5:30–10 pm, Sun &	Wheelchair Access
Tues.-Thurs.	
Till 11 pm, Fri. & Sat.	

Jose prides himself on being innovative and serving his patrons wholeheartedly. Not only does he serve native Cuban dishes, but he bakes pizza, both Cuban and Argentinean, smoked barbecued meats, empanadas, burritos, paella and enchiladas. Because the menu is compact and manageable, Jose's crew of cooks can specialize comfortably in all the dishes they concoct.

At Jose's, there are no warm-up appetizers or pre-entree goodies. You take the plunge right off the bat.

When our entrees arrived, they came all at once. Our table looked like a buffet-spread at a Cuban picnic. Straight away, we dug into the Empanada. Jose's empanada must be reckoned with as a full entree item because it certainly will engage the heartiest of appetites. A large, swollen pie of pastry crust reared up in a sizzling ramekin. Once through the golden-brown outer crust we discovered a steaming mass of juicy, boneless white meat of chicken, melted cheese, mushrooms, olives and raisins. It shimmered in a mild sauce with only a suggestion of strong spice. Very filling.

Jose's carne asada was different. Nearly hanging over the lip of the plate was a thick cut of hearty roast beef imbued with the distinctive smack of roasted garlic. The garlic flavor blended with the natural juice of the meat, making bread sopping a worthwhile effort. It was served with the Cuban staples, black beans and rice with the festive addition of plantain (banana).

After clearing off a few of the plates, we comfortably engaged ourselves with an order of Smoked Duck. The best parts of a meaty whole duckling had been smoked long until every morsel of dark meat was penetrated with a sensuous woodsy essence. The skin had been brushed with a nearly indiscernible sweet glaze, then roasted to a fatless crisp. It had a distant similarity to Tea Smoked Duck.

Our final offering was an Argentinean pizza. We ordered the Corrientes which includes ham, pork and salami. The crust to this unique pie was superb. It was made from sourdough and when fresh from the oven had a hot, yeasty, baked-bread quality with a soft, airy pliability. Topping this hefty medium pizza was a mild tomato sauce, rich dairy-fresh cheese and chunks of meat. The ham and salami took a back seat to the large pieces of spiced pork applied generously throughout. Jose also makes a Cuban Pizza with a wheat-germ crust. Personally, I prefer the Argentinean-style for its superior crust.

After a brief interlude, we ordered dessert. Jose put out two native Cuban sweet dishes that were, like everything else, impressive. We had Flan, a rich, creamy egg custard mixed with a homemade carmel sauce, and Arroz con leche – a very sweet, milky-smooth rice pudding. Probably the only thing I didn't like was Jose's coffee. It was watery and had a burnt taste.

For being probably the only Cuban restaurant in the Santa Clara Valley, Jose represents his ethnic origin with culinary vigor. This restaurant is one of those discovery places that has tremendous magnetic appeal. Jose's is a pure people pleaser.

KIKYO ★★★★
Japanese

1187-B Saratoga-Sunnyvale Rd., San Jose	Master Card — Visa
Phone: 725-1749	Reservations Taken
Hours: Lunch: 11:30–2 pm, M–Sat.	Uncomfortable Non-
Dinner: 5–10 pm, Mon.–Sat.	Smoking Section
Beer — Sushi Bar	Limited Wheelchair Access

Kikyo has been in business only a little while, and I have a strong haunch that it is going to give Azuma, Gifu and the other top-notch Japanese restaurants in the area a run for their *sushi.* Native dishes are authentically prepared and abundantly served in a novel Japanese-style setting that inspire the appetite to soar beyond its normal boundaries.

Linked to a small shopping center, Kikyo lies beneath a high A-framed ceiling where rows of tables and chairs form a neat Japanese dinner hall. Dividers of unvarnished blond wood and *shoii* create a carpenter shop-clean milieu. Angles are straight and austere and cleanliness is vigilantly maintained. Tables are closely set and the patron chatter is constant, but not distracting.

For those who require a non-smoking section, I suggest you not sit in Kikyo's non-smoking area. The room is miserably cramped even though it is devoid of second-hand smoke. The main dining room is infinitely more comfortable and adequately ventilated.

Kikyo has one of the largest, most spacious *sushi* bars I have seen. You sit front and center to the master chef who is constantly manipulating, slicing and arranging his masterful raw fish specialties. We sampled a plate of Mixed Nigiri Sushi. Displayed on a raised tray was a variety of raw and steamed fish, including tuna and prawns, set neatly onto rice molds spiked with wasabi.

After perusing the menu, we ordered a Seafood Salad. Raw oysters, steamed prawns, and scallops encircled a mound of thinly sliced cucumbers. The seafood was dressed with a rangy, rice vinegar mixture that was subtle enough not to mask the fresh flavor of the fish.

Following the customary bowl of *miso* (soup) and a lettuce salad with an uncommon, peanutty dressing, we were served a plate of chicken teriyaki in combination with a plate of *sashimi* and a plate of pork *katsu.* Portions at Kikyo are overly generous for any size appetite.

The chicken teriyaki was sliced into long, meaty strips with skin still connected, then char-broiled with a teriyaki glaze. The meat came out juicy and firm with the grill flavor cutting the sharp sweetness of the teriyaki.

I was most impressed by the freshness of the *sashimi* (raw tuna). Several silky wedges of tuna were meticulously fileted and situated in a very neat, eye-appealing formation. A large dollop of wasabi and a cruet of soy sauce accompany this course.

The pork *katsu* reminded me of an Italian veal cutlet without the olive oil and garlic. Tender pork steak was dipped in a thick batter then deep-fried to a golden crunchy texture. The meat remained juicy and filled with natural pork flavor and did not leave an oil slick on the plate or on the fingers. It was served with a gingery *katsu* dipping sauce.

Our last entree was the dish that brought the color to my pallid cheeks *yose nabe*. Before it was delivered, our waitress set up a strange looking gas rig on our table. After only minutes, she returned with a large, black iron kettle sloshing with a steaming brew of seafood and vegetables in a natural fish broth. Floating in the liquid were clams in shell, crab legs in shell, slices of scallop, chunks of white fish, oysters (added raw just before serving), egg, chard, onions, scallions, clear vermicelli, and various and sundry nutritious additions. The gas rig kept the *yose nabe* simmering through the course.

I was thoroughly pleased with Kikyo's operation. The food was excellent, the service efficient and friendly, and the prices in keeping with the quality and portion of the food.

KOKESHI ★★★
Japanese

Price Range: Moderate

1306 Saratoga Ave. in the Lucky Plaza, San Jose	Master Card — Visa
Phone: 249-6020	Reservations Taken
Hours: Lunch: 11:30–2 pm, M–Fri.	Non-Smoking Section
Dinner: 5:30–9:30 pm, M–Sat.	Upon Request
Beer and Saki	Clumsy Wheelchair Access

Kokeshi is a deep rectangular insert, hidden away at the tail end of a shopping center on Saratoga Avenue. The interior is a tight squeeze. If you have big shoulders, there is the chance you will knock over a shoji screen or a Kirin Beer sign. Though small, the place is still cozy with a tranquil setting that is perfect for long, quiet conversations.

If you call ahead, you can reserve one of three tatami style tables, secluded in the back.

For a quick meal when time is short, you can nestle your posterior on a stool lined up at a sushi bar. From here you can watch the chef slice and jockey and fry his various dishes, including a moderate selection of raw fish delectables. Service at the sushi bar is direct and fast with little or no waste of time.

When I ate at Kokeshi, my guest and I had a little extra time, so we reserved a tatami room where we removed our shoes for the full comfort of this arrangement. It was very peaceful and quiet.

Kokeshi offers a special lunch called the Bento. This item consists of several chef specialties served in a partitioned lacquer black Japanese lunch box. We had grilled strips of pickled beef, steamed eggrolls, tempura shrimp and vegetables, and two pieces of crispy fried chicken, a meaty leg and a wing. In addition, there was an attractively presented coil of sashimi (raw tuna), and a few chop stick-style cold vegetable salads. The Bento lunch is served with miso (soup), pickled vegetables, and green tea.

On several occasions I have enjoyed a simple plate of Tempura. Most notable here was the clean, almost greaseless texture of the deep fried batter, coating the shrimp and vegetables. It was light and blonde in color with no oily aftertaste. The prawns retained their natural succulence through the frying process. The vegetables, too, cooked out to a soft, firm consistency. I particularly enjoyed the batter-coated sweet potato and mushrooms. Various semi-sweet dipping sauces accompany the tempura plate and the Bento.

Kokeshi serves four Udon (noodle) dishes. The most authentic is the Tempura Udon. It presents tempura fried shrimp afloat in a clean, fresh broth packed with tender noodles. This dish would be perfect as a cure for the common cold or a nervous strain of office claustrophobia. It is healthy, wholesome, and goes down effortlessly.

Other notable dishes at Kokeshi include Chicken Teriyaki, Ton Katsu, pork cutlet, and Shogayaki Steak, beef broiled with ginger sauce. Many sushi varieties are listed on the lunch and dinner menu. Of course, there are the raw fish selections, highlighted by Nigiri Sushi and a delicious non-fish sushi, Kappamaki, cucumbers rolled in cold rice and wrapped in seaweed.

Service at Kokeshi was efficient and fully attentive to our needs. Dishes were delivered straight from the kitchen without delay.

KOMATSU ★★★
Japanese

Price Range: Moderate

---

93 S. Central Ave., The Factory,
  Campbell
Phone: 379-3000
Hours: Lunch: 11:30–2 pm, M–Fri.
        Dinner: 5–10 pm, Mon.–Sat.
        Closed Wednesday
Beer and Sake

A.E. – M.C. – Visa
Reservations Recomm.
No Non-Smoking Section
Wheelchair Accessible

Komatsu is one of the Factory's stalwart survivors. While other restaurants said adieu and shuttered their shops in this dream location, this small Japanese restaurant kept pumping out enough sushi and tempura to pay its bills and make a decent living. Komatsu earns a great deal of respect with me. It's not the best Japanese restaurant in town, but it certainly delivers the goods on a casual night out.

Komatsu is a small restaurant. It is equipped with a few Tatami rooms that must be reserved in advance, and a short sushi bar where Chef Komatsu performs his skills, making raw fish specialties. Two of my favorites are the Nigiri Sushi and the Tekka Sushi, both utilizing freshly sliced raw fish formed onto rice molds, or wrapped in brittle seaweed.

The chicken teriyaki at Komatsu always has been a masterful rendition. The breast of chicken with skin intact is cut into bite-size strips, char-grilled, then glazed in teriyaki. The teriyaki here is not thick nor candy-sweet; it is mild, loose and thoughtfully crafted.

Another dish I like here is the Korean-style beef dish, *yakiniku*. Beef sirloin again is cut into thin strips and broiled. The seasoning here is slightly hot and spicy with a strong sesame-seed flavor. The meat portion is large and filling.

Komatsu's menu is somewhat limited, but it does list a few favorite tempura combinations worth a sampling. A low-calorie selection would be tempura and *sashimi*. With this plate, we received a varied assortment of tempura prawns and vegetables with a side of fresh, neatly sliced *sashimi* (raw tuna). This dish is a bit pricy due to the seasonal availability of tuna.

Service at Komatsu is courteous in the traditional Japanese manner. Our waitress attended us with promptness, patience and a friendly demeanor.

KOREAN GARDENS ★★★   Price Range: Moderate
Korean

606 Bernardo, Sunnyvale	Master Card — Visa
Phone: 733-9535	Reservations Accepted
Hours: Lunch: 11–3 pm, Daily	No Non-Smoking Section
Dinner: 4 pm–Mid., Sun.–Thurs.	Wheelchair Access
Till 2 am, Fri. & Sat.	
	Entertainment and
Full Bar	Dancing

After a long and careful study of Korean restaurants in the South Bay, I finally discovered one that is an authentic representative of this fiery Oriental cuisine. The Korean Gardens serves Korean food exclusively.

Korean food is distinctive and highly provocative, with many of the dishes utilizing liberal doses of hot red and green pepper, garlic, onion, and other explosive ingredients. If you are not ready for the stark, spicy flavors and the unusual fresh delicacies, your first visit may be your last. For the novice, I suggest you invite a friend who knows and enjoys Korean food so that he or she can guide you through the intricate line-up of dishes.

Dinner begins with the service of three condiments. First is a plate of crispy bean sprouts and slightly cooked greens, followed by bowls of kim chee and a spicy-hot white-radish condiment powered with crushed hot-red peppers and garlic. Before proceeding, it is necessary to know that kim chee is the trademark of Korean food. Like chutney, its recipe may vary from household to household. The basic ingredients include pickled Chinese cabbage, hot red pepper, garlic and other tantalizing spices. The Korean Gardens' batch is highly aromatic, with a tangy flavor that goes well with broiled meats and fish.

For an appetizer, we ordered Din Dae Duk, a pancake of beans, pork strips and vegetables. The texture of the pancake is similar to a greaseless potato pancake, only lighter in consistency and far more flavorful.

For first-timers, I highly recommend either the Bul Go Ki or Kal Bi. Of the two, I prefer the Bul Go Ki — barbecued beef that has had a long soaking in a sweet garlic-potent marinade. The slightly chewy beef comes to the table sizzling loudly atop a black skillet used to keep the meat warm throughout the meal. I like the Bul Go Ki because it is easier to eat than the Kal Bi, which presents a sheet of short ribs of beef marinated and grilled in exactly the same manner as the Bul Go Ki. The meat clings tightly to the short rib bones. We were forced to use our fingers.

Chicken Zen presents a plate of young hen hacked into small, skin-wrapped segments. They are prepared in a very mild, almost soupy marinade that is more watery sweet than deeply flavorful. The meat of the chicken is tender, but the hacked bones pose a problem. We found ourselves nibbling carefully, too aware of the bones to fully enjoy this dish.

Like most Korean restaurants, Korean Gardens offers a host of fresh fish items guaranteed to test your love for fin fare. Commonly sea dwellers like clams, oysters, crabs and abalone abound on the menu. Balancing out the common are the uncommonly seen fish items like sea urchin, skate wings, ugliest baby octopus, sea cucumber, needle and king fish. We ordered a plate of squid with hot sauce and received instead a plate of baby octopus cooked in hot sauce. This dish will alter your expectations of this tentacle-studded ink bag. The octopus is served in a large portion with tentacles, suction cups and all sauteed in an oily red-pepper sauce that brings a quick, merciless fire to the lips and mouth. The octopus was very tender and sweet, its full flavor slightly masked by the fiery sauce it was served in.

The waitresses at the Korean Gardens are still learning English. Oftentimes, the language barrier makes it difficult to relay orders correctly; hence, we received octopus instead of squid. Phoning for information other than reservations is almost impossible. Outside of this problem, our waitress and hostess were efficient and prompt in bringing our orders to the table. Almost all of our needs were met eventually.

Korean Gardens is a restaurant that will expand your understanding of Oriental food. The dishes here are authentic and not altered for the American palate. If you're prepared when you come in, you won't go home disappointed.

LA BATONVILLE ★★★★   Price Range: Expensive
French

2807 Porter, Soquel	Master Card — Visa
Phone: 476-0599	Reservations Required
Hours: Dinner: 6–9:30 pm, Mon.-Sat.	No Non-Smoking Section
Beer and Wine	Limited Wheelchair Access

The dream of fine cuisine and vintaged wines has come true for Master Chef Leth-Madsen and his wife, Elizabeth. Their restaurant, La Batonville, is the culinary toast of the breezy village of Soquel.

Chef Leth-Madsen is a true culinary artisan, a transplant from the exquisite household of Le Mouton Noir in Saratoga. He performs wonders with wholesome, garden fresh produce, choice meats and fresh seafood. The colorful, stark, visually appealing elements of Nouvelle Cuisine are embraced by Leth-Madsen and his inspiring style of French cookery. His dishes were simple and unfettered with heavy sauces and strong, overpowering seasonings. We left his restaurant well fed, yet feeling light in the stomach.

We began our meal with two appetizers, Terrine de Volaille and a special announcement of Quenelles. The terrine de volaille presented a large slice of chicken pate with a side of homemade mustard dressing. I was impressed by the soft, airy texture of the liver and pecan puree that was easily spreadable on bread. The distinctive sharpness of the liver and the nutty aftertaste of pecans was counterpoised by the light tartness of the mustard dressing, a mayonnaise of sorts.

Our quenelles were composed of salmon puree shaped like two eggs. Their consistency was foamy and full-bodied. A heavy butter and lemon sauce seasoned with fresh dill was sparingly applied over the quenelles. Both sauce and salmon puree formed a light, appetizing union which was not filling in any way.

We were impressed greatly with our salad course. A fluff of garden fresh leaf lettuce was lightly dressed with a piquant vinaigreete. Fresh roquefort cheese was crumbled over the top for an added dimension of flavor.

Our first entree was Filet d'Agneau served with mustard sauce. An attractive overlay of lamb tenderloin slices occupied center plate. The meat was very tender with a blush pink center on each slice to indicate the perfect degree of doneness. A tangy, French mustard sauce blended with the natural juice of the lamb was poured over the meat slices. Arranged around the lamb was a garni of fresh, crisp snow peas, sauteed chard, and several potato puffs.

Our second entree selection was another red meat dish, Tournedos a la Moelle, served with a sauce Bordelaise. One, very plump, fat-trimmed filet of beef tenderloin was broiled to a juicy, red midsection. It was finished with a glistening red wine sauce seasoned with shallots, beef marrow, and fresh herbs. The sauce and the tender beef worked well in each other's company. I found the flavors to be refined, yet vocal in taste and robustness. The meat was garnished with fresh watercress. Also accompanying the meat were snow peas, potatoes, and chard.

Dessert plunged us into caloric bliss. We were presented with one of the most delicious apricot cakes we have tasted in many years. Several layers of freshly baked genoise (sponge cake) were divided by layers of fresh, fragrant apricot preserve. Each mouthful was entertained with at least one, substantial piece of apricot fruit. The cake texture was moist and soaked through with apricot juice. Topping this delightful creation was a crown of chocolate shavings, the flavor of which provided confectioner's intrigue to this cake.

Our dessert course was followed up by a plate of fresh, assorted cheeses (brie, goat, roquefort) and fresh kiwi fruit and apple slices. For those of you who want to forego the typical dessert offerings, cheese and fruit and a glass of vintaged port is a perfect way to cap off an evening.

Service complimented the quality of the cuisine and the tranquility of the environment. Elizabeth Leth-Madsen greets all of her guests, took certain orders, and even served an occasional dish. Our regular waiter was a careful tableside manager who was totally sincere in his service. Even the chef made his way out of his kitchen and into the dining room where he spoke to his guests and took comments about his food.

La Batonville inhabits a small cottage surrounded by a gravel path. The interior is quaint and homey with a quiet tranquility implicit in the ambiance. Strains of classical music are piped in softly from hidden speakers. Tables are arranged with ample room for long elbows and romancers who desire nose to nose, candlelight conversation. Guests have a tendency to speak softly, never raising their voices or laughing in thunderous repetition. La Batonville is a gentle restaurant, a restaurant infused with kindness and consideration for all.

LA BELLE HELENE ★★★★   Price Range: Expensive
French Nouvelle Cuisine

1345 Railroad Ave., St. Helena	A.E.–M.C.–V–Diners Clb
Phone: (707) 963-1234	Reservations Recomm.
Hours: Lunch: 11:30–3:30 pm, Mon.,	Well Ventilated
Wed.-Sun.	No Wheelchair Access –
Dinner: 5–10 pm, Wed.-Mon.	[upstairs bathroom]
Closed Tuesday	
Extensive California Wine List	

La Belle Helene is in a quarry-stone country abode along Railroad Avenue in St. Helena, the heart of the wine country. The stone theme carries into the interior where it is counterbalanced by rough-hewn beams and white-washed walls. The provencial savor is heightened by straight rows of colorful prints that band the walls of the main dining room. Muted conversations and the clinking of stemware convey a sense of tranquility.

Food here is French provencial brushed with the stark elegance of Nouvelle Cuisine. We started out with chilled quail stuffed with veal and pork force meat. The delicate, dark meat of the dainty bird was not overpowered by the filling.

At La Belle Helene, soup and salad are included with every dinner. Salads are served after the entree, so we were entertained with a cream of lettuce soup as our second pre-entree course. The most notable characteristic of this soup drew from the sweet, creamy essence of the blended ingredients.

The menu changes daily here, so you may or may not find the items that we sampled on our visit. However, the dishes we did enjoy bespoke a chef who follows an impeccable manner and style of cooking. All of our entrees looked clean, fresh and natural, with an emphasis on visual arrangement, the outstanding influence of Nouvelle Cuisine. Veau Poele, ila de France was a good example of "provencial Nouvelle."

Cubed white veal tenderloin had been simmered until soft and mashable in a cream sauce tasty with wine. The portion was petite, but not unfair.

Faisane Roti Marchand deVin demonstrated the chef's provencial leanings. A meaty pheasant, roasted slowly over an even heat, was finished with a dark red-brown gravy, heavy with the stout attributes of the vintage. I found the combining of the delicate pheasant with the strong wine sauce to be surprisingly complimentary.

Our fellow fish eater had a fresh salmon and was overwhelmed with what she received. The thick, blush-pink filet was moist, but pulled in long, firm pieces. An egg-light Hollandaise dappled the top of the salmon.

Porc aux Prunaux did not share the chef's careful attention as did the aforementioned dishes. The four slices of pork tenderloin were overcooked, toothy and hard to cut. A startling sweet prune sauce, nearly ebony in color, formed a glassy pool below the pork. The combination of sweet sauce and rich pork was certainly well matched, but the overcooked meat detracted from the success of this specialty item.

After a simple butterleaf salad dressed with a plain vinegar and oil, we explored the dessert ledger. The most unusual was Pashka. A cream-cheese pudding was blended with kirsch-tasting currents and topped with a bitingly sweet raspberry sauce. It was very good. For fresh berry lovers, the raspberry tart received smiles and raised eyebrows from two of my guests. A crusty pastry bottom was spread with a layer of custard cream. Set meticulously in rows on the pastry were several unbruised, bright-red raspberries. The tartness was puckering.

La Belle Helene is a well-staffed restaurant, too. There were many waiters and each made it his mission to maintain leisure pacing throughout the meal. Our waiter was never harried and always took his time to explain wines, dishes and restaurant history.

LA CHAUMIERE ★★★★★
French

Price Range: Expensive

1314 Oean Street, Santa Cruz	A.E. – M.C. – Visa
Phone: 426-2448	Reservations Required
Hours: Lunch: 11–2 pm, Mon.-Fri.	No Non-Smoking Section–
Dinner: 6–10 pm, Tues.-Sun.	[Well Ventilated]
Wine Bar	Limited Wheelchair Access

La Chaumiere is Santa Cruz's premier French restaurant. It was established by two brothers from Marseilles who brought in a Paris trained chef, Rick Scott. Since then, the two brothers have flown the coop, while chef Scott remains at the helm in La Chaumiere's kitchen. After having sampled many dishes prepared by fine chefs in restaurants from San Francisco to San Jose, it is my opinion that chef Scott is among the best in the Bay Area. His cookery is exemplified by exactness, simplicity, and a propensity for blending fine sauces.

La Chaumiere's decor presents a restful setting, ideal for those long romantic dinners. The restaurant is situated in a high gabled building just off Highway 17. Quaint fixtures blend with the knotty-pine paneling of the walls. Linen-wrapped tables are spaced for maximum comfort and privacy. Classical music drifts from hidden speakers, instilling an appetizing calm in both the lounge and dining areas.

La Chaumiere's menu is a manageable compilation of classic and creative French recipes. In addition to the regular menu offerings, your waiter will announce gourmet specials for the day. One of those specials was a cold appetizer of scallop mousse. Fresh scallops were pureed into an airy dish with a velvety smooth texture and a deep creaminess. The mousse was served with a tart, aromatic sauce made from fresh tomato puree and sweet basil. It was crowned with cured lox and garnished with cucumber slices and onions. The combination of flavors was alluring and immediate.

For our hot appetizer, my guest and I split a full order of Bouillabaisse Marseillaise. In one word, it was magnificent, one of the most sumptuous bouillabaisses I have had in a restaurant. The fish stew was delivered in two bowls brimful and resplendent with a myriad of seafood, simmering in a masterfully concocted French bouillon with saffron. There were cherrystone clams, fresh mussels, finger lobsters in shell, scallops, shrimps, and large chunks of firm, fresh white fish. The bouillon was a very tasty fish broth with pieces of tomato, herbs, and even stewed pieces of orange peel flavoring the ambrosial liquid. The dish was finished with a drizzle of Pernod. I experienced a wave of intoxication after devouring every last speck of this expertly crafted bouillabaisse.

After a brief interlude, our entrees were delivered. Quite a bargain is the Coquelet a l'Ail, or Cornish game hen in garlic sauce. With this dish, chef Scott exhibited his keen understanding for applied-heat physics. Cornish game hens can dry out easily if not attended with care. The bird I sampled here was far from being dry. It was juicy and succulent – the meat so tender that it disengaged from the bones with a simple turn of the fork. Inside the hollow cavity of the hen was a roasted, garlic-accented stuffing. Surrounding the hen was a silky brown sauce laced with fresh herbs. Whole roasted garlic cloves encircled the plate.

Served with the Cornish game hen was julienne of carrot and a row of roasted potato slices. Both side dishes were carefully arranged and provided color harmony as well as nutritional balance.

Our next entree was the Escaloppe de Veau Romano, citron vert. Two, semi-thick medallions of milk-fed veal tenderloin were crowned with spreads of melted, aged Romano cheese, butter, and a squeeze of lime juice. A complementary milk sauce was poured carefully around the medallions. The sauce possessed the creamy flavor of the veal and aided in drawing the sharp taste of the cheese and the lime into a pleasant definition.

Also for that evening, we spooned a fine vichyssoise. The recipe for this cold soup was created by Louis Diat when he was head chef at New York City's Ritz-Carlton. Chef Scott's rendition was a tribute to the original. It was made with potatoes and the white part of leeks and blended with real cream. It came to the table topped with fresh chives and seasoned with white pepper. The consistency was perfect, the temperature lightly chilled.

Our gastronomic delirium continued through our dessert course. We were so full, we ordered only one portion of Chocolate Torte. Like our waiter said, it may look small, but it's very, very rich. A thick firm wedge of deep, chocolate puree was fluffed topside with heavy cream. Because of the richness, I held each bite on my tongue until it dissolved, filling my mouth with the total essence of chocolate.

The service at La Chaumiere was efficient from our first encounter with the hostess to our last encounter with our waiter. I was particularly impressed with his knowledge of the food he was serving. When asked about the ingredients, he was able to explain in depth. He did take a little long between courses, but nothing was ever cold from having waited under the lights.

LA FORET ★★★★★   Price Range: Expensive
Continental

21747 Bertram Road, San Jose   A.E. – M.C. – Visa
Phone: 997-3458   **Reservations Required**
Hours: 5:30–10 pm, Tues.–Sun.   **No Non-Smoking Section**
         Sunday Brunch: 10–2 pm   **Wheelchair Access**
Full Bar

The culinary policy at La Foret is to employ constant innovation while using the finest meats, fish and produce available in the market. The owner is dedicated to continued research and has traveled to some of the most renowned restaurants to study. It is not uncommon to see fresh fruit sauces or brilliant demi-glaces made from long simmered stocks. No preservatives or short cuts are used in preparing any of the dishes here.

Long romantic dinners are inspired by La Foret's interior of Old Almaden elegance. Neatly appointed tables are evenly spaced and situated along a bank of picture windows. Through them, you can view the creek bed, lush with various forms of plant life. When evening comes, the dining room ignites with the flames of tableside cooking, a talent the waiters have mastered.

I have been here on many visits and have had the opportunity to sample many of La Foret's menu specialties. To keep abreast with newly introduced dishes and cooking procedures, the menu changes from time to time. Always on the menu however, has been the Medallions of Beef Bearnaise. La Foret serves two, quality filets cut from the heart of the tenderloin. They are fired to a medium rare and covered with a tarragon deep Bearnaise.

Veal is top quality. One of the House prizes is Grenedines of Veal aux Morilles. On two occasions, I have eaten this delightful dish, receiving no less than three high rise slices of veal filet, carefully fired to retain the inherent flavor and juice. The veal was glassed in a zesty Madeira rendition with those French wild mushrooms, morels.

On a more recent visit, I have sampled a succulent slab of fully boned King salmon covered with a light, fresh raspberry sauce. The marriage of flavors was an astounding achievement.

For those who enjoy tableside fires, there are such specialties as Steak Diane, Cafe Romano, and Fried Cream for dessert.

Rarely do I hear complaints about La Foret. Many of the patrons who dine here have been thoroughly satisfied and claim to return quite often. It is apparent to me that at La Foret, the patron always comes first. This is a quality I yearn for in a restaurant.

LA HACIENDA INN ★★★   Price Range: Expensive
Continental

18840 Saratoga-Los Gatos Rd., Los Gatos	A.E. – M.C. – Visa
Phone: 354-6669	Reservations Required
Hours: Lunch: 11–3 pm, Mon.-Sat.	Non-Smoking Section –
Dinner: 3–11 pm, Daily	[Upon Request]
Sunday Brunch: 11–2:30 pm	Limited Wheelchair Access
Full Bar – Piano Bar	

The grounds surrounding La Hacienda Inn make dining out a special event. The awesome girth of the forking oaks, the blossoming flora inspire the feeling of a vacation in rustic resplendence. The interior exudes memories of high-priced dinners, rings of cigar smoke and snifters of cognac.

I do offer a warning to the wise. Weekends here are packed and you may find yourself being shuffled about like a ping-pong ball. Because they are harried, the hosts and hostesses have a tendency to lose their cordiality. Rooms fill up and window seats are hard to come by. La Hacienda Inn is a different place during the early part of the week and you might find yourself having a better time then.

Through the years, the inn's menu has remained true to its original concept. You can order from the deluxe dinner side of the menu which includes with entree, an antipasto of cold cuts, relishes, and bean salads; soup or salad; fresh ravioli, which I have always found to be overcooked and pasty, and ice cream. The prices are quite reasonable when compared to other restaurants of like caliber, and the portions, in many cases, more generous. Though the complete dinner is an acceptable path to take, I prefer to order a la carte so that I can sample some of the chef's better recipes.

We commenced with a surprisingly well-crafted dish of Linguine Convongole. The linguine noodles were rather thickish, not lithe and loose. I suggest you ask specifically that the pasta be boiled al dente; we failed to do so and the noodles came out a tad overdone. Nonetheless, they were tender enough and well covered with a lip-smacking sauce of butter, olive oil, garlic, scallions and big pieces of clam with natural broth for consistency. If it wasn't for my temperate companion, I would have made the entire meal out of this pasta dish. It was very good, a classico rendition.

With our pasta, we ordered a plate of Prawns Sauteed Bordelaise. Six, succulent gulf prawns were first dusted lightly with flour, then seared quickly under a hot broiler fire. They were finished tableside in a saute of lemon, butter and spices. The sauce was a sprightly Bordelaise that sank deep into the sweet pores of the prawns.

For salads, La Hacienda Inn offers its special "Inn" salad. This grandiose concoction combines fresh slices of avocado, shrimp, crabmeat, tomatoes, scallions, and mushrooms slices – creating a masterful combination of seafood and greens dressed with a stout, red wine vinaigreete.

My opinion of the entrees varied. Our first, Tournedos Cendrillon presented thick cuts of filet tenderloin, cut from the heart and trimmed of fat. The meat was mouthwatering in itself with a rich beef flavor that well defined its expensive cut. The steaks were bedded atop crustless pieces of fried bread and finished with a sauce rich with butter and a sharp aftertaste of vino.

In the past, I have been disappointed with the Veal Scaloppine. The quality of the veal has always been fine, however. Unfortunately, the sauce that covered the veal was flat, almost totally devoid of seasoning. It tasted as if the chef had forgotten to combine his stock with the necessary ingredients to make a good scaloppine sauce. With entrees, we have been served a melange of vegetables du jour, carrots, green beans and zucchini. They were cooked properly, but haphazardly displayed on the plate. Good chefs should never get careless.

Desserts at La Hacienda are limited, yet can be impressive if you get the right waiter to prepare them. Crepes Suzette and Peaches Flambe are two of the most interesting. I do suggest after a heavy dinner, you ask for a plate of fresh fruit in season and perhaps a little cheese. Fruit and cheese aid in digestion and will make your send-off down Highway 9 a little less combustible.

LA MARGARITA ★★★
Mexican

Price Range: Bargain

2616 Union Avenue, San Jose	Master Card – Visa
Phone: 377-0254	No Reservations
Hours: 11:30 am–4 pm, Mon.–Sat.	No Non-Smoking Section
Beer and Wine – Food To Go	

Seeking out restaurants in dismal shopping centers isn't my idea of an auspicious investigation. However, despite my aversion to dining next door to auto-parts stores and kennels, I painfully admit there are many interesting eateries slotted into these lackluster storefronts. One such place is called La Margarita, a Mexican *loncheria* that brings a sparkle of sunshine to a suffering corner.

La Margarita draws its name from the famous tangy-sweet tequila cocktail so popular in big Mexican chains. In place of tequila, La Margarita uses white wine to blend its own special concoction. Although not as strong, this margarita was slushy, sweet and pleasing to the throat.

The menu here includes Mexican favorites, plus a few interesting sidelights. For example, a Salvadorean *pupusa* may be ordered as an appetizer or as a lunch entree. The *pupusa* is a very thick, homemade corn tortilla, warmed on an ungreased griddle. The center is filled with melted cheese. To eat it, you must cut down the middle and dress the pocket in each half with a cabbage salad.

Back to the Mexican menu items. We ordered a plate of *chili colorado*. The most impressive aspect of this rendition of beef and red chili was the extreme tenderness of the beef chunks. Unfortunately, the red chili gravy was too mild to evoke a tantalizing response from the tastebuds. A touch more hot pepper would have done the trick. Served on the side were Spanish rice and freshly, mashed pinto beans streaked with melted cheese.

La Margarita prepared one of the cleanest versions of the *chimichanga* I have consumed in recent years. Instead of that customary indistinguishable lump glopped with *guacamole* and sour cream, this *chimichanga* displayed the work of a conscientious cook. Each flour wrap was carefully folded around an ample spread of chopped beef, onion and spices, then deep-fried until golden brown. An avocado-fragrant *guacamole* dressed the top.

Another excellent dish is the *chili verde burrito*. Inside a large flour tortilla were several chunks of pure pork meat. The *verde* sauce presented a tasty, naturally thickened pork soup which steamed the meat in its rich flavor. The sauce was interesting and I enjoyed its departure from the more common thick varieties.

For desert, La Margarita offers that favorite Salvadorean dish of *platanos* (bananas), with fresh cream. It is worth a try.

La Margarita is a perfect little *loncheria* for a Saturday nibble which will impart a little spice to the afternoon ahead.

LA MERE MICHELLE ★★★★   Price Range: Expensive
French

14482 Big Basin Way, Saratoga   All Major Credit Cards
Phone: (408) 867-5272   Reservations Required
Hours: Lunch: 11:30–2 pm, Tu.-Fri.   No Non-Smoking Section
         Dinner: 6–10 pm, Tues.-Sun.   Limited Wheelchair Access
Full Cocktail Services

Many people ask me where I go when I'm not reviewing restaurants, when I want to relax and enjoy a dinner at my leisure. One of my favorite restaurants is La Mere Michelle. This exquisite dining establishment has always filled my needs of comfort, fine cuisine, and good wine. Consistency is the most outstanding quality here. Chef Masek and his wife, Michelle, demand only the best for their customers and refuse to cut corners. The finest meats, produce, and wines are used and food is prepared with a delicate simplicity that has become Chef Masek's culinary trademark.

The interior is provencial and elegant in authentic French style. I have always felt swept up in the rich, alluring European accents that put me immediately at ease. The focal point of the room is the dazzling dessert table, laden with freshly baked cakes, fresh seasonal fruit, usually strawberries or raspberries, and other premise-made confections. The homemade cheesecake is a must.

The menu is simple and easy to decipher. Beef, veal, chicken, and fish are all represented and prepared according to Chef Masek's native recipes. Of late, I have been ordering Original Wiener Schnitzel. Unlike the schnitzels I have had where the bread crumb coating forms leaden jacks for coarse cuts of veal, I find La Mere Michelle's to be exceptionally light. Presented is a large, expansive slice of milk fed tenderloin of veal coated in an etheral egg and bread crumb shell that fries out to a flaky, crisp consistency. This is a simple, wholesome dish served without sauces. It comes with only wedges of lemon for that added spritz of citrus.

Other quality entrees include the house specialty Filet de Boeuf Andreeff. Thick cuts of filet mignon are quickly seared to a beautiful medium rare, then finished with a stout brown sauce with a distinct, demanding flavor that fully complements the beef. My favorite chicken dish is Breast of Chicken Maison. Two supremes are flattened, breaded, and fried crisp. They are served on top of a glassy brown sauce, similar to the sauce in the Andreeff, only not as strong.

All entrees are presented with seasonal vegetables methodically cut and attractively arranged around the entree.

La Mere Michelle is a winning restaurant because the proprietors care about their patrons. They treat each customer equally and professionally. Make it a point to dine here.

LAS PALMAS TACO BAR ★★
Mexican

Price Range: Bargain

1495 The Alameda, San Jose	Cash Only
Phone: (408) 295-3132	Beer
55 Front Street, Santa Cruz	No Reservations
Phone: (408) 429-1220	No Non-Smoking Section
Hours: 10 am–8:30 pm, Mon.–Sat.	Limited Wheelchair Access
Til 7:30, Sunday	

Mary Gottschalk, fashion writer for the Mercury News, is mad at me for revealing the whereabouts of her favorite little taco bar, Las Palmas.

The Las Palmas Taco Bar has been in existence for a long, long time now and has yet to attract the aficionados of Mexican tasties. It is in a constant process of being discovered.

Probably the most inspiring, the most alluring attribute this tiny little shoebox of a taqueria offers is dirt cheap prices. The food is not to be overlooked either. It is homespun and family-style authentic, with plenty of long-simmered sauces and hot, fragrant tortillas. My favorite dish here remains the Chile Verde and Chile Colorado combination served with rice and beans and your choice of flour or corn tortillas. Tender pork chunks and tender beef chunks in a green chile sauce or a spicy, rust red chile gravy make this combo a two punch delight. Combination plates, tacos, burritos, enchiladas, quesadillas, and tostadas are just a few of the items that are offered on the wall menu.

Decor is straight out tacky. Formica topped tables are attached to skeletal legs that threaten to bend under the weight of a hefty posterior. The interior is usually littered with orange trays, taco wrappers, spent beer bottles, and well fed, lingering locals who keep themselves bemused by the cars filling up at the Shell station seen through the windows. But above all, the food is wholesome and the prices very kind.

LA TAQUERIA ★★★★
Tacos and Burritos

Price Range: Bargain

15 So. First Street, San Jose	Cash Only
Phone: 287-1542	No Reservations
Hours: 11 am–5 pm, Mon., Tu. & Thurs.	No Non-Smoking Section
To 8 pm, Fri. & Sat.	Wheelchair Access

La Taqueria comes to us via San Francisco where it has enjoyed a healthy business for many years. Its operation is strictly self-serve. The menu, anchored to the wall behind the open view kitchen, is so simple, you'll wonder how the buisness stays alive. Only tacos and burritos are served.

But they are just the reasons why La Taqueria is doing such a bustling business. Authentically crafted, these two offerings will rearrange your preconceptions about tortilla-wrapped tasties.

Long strips of dark, marinated beef, *cabeza* (beef head) and pork are roasted and sizzled over charcoal blazes.

The Taco, better known as the Shepherd's Taco, is unlike any you have had. Unlike the crispy-shelled varieties that snap apart in your hand, these are made with two hearth-warmed corn tortillas that remain firm and pliable. For the top of the line taco, the *carne asada* (grilled beef) is perfect for starters. The two corn torts are laid heavily with fresh grilled beef. Before the meat is wrapped, it is dressed with a shot of fresh pinto beans, chili and a large splash of homemade salsa. This thick, chunky blend is made with *tomatillos* (Mexican green tomatoes), red tomato, fresh sprigs of cilantro, garlic cloves, onion and other spices. It has a zesty, mildly hot flavor that brings the meat and beans into harmony.

The burritos may appear similar to other brands, but one bite will dismiss any notion that they taste the same. La Taqueria's burritos are wrapped with meats straight from the fire or the pot and include pinto beans, green chili and salsa. The taste was so fresh and spicy, I couldn't leave without having another.

My favorite burrito is a toss-up between the *carnitas* (roasted pork) or the *chili verde* (pork in green chili sauce). *Carnitas* are straight pork, roasted thoroughly without too much seasoning. As a result, the flavor of the meat is unmasked, and the meat can be a little chewy. The *chili verde,* on the other hand, is pork chunks simmered in a spicy green chili sauce. The meat, though ample, becomes a major ingredient in a very savory sauce. Either one will satisfy the pork lover.

LA TARANTELLA ★★★★
European Coffee House and Cafe

Price Range: Bargain

21267 Stevens Creek Blvd., Cupertino	Master Card — Visa
Phone: 257-5845	No Reservations
Hours: 11–11 pm, Tues.–Thurs.	Non-Smoking Section
To Mid., Fri. & Sat.	Wheelchair Access
To 5 pm, Sun. & Mon.	Seating Capacity: 64

La Tarantella is a boon to the South Bay, especially to the residents of Cupertino. This authentic European coffee house provides an interesting touch of class to the verdurous Oaks Shopping Center directly across the tree-lined boulevard from De Anza College.

The owners spent many years in Europe studying the various techniques they encountered in the coffee houses they visited along the way. In Germany, they learned the art of roasting coffee beans and grinding them down into a brewable product.

The interior is a classical melange of artistic design. Lining the rich wood walls is an inspiring collection of oils, acrylics and line drawings chosen from the Discovery Gallery. The paintings change every month. Defining the hardwood floors and high airy ceilings is a network of polished brass and copper, plus much beveled and stained glass. La Tarantella soothes the spirit and piques the appetite for a cup of hearty brew and a bite of something very special and homemade.

In addition to a line-up of coffees, ranging from the straight black house brew to those coffees frothed with steamed milk or spiked with liqueur, you can enjoy several light entrees or choose from a selection of freshly made European-style pastries. La Tarantella is an ideal place for a tranquil lunch, an early dinner or an after-the-theater snack.

On one of my visits I started with a bowl of homemade vegetable soup. One dip into this steaming liquid produced a spoonful of pulped vegetables from carrots and celery to cabbage. The flavor was immediate and wholesome with an invigorating accent of fresh lemon juice and sesame seeds.

Following this dish, I ordered one of the specialties of the house, English Meat Pie, which followed the authentic recipe. The owner is English and was weaned on such British tasties. The pie was made with a supple pastry dough, baked to a golden topside. The remaining crust remained soft and pliable yet retained the meat sauce inside without getting soggy. The filling comprised beef chunks with fresh slices of mushrooms in a beefy brown sauce.

I have also sampled a slice of LaTarantella's homemade quiche. The quiche here is made with the traditional egg base with the addition of cheddar cheese, which gives the fluffy filling a unique flavor. I found it exceptionally light with the undercrust more flaky than doughy-solid. The quiche can also be made with spinach or chicken.

Entrees can be ordered with soup, salad or fruit. I highly recommend the fruit. What I received was a marvel of a fresh-fruit display. Several varieties of in-season fruits had been meticulously sliced and arranged for maximum visual appeal. On my plate, I had apples, oranges, grapefruit, grapes, banana, strawberries and pineapple, all of which were sweet and juicy.

Service at La Tarantella is gracious and casually attentive. The management here wants you to relax, so it paces your visit accordingly. For entertainment, you can listen to the classical tunes of live guitar on weekends or enjoy the lively melodies of Flamenco guitar on Wednesday nights. At other times, classical music is piped from speakers hidden throughout the restaurant.

LA TERRASSE ★★★   Price Range: Expensive
French

3740 El Camino Real, Palo Alto	A.E. – M.C. – Visa
Phone: (415) 494-0700	Reservations Accepted
Hours: Lunch: 11:30–2 pm, M–Fri.	Non-Smoking Section –
Dinner: 5:30–10 pm, M–Sat.	[Upon Request]
Full Bar – Extensive Wine List	Limited Wheelchair Access

La Terrasse excels above all other restaurants in creating beautiful ambiance with extremely eye appealing decor. This quaint restaurant is a picture of soothing allure. The dining rooms are swathed in French provencial accents, punctuated by pale pink table linen and napery.

Though tables are closely spaced, intimacy is adroitly maintained by the subtleness of lighting and by the angles at which the tables are turned. Through a series of French doors in the main dining room, you can glimpse the outdoor patio where lunches and warm night dinners are regularly served.

One aspect of the table setting I did find odd was the placement of two full bottles of wine at each table. They are removed shortly after you are seated. It wasn't necessarily irritating, just a little senseless. It didn't really enrich the already attractive table arrangement.

We started a recent meal by dividing an entree and enjoying it as an appetizer, Saumon Joinville. We received a beautiful cloudy pink filet of salmon, poached to a firm, succulence. It was fully boned and broke against the fork in juicy chunks. The fish was served with a sauce made from cream and brandy and sweet Bay shrimps. It was an unobtrusive sauce with the cream less in evidence than the nutty flavor of the brandy and the rich underlying flavor of fresh butter. It was light and formed a perfect marriage with the delicate salmon.

Between appetizer and entree, we diverted slightly with a cup of cold avocado soup and a Belgium endive salad. The avocado soup was a disappointment. The texture was smooth and fluffy, folding to the turn of the spoon like thickened milk. The rich characteristics of avocado succumbed to a heavy whipping cream aftertaste that lingered long in the mouth.

Our Belgium endive salad was a fresh assembly of crisp, bitter sweet sprigs of endive forming a crown for a bevy of watercress. A thickened vinaigrette was unevenly distributed over the neat arrangement of greens, though the flavor was appropriately tart without a strong back bite.

When it comes to red meat, La Terrasse doesn't fool around. It serves top of the line quality and serves it in large, demanding portions. We ordered Tournedos au Poivre Vert and received one of the largest filet mignons I have witnessed since San Antonio, Texas. This solid hunk of gloriously tender red meat rose about three inches high. It was awesome and totally trimmed of excess fat. The chef roasted the meat to a turn, then flamed it in brandy, creamy mustard and green peppercorns.

Our second entree was Le Filet D'Agneau "En Croute." By all means, order this one rare because by the time it is placed in the pastry crust and has finished cooking, it may be a few degrees above medium rare. Fortunately, my lamb did not cook beyond that point, retaining a light red color and much of its natural juice. The filet of lamb came to the table enclosed in a heavy crust, resembling a freshly baked cobbler. The crust was thick and lightly browned; however, I found it to be slightly undercooked and doughy tasting in places. Otherwise, this lamb presentation was a fine rendition served with a glassy, red wine sauce that considerably defined the richness of the lamb meat.

Both entrees were served with sliced zucchini, carrots, and potatoes. All three were attractively arranged around the main course and, though slightly overcooked, were not mushy or flavorless.

Desserts are wheeled tableside on a cart laden with freshly baked tortes and cakes. Our waiter warned us about the decadence of the rich chocolate almond torte which we ordered straight away. Our waiter was right. The torte, layered with pure, dark chocolate and roasted almonds in a buttery amaretto glaze, was purely sinful. I anticipated a keen attack of sugar blues shortly after consuming that devillish dessert. We also spooned a bowl of fresh strawberries with peach brandy.

Service was a La Terrasse high point. Our waiter knew his food and explained the dishes with knowledge. He was also forthright about suggesting the dishes he considered to be the chef's better recipes. I appreciate an honest waiter who is abreast of his trade.

La Terrasse is a good French restaurant, but not yet excellent. I enjoyed the dishes I sampled, but was not particularly inspired by innovations that are setting the great French restaurants apart from those that are good. Prices are up there, so keep an eye on what you are ordering.

LE CAFE ★★★   Price Range: **Bargain**
Euoprean-style Breakfast / Lunch

---

27 Fountain Alley, (Downtown), San Jose	Cash Only
Phone: (408) 293-1919	No Reservations
Hours: 7 am–5 pm, Mon.–Sat.	No Non-Smoking Section
Beer and Wine	Limited Wheelchair Access

The opening of Le Cafe was a brave and courageous venture that helped fuel the sagging spirit of San Jose's downtown renaissance. This little, European eatery brings a touch of the Old World to a refurbished Fountain Alley. And since its opening, the hearty element that once peopled the area en masse has thinned out considerably, leaving a relatively tranquil setting in which to enjoy a cup of freshly brewed coffee and a warm, buttery croissant.

Breakfast and lunch can be relished in the rustic brick and polished wood environment of Le Cafe. Breakfast hours are permeated with the alluring scents of fresh espresso and French roast. All coffee beans are ground on the premises every half hour.

During the A.M. hours, you can enjoy such belly warmers as Belgian pancakes with melted butter and syrup or sweet fruit preserves. Oven hot croissants and sundry other pastries are also available for the sunrise set. You can even fork an egg fluffy Quiche Lorraine or get your fingers sticky on a homemade Danish.

Lunch remains primarily light and very European in style. The favorite of the House is the Stuffed Croissant. A puffy croissant is layered with thinly sliced ham, whole veal sausage, or even garlic sausage and comes warm and liquidy with melted cheese. Essentially, it is a very innovative sandwich.

Also for lunch you can savor the House specialty, Vol Au Vent. A square puff pastry is covered with such creations as Beef Bourguignonne, a wine-laced beef stew with herbs and spices. It is served with a garlicky ratatouille.

When I come to Le Cafe, I always seem to include an order of fresh, house-made pate with slices of crusty French bread. The liver pate is very delicate in consistency, but purveys a deep, nutty flavor. Several varieties of imported cheese and French pastries are also available.

When downtown San Jose finally achieves its goal, Le Cafe will be firmly situated as one of the local heartthrobs. Its location along the cobbled walkway of Fountain Alley is greatly improved. The rabble is nearly all gone and the basic complexion is becoming wholesome and airy.

LE CONCORDE ★★★★
Continental

Price Range: Expensive

14554 Big Basin Way, Saratoga	A.E. — M.C. — Visa
Phone: 867-1200	Reservations Recomm.
Hours: Lunch: 11:30–2 pm, Tues.-Fri.	Non-Smoking Section —
Dinner: 6–10 pm, Tues.-Sat.	[Upon Request]
Extensive Wine List	Limited Wheelchair Access

So far, it appears that Le Concorde has the juice to hold its own on gastronomic Big Basin Way. A great deal of professionalism is implicit in the operation here.

A fair warning to those with thin pocketbooks: the menu is exquisite and the prices are commensurate to the quality. Be judicious, but don't shy away. I believe the experience is worth the few extra ducats.

The interior is exactly what you would expect from a restaurant on Big Basin Way. It is cozy, warm and elegant, with a rich ambiance that can guide the mood and whet the appetite for fine cuisine. There are two rooms in which to dine. The first is Tudor-style, punctuated with dark beams and striking white walls; the other flaunts a wall covering, replete with flowers and dotted with classical portraiture. Linen-covered tables and stiff, white napery create settings of simple elegance for afternoon and evening dining.

Le Concorde's menu breaks from the typical. It is limited and easy to read with a strong influence from the sea. Although there are veal and other red-meat diversions, it appears the major focus here is the service of fresh fish prepared in fine continental styles.

We began an afternoon meal with a special offering of mussels. These thin mollusks were medium size, deep in color and sweet. They were steamed in a broth of natural juices flavored with fresh onions and herbs. When finished with the meat of the mussels, we removed the shells from the tureen and went to work soaking up the residual sauce with pieces of fresh bread.

From the dinner menu, we ordered Prawns Fra Diable, which proved to be a complete triumph in the preparation of the fish and the crafting of the sauce. Three juice-plump, four-bite gulfers were sauteed in a pungent sauce of butter and minced garlic. Lemon and parsley balanced the flavor. This dish also beckons the bread to dunk. Don't be bashful.

Lunches and dinners come with a choice of soup or salad. We sampled both. The soup was a puree of fresh vegetables made from real cream with no flour thickness. It spooned up nicely. The salad brought a small serving of leaf lettuce drizzled with a mild vinegar and oil. Simple.

The most outstanding entree for that day was the Salmon with Sorrel. A fully boned filet of fresh, pink-fleshed salmon was broiled ever so lightly and streaked with a buttery sauce, flavored with sorrel. What I liked most about the fish was its moist flakiness, a sign of correct preparation.

Our second dish was an average offering of veal sausage and pasta. A ramekin was filled with ziti-style pasta, dotted topside with diagonally cut pieces of veal sausage. The sausage was lightly spiced in keeping with the mild flavor of the young calf meat. The sauce was a brothy onion-and-beef-flavored concoction that could have been thicker. I found this dish filling, but not special.

The service at Le Concorde was exceptional. The waiter was perhaps one of the best I have had. He was sincere, amiable and always willing to serve the patron first, never once cutting corners or making excuses. The proprietor made it a point to greet his patrons, pour wine, serve plates and even bus tables.

Though the prices are somewhat high, Le Concorde has what it takes to become a success on Big Basin Way. The total package is worth the price.

LE MOUTON NOIR ★★★★   Price Range: Expensive
French

14560 Big Basin Way, Saratoga   All Major Credit Cards
Phone: (408) 867-7071   Reservations Required
Hours: Lunch: 11:30−2 pm, Tu.-Fri.   No Non-Smoking Section
         Dinner: 6−10 pm, Tues.-Sat.   Wheelchair Access Limited
Beer and Wine

If you are still befuddled by Nouveau Cuisine and its many forms and complexities, take a trip to Le Mouton Noir for either lunch or dinner and get the facts straight. Le Mouton Noir is perhaps the only French restaurant in the South Bay to serve Nouvelle Cuisine in its purest form. The chef here follows the tenets of this inspiring mode of French cookery by offering dishes that are simple, visually striking, that utilize only the finest meats and vegetables the market can procure.

I have been to this quaint French restaurant tucked along Big Basin Way in Saratoga Village on many occasions. My last visit was a celebration of one's birthday. Every aspect of our meal from service to ambiance to food completed the celebration. My evening here was flawless. My guest grew a year older in fine style.

In addition to a rather limited menu, Le Mouton Noir brings the patron several specials, including appetizer specials, entrees, and even seasonal desserts. On one occasion, we began our meal with an order of mussels in season. The large meaty mollusks were simmered in a brothy sauce rich with cream and sprightly accents of garlic. With this dish, I made good use of Le Mouton Noir's delicious rolls by dunking chunks of bread into the hot broth. Another visit, we had an order of shiitake mushrooms. They are broiled with a glaze of olive oil, dressed with a light vinaigrette and cut into long sections. The flavor imparted a subdued earthiness, tender outside, soft and fleshy inside.

Entrees comprise exquisite milk fed veal dishes, lamb tenderloin offerings, beef, fish and sometimes pork. On an earlier visit, we had Filet D'Agneau en Croute. Nestled inside a flaky pastry shell was a thick slice of lamb tenderloin. It was served with a glassy brown sauce laced with Madeira which highly complimented the deep flavor of the lamb.

Duckling preparations may vary from night to night at Le Mouton Noir. Once we had an creative duck rendition which delivered a roasted duckling caped in a sauce composed of tart kumquat and green pepper-corns. Another visit, we had the traditional duckling with orange sauce. Both recipes were deliciously prepared.

Many veal entrees are offered from the highly creative veal with morel mushrooms to the veal in light cream sauce. I have always been notably impressed by the milk fed delicateness of the calf. It has never been overcooked or over-sauced.

Side dishes like vegetables, rice and potatoes are always fresh, color-ful and artistically arranged around the main entree. The chef here has an eye for balance, bringing forth the beautiful aspect of food as well as the inherent flavors.

Le Mouton Noir is no black sheep. It belongs at the top of the heap with the greater restaurants of the South Bay. It is a shoe in for con-tinued success.

LE PAPILLON ★★★★★   Price Range: Expensive
Continental

410 Saratoga Avenue, San Jose	A.E. – B.W. – M.C. – Visa
Phone: (408) 296-3730	Reservations Required
Hours: Lunch: 11:30–2:30 pm, M–Fri.	No Non-Smoking Section
Dinner: 5–10 pm, Mon.–Sat.	Limited Wheelchair Access
Full Cocktail Service	

The first time I ever walked into Le Papillon, it was totally empty. My wife and I were the only two customers. Since that time several years ago, Le Papillon has grown tremendously. Business is booming. Not only is Le Papillon successful in bringing in a constant flow of business, but it has groomed influence among other restaurant owners who look up to it as one of the best.

One of the most salient factors that keeps Le Papillon a solid best restaurant contender is the proprietor's keen attention on his business. He never lets things go astray and always places the patron on a ped-estal. You will feel important when you dine here, the way it should be when you put down your hard earned dollars for a meal.

The cuisine at Le Papillon has also developed. The proprietor keeps abreast of culinary innovation and constantly employs new methods. Like its compatriot restaurant, La Foret, the dishes here now embrace the beautiful elements of nouvelle cuisine. Fresh produce, meats and seafood are simply prepared and laid out in visually stunning presenta-tions. I have always been impressed with Le Papillon's Prawn Cocktail.

The prawns are very large and succulently prepared. They come to the table hooked over a tuliped glass dish filled with ice and a side of spicy cocktail sauce. The freshness of the prawns has been very striking, the flavor deep with a light whisper of the sea.

Other appetizers I enjoy are the Fettuccine Alfredo and the Fresh Oysters when in season. The ribbon noodles in the Fettuccine are tender and not overcooked. The sauce is creamy rich and adheres to the pasta in thick, glistening coats. Beware of the calories.

Le Papillon conducts tableside cooking without theatric pomposity. There are explosions of fire, but there is purpose to these explosions. Steak Diane and Cornish Game Hen are brilliant tableside entrees. The Steak Diane, especially, will satisfy the desire for red meat in classic continental preparation. Meat and seasonings are prepared before your eyes then flamed in the finale with a dousing of cooking brandy. The flavors are demanding and complex. Your palate will have a good work-out.

On a more recent visit, we indulged on a piece of fresh Salmon, the likes of which I only see in photographs. The focus of this dish honed in on the freshness of the fish and its pale pink-orange color. The meat of the fish flaked in large, moist pieces. A light, clear port sauce with seedless green grape halves surrounded the filet. On the center of the filet rested a dollop of fresh Hollandaise garnished with caviar. Accompanying the fish were fresh Chinese green beans, and julienne of carrots, cooked al dente.

Desserts include an exquisite Grand Marnier souffle, plus an assortment of fresh fruits and berries. There is also a limited host of flambe desserts like Baked Alaska and Cherries Jubilee.

There are very few people who dine at Le Papillon and leave dissatisfied. The restaurant is designed to make you happy with excellent cuisine and professional service.

LEXINGTON HOUSE ★★★   Price Range: Bargain
Breakfast / Lunch

---

337 North Santa Cruz, Los Gatos	**Cash Only**
Phone: (408) 354-3220	**No Reservations**
Hours: 6 am–4 pm, Daily	**Non-Smoking Section**
	Limited Wheelchair Access

When Alex died, there was talk that the Lexington House was finished. How could anybody replace the venerable, world traveler, Alex, with his bottomless bag of culinary escapades?

But Alex has been gone a while now, may he rest in peace, but The Lexington House still prevails. Grantedly, the whacky frenetics have been dismissed, but the food is still good, in some aspects, much better. The kitchen crew have a real hand on their trade and cook food with a much lighter touch than Alex ever did.

The Lexington House is one of the better breakfast nooks in the area. The cooks here are A.M. artisans, performing wonders with the simple egg and the sizzling griddle. Breakfast dishes like the Country Scramble, made with three farm fresh eggs, diced ham, and melted cheese, have become a Los Gatan morning heartthrob. In addition, omelets abound, as well as the basic bacon and egg style match-ups.

My favorite here is the Egg Benedict. The eggs have always been perfectly poached so the yolks are loose, but not mucusy. The Hollandaise is an etheral, buttery blend that glistens creamily over the eggs and does not become leaden in the cooling process.

Lunches are hearty and very filling. Hot Open Prime Meat Sandwich Platters are highlighted by the Hot Roast Sirloin of Beef or the Sliced Kosher Style Corn Beef. The Chef's Salad Bowl is a colorful and healthful composition of greens, julienne of turkey, ham and cheese. Portions are usually large, almost too large.

Outside of the New Yorker Hamburger, which includes cheese, bacon, and a large beef pattie, I have been put to sleep by the other burger alternatives. They are just too typical.

To those who have stayed away from The Lexington House because Alex isn't there anymore, I can only say the food is still very good.

LIEN'S CAFE ★★★   Price Range: Bargain
Vietnamese

---

360 West San Carlos, San Jose	Cash or Checks Only
Phone: (408) 298-2483	No Reservations
Hours: 9:30 am–9 pm, Tues.–Sun.	No Non-Smoking Section
Beer and Wine	Limited Wheelchair Access

I am so glad Lien's has cleaned up its act. After my first review of this excellent Vietnamese restaurant, I received letters telling me that the place was filthy and totally unfit for dinner. In my first review, I explained that the decor was run down, tacky and unsavory. I even mentioned that there was a starry-eyed boy in cutoffs dancing through the dining room killing flies against the tables. All of these drawbacks have been done away with. Lien's is now a clean, little cafe with linen covered tables neatly arranged and evenly spaced. The starry-eyed youth is no longer around, thank God.

When it comes to food, however, Lien's rests at the top of her class in a growing number of Vietnamese restaurants. I have had a chance now to compare Lien's food to other Vietnamese recipes cooked up at other restaurants. Lien exhibits a certain flair that the others cannot equal. For example, Ga Rang Xa Ot (Lemon Grass chicken) is deeply laced with the zest of lemon. You can taste it in every bite of the tender, fully boned chicken squares. The sauce is a loose brown sauce made fiery with hot pepper and plenty of lemon grass.

Nem Muong is one of Lien's specialties and a true Vietnamese favorite. A plethora of grilled meatballs are served with a beautiful garnish of fresh cucumber slices, carrot shreds, lettuce, fresh corriander, pickled leeks, and dipping sauces. To eat, you must wrap the meatballs and vegetables inside a sheet of hot rice paper. Sweet, spicy, bland, and tangy worked simultaneously against the palate.

I am also fond of the Tom Rang Man or roasted prawns. Several prawns, still in shell, fan a bed of sauteed onions. They are prepared in a glazy sauce of garlic, oil and sugar, and finished with a sprinkling of corriander.

For appetizer, don't miss Lien's Cha Gio (Imperial Rolls). Wrapped in dried rice paper fried to a transparent crispness, was a mousse of shrimp, pork, and vegetables. Served on the side for dipping was the celebrated Muoc Mam, a delightfully piquant fish sauce blended with garlic, hot pepper, and fresh lime juice.

You no longer have to fear Lien's decor. It has been redone and cleaned up. The food here can be considered cuisine. There has always been a balance and a careful hand exemplified in the cooking of Lien's many Vietnamese dishes. If you're looking for something different, perhaps exotic, give Lien's a try.

LOON WAH ★★★   Price Range: Moderate
Chinese

1132 Saratoga-Sunnyvale Rd., San Jose   Master Card – Visa
Phone: (408) 257-1642   Reservations Recomm.
Hours: 11:30 am–9 pm, Mon.–Thurs.   Non-Smoking Section
         11:30–10 pm, Friday   Wheelchair Access
         4–10 pm, Sat. & Sun.
Beer and Wine

When I first dined at Loon Wah, I was extremely delighted with its unique list of Chinese specialties. The great majority of the dishes I sampled were prepared by a real chef, who knew the balance and complexities of Chinese cooking. On subsequent visits, I was also impressed;

however, I did run into a few inconsistencies that were not present on my first visit. The Twice Done Pork, for instance, was much too hot, the peppers this time defeating the subtle spiciness that I remembered from the first sampling.

The decor, however, remains a beautiful presentation that eases the appetite and allows one to sit back and relax. Stunning, hand-embroidered screens, chandeliers and wine cabinets blend elements of provencial France with the understated elegance of the Orient. Tables are linen covered and are spaced for privacy and quiet discussion.

A great way to open up a meal at Loon Wah is to order the House Special, Loon Wah's Lettuce Blossom. This dish brings a dice of lean pork, mushrooms, onions, water chestnuts and bamboo shoots, cooked together into a colorful melange. To eat, you first brush the inside of a lettuce leaf with hoison, then fill with the pork mixture. Roll tightly and eat. The watery crunch of the lettuce cools the palate while the pork and hoison stimulate it with flavor.

Loon Wah's menu lists the commonly seen Chinese specialties like Chicken Chow Mein, Egg Foo Young, and Pork Fried Rice. I recommend you explore further and taste the more intriguing dishes. Sauteed Scallops are worth a try. When fresh, the scallops are large and firm with a rich sweetness that absorbs the seasonings applied during the cooking process. Any of Loon Wah's Kung Pao dishes are done with traditional savor and include the Kung Pao trademark of hot red peppers and peanuts. I particularly like the Kung Pao Prawns.

On each visit here, I have ordered a plate of Roast Duck. Loon Wah follows the Cantonese style of barbecuing the duck until the skin is golden brown and the dark meat is juicy and succulent. The duck is always neatly cleavered into manageable pieces that are better eaten with the fingers rather than the sticks.

Loon Wah is a quality Chinese restaurant. The inconsistencies are few. I have always been pleased and well fed.

LOS PERICOS ★★★   Price Range: Moderate
Salvadorean

---

33 So. Central Ave., (The Factory),   M.C. – Visa – Checks
  Campbell   Reservations Recomm.
Phone: 866-9918   Non-Smoking Section
Hours: Lunch: 11–2 pm, Mon.-Fri.   Wheelchair Access
           Dinner: 5–9 pm, Mon.-Sat.
Beer and Wine

Los Pericos deserves to be recognized. Salvadorean cuisine is unique, light, and a refreshing switch from the heavy sauces and stewed meats of Mexican food. Confusing the two would be a mistake.

The interior is restfully quiet, spacious and airy. Waxy green ferns blend with white-washed walls hung with pictures of rainbow-colored tropical birds. Nothing is overdone.

Salvadorean dishes are more intricately cheffed and less sauced than Mexican, relying more on natural flavors, than overbearing spiciness. A traditional favorite in El Salvador, offered as an appetizer here, is the Pupusa. Fresh homemade corn tortillas are plated together, filled with cheese, then pan fried to a golden brown on both sides. To eat, the center is sliced then filled with curtido, a piquant cabbage salad with tomato chunks, fresh cilantro and raw onions. I was particularly impressed with the lightness and the mellow flavors of melted white cheese and corn.

A dish we sampled as a second appetizer, although listed as an entree, is the Yucca Con Chicharrones. Yucca root has the firm consistency of boiled potatoes. In this dish it was cut into thick cubes and served warm in a salad of curtido and crispy fried pork chunks. Drizzled onto the root was a deep-red tomato sauce, tasting of a fresh tomato puree.

On my first visit here, I savored a plate of Lengua En Salsa Y Crema. Lengua translates beef tongue. It is sliced thinly and splayed on a platter. A creamy sauce made with tomato, onion and sour cream covers the tongue, complementing the mildly beefy taste with a tomato tartness.

Pollo Encebollado was a disappointment, after expecting something "exotic" as stated on the menu. Three medium-size pieces of chicken were sauteed in a sauce not unlike that served with the tongue. The result was a latin rendition of chicken cacciatore without the spicy zest.

For the light diner or weight-conscious lunchnik, the Sopa de Camarones will not threaten the waistline. We tried a bowl of steaming hot prawn soup made from vegetable stock. It was chock full of fresh prawns, carrots, cabbage, celery, zucchini and a gratuitous chunk of corn on the cob.

For dessert, Platanos Solo Crema can't be missed. Slices of ripe *platains* (bananas) are lightly fried, then streaked with fresh, sweetened cream. The sugar was a whisper in this dessert, providing the perfect nightcap of sweetness.

MADDALENA'S ★★★★★
Continental

Price Range: Expensive

---

544 Emerson St., Palo Alto
Phone: (415) 326-6082
Hours: Lunch: 11:30–2:30 pm, Tu–Fri.
         Dinner: 6:30–10 pm, Tues.–Sat.
Full Cocktail Service

All Major Credit Cards
Reservations Required
Non-Smoking Section
Limited Wheelchair Access

I said it once and I'll say it again. Freddie Maddalena is, perhaps, the best restaurateur on the Peninsula. He has created one of the most beautiful dining rooms I have yet to encounter. One step through the portals of his prize restaurant and you are swept up in unprecedented elegance. The decor will fill your eyes with lavish sights. A milieu of antiques, linen, candlelight, palms, and intriguing art await the unsuspecting diner.

In addition to the more popular Main Dining Room, Maddalena's is equipped with an upstairs mezzanine where a harpist plucks soothing strains on her instrument. For the lovers wanting complete privacy on a very special occasion, Maddalena's also offers The Private Room. It is set up for one party. A party of just two, or a party of ten. I had the opportunity of dining here with my wife on our first wedding anniversary. It was an experience we will never forget. The lay-out, the food, the wine, the guitar serenade formed the ideal repast for this special day.

Freddie Maddalena does not disappoint in the food department either. He has a master chef piloting his stoves who prepares cuisine comparable in quality to the decor in which it is served. I am particularly fond of the Tournedos of Beef Bearnaise. On both samplings, I was served two thick cuts of beef tenderloin on beds of toast. The Bearnaise was a smooth, loosely concocted blend with a distinctive flavor of tarragon. Maddalena's has also offered the Tournedos Henry IV. This includes a capping of artichoke hearts with the beef and the Bearnaise.

On both the lunch and dinner menu, you can have the opportunity to sample one of several exquisite pasta dishes. The Linguine Vongole is my favorite. Tender pasta is boiled to the perfect al dente degree. A clean, brothy sauce made from natural clam juice, butter, garlic, and chopped parsley is then applied. Six whole clams in shell formed an attractive circle around the portion of steaming semolina. A sprinkle of freshly grated cheese, a dash of coarse ground pepper and you have something to write home about. Don't forget to spoon the broth at the bottom of the dish. It will give your id a spark of energy.

Of course, you will find a cast of milk fed veal specialties on Maddalena's menu. The veal here is the finest quality as indicated by its pure white color and its creamy flavor and finely grained texture. To fully appreciate the attributes of the veal, the Veal Piccata is a good choice. Veal scallops are sauteed in butter, lemon and capers. The tartness of the capers balances well with the milky veal.

In addition to beef, veal, pasta and lamb, Maddalena's offers fresh fish specialties, some of which are announced tableside.

Maddalena's is one of the best restaurants in the South Bay area. Oh, excuse me, I meant to say in the Peninsula. An evening here will etch fond remembrances deep in the grey matter.

MAIN ST. ★★★★
Seafood and Steak

Price Range: Moderate

169 Main St., Los Altos	A.E. − M.C. − Visa
Phone: (415) 948-4332	Reservations Recomm.
Hours: Lunch: 11−3 pm, Mon.-Fri.	No Non-Smoking Section
Dinner: 5−10:30 pm, Mon.-Sat.	Limited Wheelchair Access
Closed Sunday	

Full Bar

Mac's Tea Room has finally gotten some competition. Main St. is beginning to draw a large clientele from the gentry of Los Altos. And rightly so. I was astounded to discover how generous the portions were and how reasonable the prices. It's almost a steal, especially when you consider you are eating in classy environs, surrounded by a suit and tie clientele. The place is rich and it's friendly to the pocketbook.

Lunch time is one of the best times at Main St. The kitchen here bases its output on straight forward dishes without calling on gimmicks and subterfuge to reel in the customers. The lunch and dinner menus are strongly influenced by seafood, fresh and delicious seafood. If you like freshly shucked clams or Blue Point Oysters, this is the place to do your slurping. The prices for these fleshy, sea sweet delights is tearfully cheap. I felt as though I had entered a dream thrusting me back to the clam bars on the streets of Buffalo, New York. I just kept slurping and slurping until I was fully sated.

The menu highlights, in addition to seafood, a huge, fist-sized Club Sandwich, the likes of which you have not seen in a country club. This sandwich is cut simply in half and not in the traditional quarters. It is layered with fresh turkey meat, morning fried bacon, lettuce and mayo. The flavors are simple and memorable. Look for this item at lunch time.

For dinner, go for the red meat. The steaks here are large and thick in terms of inches, not micro-meters. The New York is an honorable cut that requires a sharp knife to cut through its charbroiled bulk. Prime rib is also a good choice. The meat is always roasted to perfection and cut in thick juicy slabs.

Main St. brings you fresh fish specials for both lunch and dinner. Seasonal catches like Sole, Salmon and Halibut, come and go on a rotating basis. Though the kitchen staff cannot boast having a master chef at the burners, the cooks are capable in grilling fish properly. The fish I have sampled here has never been overcooked or oversauced.

Main St. presents a sophisticated setting with a long row of very private banquettes, perfect for business discussions or romantic couples seeking to hide away from the dining room milieu.

I was definitely surprised by Main St. I was expecting average eats at high prices. Instead, I stumbled onto a great find, a restaurant with a heart for the hungry masses.

MAMA TRIED ★★
Philly Cheesesteak

Price Range: Bargain

2655 El Camino Real, Santa Clara	Master Card — Visa
Phone: 296-1224	Seats 200
Hours: 11:30 am—Midnight, daily	Non-Smoking Section
Full Bar	Wheelchair Access

Mama Tried is a Philadelphia-flavored restaurant with a full cocktail bar and a cast of interesting edibles like Philly Cheesesteak and hoagie sandwiches, all made according to authentic specifications with only the best ingredients.

Though its name has a special attraction, with the blink of a slow eyelid the average driver could easily miss Mama Tried on El Camino.

The interior unfolds a warm, inviting picture of the new-wave sandwich shop where coziness is punctuated by a circular bar and an in-view kitchen. Those who don't want to swill and eat along a resined bartop may choose a hiding place at a table. For game junkies, Mama Tried offers a pool table and a pair of electronic games.

The gastronomic hook here is, without a doubt, the Philly Cheesesteak and the Philly Hoagie. After sampling the Cheesesteak at Jersey's (1781 Winchester Blvd., Campbell), I couldn't wait to taste the diversions the Philadelphians had conjured up for this legendary back-East sandwich.

The most striking feature of Mama Tried's cheesesteaks is the bread that contains the griddle-fried sirloin and cheese. The dough is brought in from the East Coast, and the rolls are baked daily. The quality is commendable. Baked to an near-croissant flakiness topside, the rolls are light, yet doughy and firm enough to form sturdy pockets for the juice ingredients.

The fillings consist of thinly sliced steak fried to a springy texture, liquidy melted cheese, sauteed onions and relish of Italian-style tomato sauce. Six variations exist, including the popular Pepper Steak which uses strings of pungent green peppers.

The Philadelphia Hoagie is Mama Tried's answer to a Togo's No. 17 submarine sandwich. The Italian Hoagie presents a roll full of neatly sliced Genoa, capacolla, prosciutto with the addition of provolone, tomato, lettuce, raw onions and a light olive-oil dressing. The lightness of this sandwich was most outstanding.

MANNY'S CELLAR ★★★   Price Range: Moderate
Italian

175 West St. John St., San Jose	A.E. – C.B. – D.C. – M.C. –
Phone: 286-5990	Visa
Hours: Lunch: 11–2:30 pm, Mon.–Fri.	Reservations Taken
Dinner: 5–10 pm, Wed.–Thurs.	No Non-Smoking Area
Till 11 pm, Fri. & Sat.	Clumsy Wheelchair Access
Full Bar	

Manny's Cellar has developed a multi-dimensional character, infused with the whackiness of a comedian friend. For more than a century, it has continued a long and rollicking service to the residents of San Jose. Stepping down the worn, narrow steps into the subterranean den of this Italian cellar is like entering a living restaurant museum.

As the new downtown complexes reach far into the sky, Manny's holds tough to its roots as it becomes slowly buried in the monolithic shadows of progress. No matter what happens, I've got a strong notion Manny's will remain an immovable force in the emerging cityscape. Located literally in the cellar of a very old building that was a boarding house for Italian immigrants in the late 1800s, Manny's manages to dodge the wrecking ball.

The interior is a vision of age-old memories, of forgotten nights when locals were elbow-deep in whiskey and spaghetti. Spirited dialogues and incessant tinkling silverware assault the ears from the moment you enter the door. A disorderly array of red-cloth-covered tables, chairs, stools and a popcorn machine create a picture of riotous dining and booze swilling. Pabst Blue Ribbon lamps, attached to cellar support posts, lend a weird touch to the overall motif. Blue-collar workers, executives, high-society diners and street dwellers blend in the ambiance like a fat hand in a tight glove.

Meal time at Manny's draws its merit from reasonable prices and engaging, multi-course dinners rather than its quality. I have never been impressed by any great display of cuisine at Manny's. The food is OK — always hearty and generously portioned.

All dinners include soup, salad, entree and ice cream. On our night here we sampled a field hand's brew of hearty minestrone. Simmering in a very loosely based vegetable broth were large pieces of overcooked rigatoni, chunks of celery and carrots, plus other odds and ends of vegetables. I was delighted by the salad, a common mixed green with a very tasty bleu-cheese dressing.

With soup and salad courses, we were supplied with baskets of fresh Italian bread, the kind Italian bakers get up at 2 a.m. to make.

Highlighting the menu Friday and Saturday is what our waitress regarded as the specialty, Prime Rib. I was expecting more than I received. I'd had visions of a large, juice-dripping slab of meat; what came to the table was a pedestrian cut of prime rib with average tenderness in an adequate pool of natural juice.

After being tipped that the Sausage and Rigatoni was a winner, we ordered it with high hopes. I can't say I was thoroughly disappointed, but I will say I've had much better at lesser-known establishments. A heavy portion of sauced rigatoni tubes occupy most of the plate. Squeezed to the far edges of the dish are two medium-size, tightly packed Italian sausages, rich with a fragrant pork flavor. The sauce covering both pasta and sausage is unique to Manny's Cellar. It's a glassy brew with a beef-bouillon flavor and a brownish color. Interesting.

Intuition led us into ordering the Veal Scallopine. The veal used in this robust rendition requires action with a sharp knife and a few extra chews with the choppers. It is a rough cut, seemingly from a maturing calf. Enhancing the heartiness of this scallopine recipe is the deep-brown wine sauce in which the veal slices were sauteed.

Our last entree was the Scalloni. This star-crossed fish dish blends scallops and abalone pounded together, forming good-size filets, dipped in egg batter, then sauteed in butter. The rich flavor drew from the sweet creaminess of the scallop while the texture came from the firm tenderness of the abalone. Served alongside is a generous helping of tartar sauce.

Side dishes include spaghetti, rigatoni and baked potato. All three were adequate, though somewhat unnecessary because of the large amount of food served in the entrees.

Manny's Cellar is staffed by a vintage crew. Veteran waitresses attend their tables like troopers. Most have been here as long as Manny's has been strictly a restaurant, and they have developed endearing personalities that make your dinners flow without error.

MAXWELL'S PLUM ★★★
Continental

Price Range: Expensive

Ghiradelli Square, San Francisco	A.E. – C.B. – D.C. – M.C. –
Phone: (415) 441-1161	Visa
Hours: Noon–2 am, Mon.-Fri.	Reservations Required
From 11 am, Sat.	No Non-Smoking Section
To Midnight, Sunday	Wheelchair Access
Full Bar — Extensive Wine List	

When I entered Maxwell's Plum I felt as though I had entered a jeweled treasure chest. Each room presented a dazzling display of sparkling brass, copper, chandeliers and boundless murals of glittering stained glass. There are five menus representing the theme of various rooms (The Bay Room, The Cafe, The Cafe Luncheon, The Bay Room Luncheon, The Weekend Brunch). We were seated in the more elegant Bay Room overlooking Aquatic Park with a grand background of Bay Water. The overhead must be stupefying. I couldn't help wonder what is in store when the tremendous curiosity business wears off, leaving Maxwell's Plum as yet another one of San Francisco's upper echelon restaurants.

While the interior titilated my imagination, the food brought me back to Earth. The entrees we sampled were good, but not nearly as impressive as the decor and ambiance. I did find the prices reasonably competitive and the visual presentation of each dish to have huge eye appeal. I believe the chefs here are well trained in the culinary arts and take their time in preparing their specialties.

Our dinner began with a pasta appetizer called Paglia e Fieno. Both white and green ribbon noodles were boiled to a firm, starch-clean tenderness, then tossed with pieces of Italian sausage and sweet peas in a cream sauce, moderately sharp with Romano cheese. The sauce had a smooth consistency that clung evenly to the noodles.

Following the pasta, we explored Maxwell's salad repertoire. All entrees are a la carte and salads are extra, but worth the sampling. With such a large variety of salads, I recommend that you avoid the common dinner green. It was mundane in comparison to its fancy menu mates. The one that we all agreed was the best was the avocado tomato, bacon and Roquefort. The vegetables in this salad were vibrantly picturesque. The deep-red tomato slices glistened with juiciness and were arranged in a half crescent on the plate. Crumbles of pungent Roquefort, real bacon pieces and a clean, ripe avocado half were banked along the row of tomatoes. A subtle vinaigrette was applied by our waiter.

After a long interval, our main courses were delivered. From "Entrees," we ordered the Wild Boar which came to us in large, hefty high-rise chops. The texture of the boar was tough, but the flavor of the meat purveyed a gamey savor that was unique and tantalizing. A fruity brown sauce covered the boat chops and sauteed apples were served alongside.

Our second entree was Maxwell's version of veal picatta, one that closely followed the traditional recipe. The escalopes of white veal were sauteed to a fork tenderness in a rich butter, then finished with a squeeze of lemon juice. The sauce was simply crafted without excesses and worked well with the delicate flavor of the meat.

We also sampled a slab of fresh salmon that received a little too much fire. Though the meat was somewhat dry, it retained its fresh sea taste as well as a nice pink hue. The dryness lost its edge when the waiter applied a very smooth bearnaise topside. Maxwell's bearnaise was creamy and light and speckled with flecks of tarragon. This exquisite bearnaise was also offered with the Filet Mignon.

For dessert, we opted for fresh fruit and went with the fresh strawberries and raspberries (seasonal). Topping the berries was of Schlag or Devon Cream with brown sugar. We had schlag, a sweet, heavy cream, that was not sweet enough to balance the severe tartness of the berries. I suspect that they were not at the peak of their ripeness.

Maxwell's Plum is a fantasy restaurant, certainly worth one visit this summer to San Francisco. So far, business is on the verge of exploding. I'm sure Ghirardelli Square is doing somersaults over all residual business this plum will bring.

MENARA ★★★★   Price Range: Expensive
Moroccan

---

41 Gish Road, San Jose	A.E. — M.C. — Visa
Phone: 998-1583	Reservations Recomm.
Hours: Lunch: 11–2 pm, Mon.-Fri.	No Non-Smoking Section
Dinner: 6–10 pm, Mon.-Sat.	Limited Wheelchair Access
Full Bar — Entertainment: Belly Dancing	

Menara has preserved the marvel of its decor. The proprietors have well maintained the mystery and the beauty of their restaurant, keeping the fixtures clean and sparkling. You enter into a spacious foyer where the gentle bubbling of a floor fountain immediately fills your ears. To the left is a full bar. To the right are several velvet couches and pillows where romancers can sip cocktails and converse before dinner.

Through a Moorish archway lies the central dining room. It is a vast, well ventilated area plush with red carpeting, more velvet couches, big pillows, and brass tables. Large rotary blade fans whir hypnotically overhead, stirring the deep blood reds and dark blues cast from ornate

Moroccan lamps. Don't be shy at Menara. Get totally involved. Let your senses dance.

Because the tradition of eating with your fingers is encourarged here, you will be entertained with a hand-washing ritual before dinner is served. A waiter will perform the rites by having you place your hands over a portable basin and then pouring warm water over the fingers. He concludes by spraying you with rose water.

Shortly, thereafter, you are presented with your first course. The best way to enjoy the wonder of Moroccan cuisine is to order a combination dinner. At Menara you can have such feasts as the Diner Rabati or the Le Diner Menara. We went with the Rabati.

The commencing dish was the traditional Moroccan salad. A ring of marinated tomato dressed with lemon, olive oil, and cumin circled a ring of diced cucumber in a smooth avocado puree springing with lemon. Forming the center was a cold stew of eggplant strong with cumin. With this salad, you are served fresh Moroccan bread with which to scoop the liquidy ingredients.

Following the salad, we received B'stilla. Neslted within layers of crackling crisp filo pastry is an assemblage of chicken, raisins, and cinnamon. The surface is dusted with powdered sugar with the words "Enjoy Menara" written in the covering of white. Unfortunately, the B'stilla, this time around, was over-baked, resulting in a very dry consistency. The chicken was also very dry, lacking the moistness that I am used to in this recipe.

After a brief respite that included the quaffing a heady Algerian wine, our third course arrived in a puff of lemony steam. Tajine de Poulet Aux Citrons. Several native Moroccan dishes are braises called Tajine (simmered long in a conical pot). This course exemplified this process. Resting in a large sunken dish were two, fat, meaty hens. The hens had been stewed in a strong liquid rich with the full-bodied essence of citrus which purveyed an enjoyable aftertaste. Woven into the flavor was fresh clove. This aromatic spice had a striking influence on the overall taste.

Probably, the most memorable quality of this chicken was the wonderful succulence of the meat. It was so tender, it tore effortlessly from the bones.

Our final two courses came on the heels of each other. The first to arrive was a platter of Cous-Cous or cracked wheat. This traditional Northern African dish combined mouthwatering grains of semolina with an assortment of vegetables, raisins, nuts, and flavored with herbs and spices. The bits of zucchini and carrots present in this offering tasted as though they were plucked from the saute pan of an Italian chef. They just didn't assimilate with the buttery flavor of the wheat.

With the Cous-Cous, we received a plate of lamb chunks braised in honey. The honey saturated the meat and its cloying sweetness sent jarring impulses to the brain. My first bite nearly pushed my face into the carpet. The meat of the lamb wasn't nearly as succulent as the chicken, yet it could be torn apart with little problem.

For dessert, a bowl of fresh fruit and cups of mint tea are presented. The mint tea is traditionally poured from an exaggerated height. We prodded our waiter to extend the customary distance. With a smile, he raised the tea urn much higher and poured the sweet, green libation directly into the cups. The pouring process brings an uplifting aeration to the tea.

During our meal, a belly dancer entertained for the many customers reclined on pillows in the dining room. She was very adept in her art and performed a variety of belly dances from different countries throughout the world.

Though I was a little disappointed with the food at Menara, I was fully compensated with exotic atmosphere. Sometimes, though very rarely, the trade-off is acceptable.

MEKONG ★★★
Vietnamese

Price Range: Bargain

288 Castro St., Mountain View	Master Card – Visa
Phone: (415) 968-2604	No Reservations
Hours: Lunch: 11:30–2 pm, Tues.-Fri.	Non-Smoking Section
Dinner: 5:30–9 pm, Tues.-Sun.	Limited Wheelchair Access
Beer and Wine	

Mekong was around long before the influx of Vietnamese restaurants hit the Downtown San Jose Area. In fact, this Castro St. restaurant has been around for many years, surviving the erratic and constantly changing conditions of the fickled restaurant trade.

I had nearly forgotten about the Mekong when I saw its markee while doing research along Castro Street's famed Chinese restaurant row. It made me feel good to see that it had come through the hard times with the doors still open for business.

The menu includes many of the classic Vietnamese dishes, plus several new additions that were not on the menu when I first reviewed this restaurant. Current additions include several brochette items. A masterful seafood brochette comprised of a skewer of prawns and scallops is served in a simple, wholesome manner. Spicy hot dipping sauces are available. Just ask. There is also a hearty Beef Brochette and a Pork Brochette. I prefer the seafood variety.

For those seeking a switch from the traditional Imperial Rolls, the Mekong now offers Spicy Beef. This is made up of marinated beef rolled up in tender grape leaves. An explosive dipping sauce packed with red peppers comes along side. Of course, the Imperial Rolls are still very good here. A puree of vegetables and meat are rolled up in rice paper, then fried in oil until transparent and ringing crisp. They are served with the tangy fish sauce, Muoc Mam.

The Beef Curry is among my favorite dishes at the Mekong. This curry recipe calls for tender slices of beef in a pungent curry blend that echoes the aromatic flavor of East Indian curries. The spices thoroughly enhance the beef taste, while creating a quality that is at once different and refreshing.

The Mekong is a good choice when considering a Vietnamese restaurant. The food is authentic, the atmosphere still funky Western, and the service warm and friendly, though sometimes slow.

MEYBERG'S ★★★   Price Range: Bargain
Jewish Deli

1002 Town & Country Village, San Jose	Cash Only
Phone: 243-7195	No Reservations
Hours: Open from 7 a.m.	No Non-Smoking Section
Beer and Wine	Limited Wheelchair Access

Through the long, hard years, Meyberg's has established itself as the South Bay's most cherished Jewish deli. With an endless line-up of wholesome hot plates and mouth-watering sandwiches at reasonable prices, patrons continue to file in throughout the week, seeking sustenance in traditional Meyberg style.

For those not hungry for the typical deli sandwich, I recommend you try a plate of beef bratwurst made by Mr. Meyberg himself. A bratwurst plate consists of two, large, meaty sausages, packed tightly with beef and spiced with clove and other alluring seasonings. The sausages are barbecued over charcoal which imbues the beef with a pleasant smoky flavor. With all hot plates, you have your choice of one hot side dish and one cold salad. They include such items as noodles with gravy, rice, red cabbage, plus a host of salads, highlighted by the German style potato salad.

Another interesting deli alternative at Meyberg's are the short ribs. Meyberg first grills the meat, then braises it until the beef falls from the bones in succulent chunks. A brown, glazy sauce accented with Madeira strikes up tasteful harmony with the ribs. A side of noodles and a scoop of potato salad make the perfect accompaniments.

Sandwiches at Meyberg's are crafted on the spot by a cast of counter clerks who are generous when loading up the bread with meats. I have recently enjoyed a juicy hot pastrami with a sheet of swiss cheese. The thin folds of lean, tender pastrami were mounded onto slices of fragrant rye with only a brush of mustard. If you don't like rye, you have your choice of various styles of bread, including French roll.

Meyberg is very generous with his dill pickles. Located at the end of the counter in close proximity to the cash register is a tray of dill pickle chunks. So far, nobody has stopped me from taking as many as I want. I love the taste of dill pickles with pastrami or corned beef.

The Meyberg prize sandwich is by far the Reuben, crafted with enormous savor by the sandwich makers. Pastrami, corned beef, sauerkraut, and Swiss cheese are applied onto rye bread in a great amount. It'll take a big mouth to envelope a biteful of this sandwich. Regular mustard, hot mustard, and bottles of fresh horseradish are standard condiments on all tables in Meyberg's. Use at will.

MINATO SUSHI ★★★   Price Range: Bargain
Japanese

617 North Sixth St., San Jose	**Master Card – Visa**
Phone: 998-8711	**Reservations Taken**
Hours: Lunch: 11–2 pm, Tues.-Fri.	**No Non-Smoking Section**
Dinner: 5–8:30 pm, Tue.-Thurs.	**Limited Wheelchair Access**
Till 9 pm, Fri. & Sat.	
Beer and Wine	

Minato Sushi is a no-frills establishment. Many locals come here to eat, fill their bellies, and get on their way. Lingering after a dinner doesn't fit into the program, unless you want to read the newspaper or chat with one of the workers. Service is fast and efficient. The food is basic, wholesome, sparingly seasoned, and direct. What comes from the kitchen is what you might see steaming on a table in a Japanese household. Nothing jazzy, no high-gloss cuisine.

We started with a spread of appetizers. Gyoza, the Japanese ravioli, was unlike the more delicate varieties I have sampled. Here they were larger and bulkier, somewhat like the Chinese pot sticker. The dough was slightly dry to the bite and chewy. The filling of chopped meat and vegetables were pervasively spiced and grew tangy when dipped in soy sauce.

Sharing space with the gyoza was a plate of Sushi Mix. A limited selection of raw fish had been molded into glutinous rice forms. The most impressive presented a wheel of seaweed-wrapped rice with a center of raw eel, egg, spinach. Also displayed were thin slices of raw tuna on beds of molded rice, and raw abalone, also on rice. The flavors of the fish and rice were fresh and clean. I did miss the service of the hot and tingling green mustard which is traditionally served either inside the sushi or on the side.

With most dinners, you receive a complete lineup of pre-entree teasers. Before we could even get adjusted to our seating, we were served our first course, tsukemono (cabbage salad). After our appetizers came our miso soup and salad, a bowl of crisp iceburg lettuce drizzled with a vinegar-potent, Japanese-style dressing.

Those who like their entrees plain and straightforward, will revel in Niku Mizutaki. The presentation of this stark soup exalts Buddhist simplicity. A clear, nearly unseasoned broth, stocked with vegetables and meat, is served up in a black iron pot. There were complaints at my table that it was bland. Indeed, it is bland, and if you hanker for spicier fare, Niku Mizutaki is not for you. It is an uncomplicated soup that will purge the impurities from your body, leaving you fresh and alive.

One of Minato Sushi's most outstanding attributes is the service of generous portions. This fact was established by the Chicken Teriyaki. A long platter was filled with strips of char-grilled chicken. The chicken pieces were still clothed in their skin, which was sizzled black from the searing charcoal blaze. The grill flavor thoroughly penetrated the flavor of the meat and dominated the weak, slightly soupy teriyaki marinade. There was so much chicken, you could have shared it with your friends and still had an ample portion for yourself.

Our last entree was a combination of Tempura and Sashimi. Minato Sushi restores my belief that the Japanese are the masters of the deep-fry, a technique they perfected from the Portuguese many, many years ago. Large, jumbo prawns and an assortment of fresh vegetables are dipped in batter, then deep-fried until crackling crisp. Tempura deep-fry presents a blond-colored batter jacket that is light, airy, and nearly greaseless when fully fried. The process seals in the natural juices of the prawns and retains the nutrients of the vegetables. I bit into a fried mushroom and my mouth was filled with its full, unmitigated flavor.

Rounding out this combination plate was a tray of sashimi. Raw tuna was displayed in accurately cut rectangles set in neat rows. The fish had a deep pink hue and a clean, immediate savor. With a dip in a spiked soy sauce, the marriage of fish and marinade was truly fulfilling. For those conscious of their weight, sashimi is very low in calories and high in nutrients.

Service at Minato Sushi was efficient. Waitresses do things by rote here and disappear after they serve a dish. If you want another beer or saki, you'll have to flag one of the waitresses down. They rarely come to you. When we were finished, nobody told us that we had to pay our bill at the counter. It is up to you to figure it out.

MINI GOURMET ★★★   Price Range: Bargain
American

---

599 So. Bascom Ave., San Jose	Cash Only
Phone: 275-8973	No Reservations
Hours: 6 am–9 pm, Mon.–Fri.	No Non-Smoking Section
7 am–3 pm, Sat. & Sun.	Limited Wheelchair Access

Breakfast is a meal that is often overlooked by restaurant reviewers. And I must admit, I have been negligent in my morning-meal research. Lately, though, the Mini-Gourmet came back into view, stirring fond memories of piping hot omelets and Saturday basketball games at Lincoln High School. This steamy, always smoky little diner, hugging the corner of Bascom and Moorpark for over 11 years, has become an essential inclusion in San Jose's growing treasure chest of restaurants. The Mini is no fluke; it has so much going for it that breakfast alone would not do justice to its long list of basic food merits.

Breakfast, however, will leave you breathlessly awake and fully satisfied. A morning meal here will drive away any notion of having lunch. Meals run hearty, which often means large portions and a lot of carbohydrates. The best way to describe the food at the Mini is to say it is American, downhome-style grub. Sit back and fill your bucket.

For a breakfast visit, I sat down to a nutritious plate of bacon and eggs. This meal includes two eggs to order, three bacon strips, hash browns and toast and jelly. I ordered my eggs over easy and received them with that desirable opaque yolk surface. The griddle masters at the Mini have been frying eggs for a long time and rarely mess up an order. The bacon strips were long and lean. For me, the sign of a top notch breakfast cook lies in the quality of the hash browns. The Mini's potatoes were fried to a crispy, golden topside while the potato shreds below the surface remained moist and potato rich.

For lunch, I highly recommend either the patty melt or the Reuben. The melt is a gourmet-style hamburger set between toasted rye bread with grilled onions and melted cheese. The Reuben is prepared with traditional savor, featuring thinly sliced corned beef also between rye with a generous helping of sauerkraut and Swiss cheese.

Dinners uphold diner quality at the Mini. All entrees are served with your choice of soup or salad, potatoes, vegetables, rolls, and ice cream or sherbet. Pork Chops with mashed potatoes and spiced applesauce won't disappoint your expectations. For those on light diets, a bevy of freshly made salads and seafood salads are offered daily.

The Mini Gourmet is here to stay. It has proven itself to the hundreds of faithful customers who swing through the doors daily.

MOTHER LODE ★★ Price Range: Moderate
American Melting Pot

Corner of Wolfe & Stevens Creek, Cupertino	A.E. — M.C. — Visa
	Reservations Taken
Phone: (408) 253-3334; 253-3335	Non-Smoking Section
Hours: 11 am–10:30 pm, Daily	Limited Wheelchair Access
Beer and Wine	

The old, weather-worn location at the corner of Wolfe Road and Stevens Creek Blvd. was built with one theme in mind: The Mine Shaft. Mother Lode is the third restaurant to stake a claim in these mining haunts. It is my recommendation that if Mother Lode fades out, as did the former two tenants, the current proprietor should get smart, board up the kitchen and dig for gold right through the dining room floor.

The interior of this miner's culinary stop off is shadowy and difficult to navigate if you are space blind. Aisles are narrow and tables are hidden away for the ultimate in privacy. The first time I was here I needed assistance to find my way out the door. Not only that, I felt as though I had been nailed up in a tunnel with only a candle and a varnished table to keep me company.

The menu is a mish-mash of California favorites. Pasta, seafood, Mexican food, omelettes, burgers, quiches, steaks, and a limited selection of BBQ items co-mingle in harmony on one single menu. I pray for the chef every night.

The best item on the menu is the Baby Back Ribs. They are definitely worth the price of admission. These pork rich, succulent ribs are portioned generously. A plate will deliver over 10 meat-laden ribs Barbecued over a charcoal blaze. The pork is so tender it tears from the bone shaft with a simple tug of the teeth. The ribs are served with a vinegar tart BBQ sauce, a cobette, and an order of rice pilaf. With your dinner you have a choice of soup or trip to the salad bar. Go for the salad bar. Though not as inspiring as some I have seen, the greens were fresh and the dressings flavorful, not bottled tasting.

The Mexican food items are few. Of the four offered on the menu, I suggest the Quesadilla. This item plies two large flour tortillas together with a center of melted cheese. The top is garnished with guacamole, salsa and sour cream. The quesadilla would make a filling, meatless alternative to a burrito or a tostada, the other two Mexican offerings on the menu.

As for the omelettes and the quiches, I can only say they make good bed-time food. The vegetable omelette was big and boring. It was a bear paw of fluffed egg filled with mushrooms, onions, zucchini, and carrots. The ingredients were very healthful, but flavor was on furlough. Stick with the BBQ items.

In my heart, I know that Mother Lode has the odds stacked against it. Two restaurants with the same exact theme have bitten the bitter dust. I only hope that the Mother Lode can find gold where the others found chalk.

NICOLINO'S GARDEN CAFE ★★★
Italian   **Price Range: Moderate to Expensive**

1228 Reamwood Ave., Sunnyvale	A.E. − M.C. − Visa
Phone: (408) 738-5325	Reservations Required
Hours: 11 am−11 pm, Mon.–Fri.	No Non-Smoking Section
4−11 pm, Sat.	Full Wheelchair Access
10 am−11 pm, Sun.	
Full Bar − Sunday Brunch	

Musicians, tableside technicians, pizza makers, fast talking hosts, glamorous hostesses and Magicians cavort amidst the quasi-elegance of Nicolino's Garden Cafe. While we swallowed our fettuccine, we watched sponge balls disappear from sight, flames explode from copper pans, and waiters zig-zag in string art patterns throughout the dining room. A din of laughter and spirited dialogue punctuated the smooth plunking of piano keys ever present in the ever crowded Nicolino's. The owners of Giorgio's and Frankie, Johnny and Luigi's have built themselves a winner.

If you want to eat well at Nicolino's make your desires known. For instance, one of the innovative items of the pizza kitchen, visible from the main dining room, is the Sausage Bread. Make sure you ask your waiter when the sausage bread was pulled from the oven. When it's hot and the cheese is melted, the sausage bread is an excellent item. After having been out of the oven for some time, the sausage and the cheese woven into the bread dough grows hard and loses flavor. This goes for the Spinach Bread as well. Make sure they are hot and you will be satisfied.

Nicolino's kitchen will accommodate special orders. Pan Fried Calamari is listed on the menu as an appetizer. On my first visit, I found the fried squid such a good item, I promised myself to order it as an entree when next I came. Though the Calamari isn't listed as an entree, the kitchen accommodated by making a larger order. The squid here is very tender and fresh. The filets are breaded and pan fried in garlic and olive oil. A very simple and zesty rendition.

Contrary to what you may think, Nicolino's is somewhat deficient in the pasta department. Only a few specialty pastas are offered like Fettucini with Clams and Mostacioli Suprema, The cream sauce is used more frequently with the pasta then the red sauce or the simple garlic, oil and herb. The cream sauce works well with the Mostacioli Suprema, a platter of tubular pasta with seafood (prawns, baby shrimp, king crab). It was light and milky with a distinctive infusion of the sea. I missed the tastier clam broth, garlic and oil sauce with the Fettucini with clams. The dairy rich sauce did not bring a balance of flavor to the fresh clam and al dente boiled pasta.

One of my favorite dishes here is the Prawns Stefano. Succulent, jumbo prawns are butterflied and flattened, breaded, and pan fried in olive oil and garlic. The flavors are intense.

Another prawn specialty when offered is the Prawns Bordelaise. If you get the right person to make it, you will be totally satisfied. On one visit, the master renzo of the House performed his tableside magic on six jumbo prawns. He did them just right in a sauce that was garlic potent, yet well balanced.

Nicolino's is in the fast lane to success. Lunches are impossible to get a table and dinners are picking up very quickly.

THE 19TH HOLE ★★★★★   Price Range: Bargain
Hamburgers

Stevens Creek & Lawrence Expwy.,   Cash Only
  San Jose   No Reservations
Phone: (408) 296-9219   No Non-Smoking Section
Hours: Lunch (only): 11–2:30 pm,   Limited Wheelchair Access
            Mon.-Sat.
Full Bar

The 19th Hole makes the only 5 star hamburger I can think of in the South Bay. Kirk's and Clarke's are great, but the Hole's beef pattie on bun takes the cigar.

The Hole's burger is an architype in itself, the type of meal childrens' dreams are made of. Each pattie weighs in at 1/3 pound of pure, unmitigated beef and is fired over an open flame by sizzle queens Nina and Irene. There is minimal shrinkage of the pattie from loss of fat and juice. When you sink your teeth into this massive burger, you're going to taste a lot of beef.

What makes this burger so good is the simple, homestyle manner of its preparation. The sesame seed buns are fresh and the condiments applied are not tainted with flavor adjuncts and crazy, gloppy additives. You get meat, bread, with a swash of mayo, plenty of juicy dill pickles, a thick wheel of fresh onion, a dash of salt, and a dash of pepper. You apply ketchup and mustard.

With the hamburger, don't forget a basket of Nina's special French Fries. They are long, thin potatoes, fried to a crisp exterior and a moist, soft interior.

Go for it!

THE NOODLE PALACE ★
Spaghetti

Price Range: Bargain

140 North Santa Cruz, Los Gatos	M.C. — Visa — Gold Card
Phone: 354-0555	No Reservations
Hours: Lunch: 11:30–2:30 pm, M–Fri.	Non-Smoking Section
Dinner: 5–10 pm, Mon.-Thurs.	Wheelchair Access
Full Bar	

The Noodle Palace is a great place to hang loose with the kids and fill up on big portions of pasta. As for the quality of the pasta dishes I have sampled here, I can only say I have been consistently unimpressed.

Nobody seems to complain about The Noodle Palace, however. The place maintains a healthy trade. The reasons are simple for its success. As a family restaurant, The Noodle Palace succeeds enormously. Children like the place. The profusion of turn-of-the-century geedunkery gives them plenty of visual entertainment. There are even video games in the foyer. Personally, I find the presence of video games in a restaurant like this to be distasteful. How much beeping, crooning, electronic warbling can humankind take before we all go mad? The sounds were nauseating.

Nevertheless, portions are big and prices are low. You can feed the whole family and still have a few dimes left over.

The menu is very simple, comprised mainly of pasta dishes. Various sauces and toppings provide variation with your semolina. Probably the best entree here is the basic Spaghetti with Meat Sauce. I must say the sauce was pretty good. It had a sharply defined tomato tartness tempered by the flavor of the hamburger. The presence of the beef made the sauce very thick and chunky. It hung to the spaghetti strands and didn't dribble down to the bottom of the plate.

As I feared, however, the pasta was overcooked. I understand that at restaurants where the main output is pasta, the cooks must employ techniques which enable them to get the orders out fast. I didn't expect al dente, but I didn't expect soft, mushy spaghetti either.

An interesting pasta dish that The Palace serves is the Kasseri Cheese and Pasta. A thick coat of Greek white cheese and melted butter covers a heaping portion of spaghetti. The richness of the cheese and butter combination gives the overboiled pasta a needed boost. I do recommend that you don't dally over this dish. Eat it reasonably fast. The melted cheese has a tendency to congeal into a rubbery mass.

All spaghetti dinners come with a salad of iceburg lettuce, and a small loaf of warm sourdough bread.

Service at The Noodle Palace is well meaning, but consistently slow. Waitresses have a tendency to wander about even in the thick of business. All entrees have always been served hot from the kitchen however. At times, the management has been aloof and slow in bringing your check.

OKAYAMA ★★★   Price Range: Bargain
Japanese

565-A North Jackson St., San Jose   Master Card — Visa
Phone: 279-9920   Reservations Taken
Hours: Lunch: 11–2 pm, Thurs.-Tues.   No Non-Smoking Section
         Closed Wednesdays   No Wheelchair Access
         Dinner: 4:30–8:30 pm
Beer and Wine

Like most of the cafes around Japan Town, Okayama presents a personalized version of the Japanese coffee shop, equipped with Coca Cola menu, counter, exposed ice box and plastic-covered tables with kitchen chairs. Japanese lanterns, a few 3-D prints and several well-placed Asahi beer decals are about all the ethnic decoration you'll find here. But this bacon-and-eggs image goes no further than the decor. The food, prepared and served in the traditional Japanese manner, is all wholesome and healthful.

We commenced with a plate of Nigiri Sushi. The quality of these rice tasties exceeded the reasonable price tag. Placed on top of molded rice were three varieties of primarily raw fish. The middle row displayed raw tuna or Sashimi, thinly sliced to fit the contour of the mold. Raw abalone and partially boiled shrimp completed the sushi plate.

The Japanese are noted for their hearty noodle dishes which are always found under the heading, Udon. Okayama offers nine different Udon selections, each large enough to suffice as a meal in itself. We sampled the Tempura Udon, dividing it four ways as an appetizer. Thickly coiled into a bowl of steaming broth were long, fat noodles, similar to spaghetti, only heavier. Topping the soup were two, tempura-fried shrimp and a handful of scallion rounds, added for distinctive flavor. The characteristic crisp tempura batter had softened in the hot broth; however, the butterflied shrimps retained their tenderness in the natural simmering heat of the soup.

All entrees are reasonably priced and all prices remain the same through lunch and dinner. Our most expensive item that evening was Salmon Nizakana. Simplicity is the outstanding characteristic of this fish offering, perfect for the calorie counter. A filet of salmon was delicately cooked in a seasoned soy sauce that was sweet like teriyaki. The fish was fork tender and flaky, releasing a bouquet of the sea with each bite. Served with the salmon were three squares of tofu.

Chosen-yaki was our beef concession for the evening. Laid in congruent rows were several slices of char-broiled beef tenderloin. The meat had been lightly marinated in, again, a sweet soy mixture, pleasantly distilled by the charcoal flavor of the grill. A spicy, Korean-style dipping sauce came with this dish, the hotness of the pepper pods adding a stimulating touch.

All entrees are complete dinners and include soup, the traditional Mizo, steamed rice, Tsukemono, Japanese pickled cabbage, tea and fortune cookie. No desserts other than fortune cookie can be purchased.

Service is executed by sweet-natured cafe matrons, kimono clad and tranquil. Dishes arrived to our table steaming hot from the kitchen. Never a delay between courses. The only delay we did encounter came when the meal had ended. The presentation of our bill was held up because the staff at Okayama was making ready to sit down and eat, family style. This type of casual attitude is part of the homey atmosphere at Okayama, one that you will find at almost all of the Jackson Street restaurants.

ORIGINAL JOE'S ★★★★   Price Range: Moderate
Italian

301 South First St., San Jose	Cash Only
Phone: 292-7030	No Reservations
Hours: 11 am–2 am, Daily	No Non-Smoking Section
Full Bar	Limited Wheelchair Access

Criticizing Original Joe's is like criticizing Paul Bunyan and Babe the Blue Ox for ravaging America's tree-studded wilderness. Original Joe's is a legend in its own time, a landmark, one of the most popular restaurants in San Jose. Forty-four years in business is a monumental achievement.

I have reviewed Joe's on several occasions. I once wrote that the waiters were surly and wore tuxedoes spotted with food. They've cleaned up their act since then. On my last few visits, they have been very accommodating and neatly clad in clean penguin suits.

On any given night, plan on a twenty-minute wait, or else squeeze onto a stool at the long counter where you can heat your cheeks on the flames shooting up from the chefs' sautee pans.

People love this place; they love to watch these chefs create their specialties along the open-view kitchen. Again, I am not inclined to speak hyperbolically about Original Joe's, unless it's about the amount of food served with each dish. The portions here are huge.

One night we sat down to a dish of spaghetti and meatballs that left me nearly gagging from over-indulgence.

The platter was heaped with a mass of springy spaghetti, built higher with a thick coat of hamburger-chunky, beefy-tasting spaghetti sauce. Anchoring the ends of the platter were two baseball-sized meatballs I don't think Joe DiMaggio could have clubbed out of Yankee Stadium.

Big portions are what New West (now California) magazine once said San Joseans had a penchant for. Original Joe's embraces this opinion and never seems to disappoint its customers.

The menu here is extensive. You can order anything from Continental specialties flamed with wine to a quality-cut 18-ounce New York steak to one of the best hamburgers in town. Joe's hamburger sandwich is a weighty slab of ground beef packed onto an even bigger Italian roll. A mouthful of this sandwich delivers pure beef flavor and enough natural juice to make an embarrassing mess. Other notable sandwiches are roast lamb and roast pork.

My favorite dish at Original Joe's is the Osso Bucco for lunch, served Wednesdays and Saturdays only. These meaty veal shanks, packed with that sauce-defining, suckable marrow, are simmered slowly in the authentic mood. With a basket of fresh Italian bread and side of mashed potatoes, this dish cannot be topped. It is unfortunate Osso Bucco comes only twice a week.

For alternatives that are always on the menu, day or night, you won't be disappointed with any one of Joe's famous sautee dishes. Veal scallopine with mushrooms, sweetbreads saute, and calf's liver saute, Venetian style, are just three of the appetizing dishes flamed up on the open-view burners.

At Original Joe's be prepared to dig in. There are no rules of dining etiquette here to follow. This restaurant is not given to daintiness or candle-lighted evenings. It is loud, sometimes abrasive, but always active and well-peopled with every sort of person you can imagine. I once saw a punk rocker with greenish hair chowing down on a meat-ball sandwich. That's Original Joe's. And just think, you can get a full meal up almost untl about 2 a.m. You can't beat that with a stick.

PAOLO'S ★★★★★   Price Range: Expensive
Continental / Italian

South 12th & Santa Clara, San Jose	All Major Credit Cards
Phone: 294-2558	Reservations Required
Hours: Lunch: 11:30–3 pm, Mon.-Fri.	No Non-Smoking Section
Dinner: 5–11 pm, Mon.-Sat.	Wheelchair Access
Full Bar	

Paolo's is San Jose's continental anchor. It was the first restaurant in its class to open in the South Bay. Jack Allen, known to many as the patriarch of continental dining, keeps a tight rein on his operation, making sure his foods are the finest he can procure in the marketplace. Having worked in the canneries as a young man, Allen has a direct line on probably the freshest, the ripest produce in the area. Vegetables and fruits are always deep in color and abundant with natural sweetness.

Though I have met with some inconsistencies at Paolo's, generally in the area of service (I recall vividly the famous cannoli toss), I find the food to be prepared with continued excellence. Veal and pasta are among the most desired dishes presented on the menu. Allen serves only the best Wisconsin milk fed veal that is always cooked to the correct degree. Veal Pizzaiola, Veal Cutlet alla Milanese, or plain broiled veal steak reveal the rich attributes of high grade veal. Sauces are applied sparingly so that the full flavor of the meat blossoms forth.

Pastas number over 20 on Paolo's extensive menu. Almost every shape and size of semolina can be ordered. The pasta here is continually and vigilantly cooked tender with the most pleasant resistance to the bite. On several occasions, I have twirled into plates of Linguine with Clam Sauce. This dish comes with either the red or the white sauce and uses only fresh clams, not canned. Gnocchi are homemade and come out light and airy, not pasty and heavy on the digestive tract.

When it comes to shellfish, Allen has proven his aptitude for attaining only the best, always the freshest. Such shellfish appetizers as Clams Oreganata, Mussels Oreganata, Danish Scampi, Oysters or Clams on the half shell, or even soft shelled crabs are a few of Paolo's most delightful seafood amenities.

And for dessert, you can't go home without a serving of homemade gelati. This fresh, creamy, smoothly textured Italian ice cream is made daily on the premises. In addition, Paolo's glorious fresh fruit display offers just about every variety of melon:, raspberries, grapes, including the Concord grapes, and other tree ripened fruits for your choosing.

Paolo's has been consistently honored with the Travel-Holiday Dining Award. Though I am less than taken with the impressiveness of this award, I do feel that generally it classifies some of the best restaurants across the U.S. Paolo's is certainly one of them.

PARADISO'S DELI AND ITALIAN GROCERY ★★
Italian Deli   Price Range: Bargain

791 Auzerais St., San Jose	Cash Only
Phone: 295-6459	No Reservations
Hours: 8 am–5 pm, Mon.–Sat.	No Non-Smoking Section
Inside (Outdoor patio more accessible)	Very Limited Wheelchair Access

Through the haze and dust of industrial Auzerais Street, you can almost smell the stout Italian aromas wafting from Paradiso's Deli. In a location that would have doomed the weak-hearted, Paradiso's has survived like a trooper, entrenching itself as one of the best little Italian eateries in town.

During business hours, Paradiso's stirs with activity. I have seen gardeners with turf under their nails to high tech executives to secretaries in floral patterned dresses sharing space as they eat a hot lunch special or a freshly made sandwich. The seating arrangements are makeshift and tightly spaced. Oddly enough, however, I have always been able to find a table despite the crowds. People rarely linger here. They come to eat and then leave.

The menu fare is mainly Italian, from freshly sliced cold cut sandwiches to pasta dishes smothered with homemade tomato sauce. Lunch specials are offered daily. More than once I have had the Veal Parmigiana Special. It comes with entree, a side of spaghetti, and a salad with your choice of dressing. The veal here isn't the best. It has a coarse, tenderized texture, but the flavor is good. The meat is heavily breaded, covered with melted cheese, and finished with tomato sauce.

With the entree, I had spaghetti that was slightly overcooked. The sauce however, was an excellent brew with a deep, savory flavor. The salad was nothing special.

Hot sandwiches are worth a mouthful. The Meatball provides one of the better examples. First of all, the meatballs here are made with good beef and not some breadcrumb mixture. They cook out juicy and firm and fill the mouth with bouquets of garlic. The meatballs are sliced and carefully molded onto a sweet dough Italian roll, then lightly topped with sauce. Paradiso's makes one of the only meatball sandwiches you can eat with your hands and not stain your pants with sauce. For an extra wallop ask to have a jalapeno pepper added to your sandwich.

Other specials that frequent the blackboard menu are eggplant dishes, enchiladas, and Italian sausage plates. The sausages here are long, fat links, fully packed with ground pork and flavored with fennel. They do spend much time simmering in sauce which overcooks the meat, making it slightly soft and breakable. But never tasteless.

PATISSERIE BOISSIERE ★★★   Price Range: Moderate
French / Pastry

Mission St., between Ocean and   Cash Only
  Seventh, Carmel   Reservations Recomm.
Phone: 624-5008   No Non-Smoking Section
Hours: 9:30 am–9:30 pm, Thurs.–Tues.   Limited Wheelchair Access
Extensive French Wine List

For dinner one night in Carmel, we visited a restaurant we had always sampled for noon-time snacks, Patisserie Boissiere. Located in a quaint, European-style niche near several art shops, this restaurant is truly authentic. The proprietors are from Orleans, France, and cook in a style characteristic of their native home. Most of the entrees are simple renditions, following family recipes. The specialty of the house will lead you into caloric sin. Authentic French pastries line a glass counter as you enter. They are all premise baked, very rich, and very sweet.

The lunch and dinner menu is identical except for price. Dinner prices are slightly elevated, though still reasonable. With a salad and/or an appetizer, prices are still reasonable when compared to other French establishments.

If you desire an appetizer, I highly recommend the Petit Pate Parisien. This item brings the splendid pastry into play. Nestled in the thin, flaky folds of a golden baked roll is a veal and pork sausage. It crinkles to the touch of a fork. Served with this light item is a crock of spicy dijon mustard. Just a dollop will intensify the flavor, bringing all into a savory balance. As a light entree item, the petit pate is served with a small salad.

If you just want a salad and a glass of white wine, the Marie Antoinette is perfect. It presents a vine-ripened, naturally sweet tomato, stuffed with whole, sweet, bay shrimp and hard-boiled egg halves on a bed of butter leaf lettuce. A tart, creamy vinaigrette makes the most complementary dressing.

Out of the four full entrees we sampled, I highly recommend two, Roulade de Celeri and the Poulet Provencale. The roulade is unique in every aspect. Wrapped around aromatic shafts of celery hearts are several thin layers of lean ham. The three rolls are baked with a covering of cream sauce and Swiss cheese, neither of which were overbearing or too thickly applied.

With the poulet Provencale, I found myself dunking a considerable amount of bread into the sauce. This dish brings you chicken breast, fully boned, and cut into forkable pieces. The chicken is simmered en casserole with a sauce made of white wine, fresh tomato chunks and black olives. The flavor of garlic was also well instilled. This dish was described as one you would find served in a small cafe along a country road in France.

Dessert and coffee should not be missed here. Even if dessert and coffee is all you want, this is the place to stop for it. At dinner, a tray of pastries is brought to the table by your waitress. From there, you choose what you most desire. All the pastries are made by Pierre Boissiere, a master pastry chef in the strict French tradition. Some of his famous pastries are the rich almond and rum Pigalles, the classic Napoleons, or his lemon cheesecake. With a cup of French-roast coffee, you'll find perfect dessert harmony.

PEAR WILLIAMS ★★★★   Price Range: Expensive
French

---

150 Middlefield Road, Menlo Park   Master Card – Visa
Phone: (415) 323-8445   Reservations Required
Hours: Lunch: 11:30–2 pm, M-Fri.   Non-Smoking Section
        Dinner: 6–9 pm, Tues.-Sun.   Full Wheelchair Access
Beer and Wine – Sunday Brunch

Chef McCombie of Pear Williams Restaurant has always been an exciting master of French cuisine. His cookery is manifestation of a man who does not rest on his laurels, who takes praise and then continues to serve the same menu, the same dishes for years on end. McCombie ventures out, embracing creativity in cuisine, incorporating new techniques into his own delicious style.

At first when I came to Pear Williams, I would explore McCombie's exquisite puff pastry entrees and desserts. Puff pastry was and still is one of his specialties, a specialty that many chefs dabble with, but never master. I recall the fine puff pastry item, Supreme de Volaille aux Morilles. Succulent morsels of chicken breast were sealed into the moist, buttery pocket of a feathery light pastry shell. The crowning glory of this dish was a smooth brandy laced sauce balanced with those rich, alluring French mushrooms, the morels.

Of late, I have sampled McCombie's more provencial dishes, particularly his stews. Every month, if you put your name on a mailing list, Pear Williams will send you a special menu, comprised of unique dishes created by McCombie. Following up one of these menu tips, I enjoyed an excellent Raoug D'Agneau aux Aubergines. It was a rich lamb stew in a wine deep sauce with spices and fresh pieces of tomatoes. With the lamb were several slices of fleshy eggplant. A great combination. Another stew that comes around once and a while is the Veau Marengo. McCombie follows the classic recipes, combining tender veal chunks with fresh herbs, and orange in a tomato-based sauce. The sauce was not too thick and could be spooned with ease.

If you leave Pear Williams without sampling dessert, you have made a tremendous error. Turn around immediately and go back. If you want to rack up many caloric sins you must order Feuilletage des Poives (allow 20 minutes for preparation). The buttery rich pastry shell rises in glory here. It is filled with a silky custard cream then topped with sweet poached pears and a mound of creme chantilly. Ahhhhhhh. With a cup of special roast, you may slip into gastronomic nirvana.

The restaurant itself presents a peaceful picture of chic country elegance. Most striking are the wood carvings that divided the booth, plus a series of framed art pieces set against pale wine colored walls. Service has been off on occasion, but mostly, it has been attentive and efficient. Pear Williams is a must try restaurant.

PEDRO'S ★★   Price Range: Moderate
Mexican

3935 Freedom Circle, Santa Clara   Master Card – Visa
Phone: (408) 496-6777   No Reservations
Hours: 11 am–10 pm, Sun.–Thurs.   Non-Smoking Section
         11 am–11 pm, Fri. & Sat.   Full Wheelchair Access
Full Bar – Sunday Brunch

Pedro's has become the symbol of Mexican dining in the South Bay. Its history weaves a tale of success that would make any restaurateur green with envy. It began as a small Mexican eatery in Los Gatos where it captured the hearts of many diners seeking a switch from the steak and potato humdrum. From there, it expanded, added more tables, a bar, and before Pedro and his family knew it, they had gleaned a cult of followers. And at Pedro's people love to wait. Waiting is part of the Pedro experience. On busy nights. you will see Los Gatans with cocktails in hand waiting along the street, soaking up the evening air. Pedro's is a happening.

Recently, the big Pedro machine opened a second store in Santa Clara. This place is the big daddy, the dream boat, the ultimate symbol of their success. It is a palatial hacienda done to the nines with beautiful Mexican fixtures, inlaid tile, wrought iron, and stained glass. And like the old Pedro's, the place is constantly jammed with patrons. It is uncanny, because I have never found the food to be very inspiring. It's the experience more than the food that people come here for.

Pedro's menu is a typical compilation of Mexican favorites with a few creative departures like the crab enchilada which I have never enjoyed. It has always been soggy and overly sauced.

The dishes I enjoy here are the basics. Chile Verde is one of the best I have sampled in a restaurant of this magnitude. The pork chunks are large and juicy and the chile sauce a spicy blend of herbs and green peppers. Though not hot, the spice does leave a refreshing buzz along the lips. Recently, I enjoyed a plate of Carnitas. The pork was roasted tender and moist then heaped onto steamed corn tortillas. Served along side was a piquant, homemade salsa chunky with fresh tomato, onion, cilantro and plenty of garlic.

The other basics like tacos, enchiladas, chile rellenos are pedestrian offerings that usually put my tastebuds to bed. They come diluted down, strictly gringo fare.

If you don't want to eat, Pedro's is a fine place just to sit and have a cocktail and a basket of chips. The surroundings are plush and the interior comfortable. Perfect for singles on the prowl.

PIKO'S BAR AND GRILL ★★★★

California Cuisine

Price Range: Moderate

1523 West San Carlos, San Jose
Phone: (408) 295-5313
Hours: Lunch: 11 am–2:30 pm, M–Fri.
       Dinner: 5–10 pm, Daily
Beer and Wine

Master Card – Visa
Reservations Recomm.
Non-Smoking Section
Limited Wheelchair Access

Piko's Bar and Grill serves the first California cuisine in San Jose, a refreshing innovation for this area.

"California Cuisine?" You ask. Sounds like a fad. From what I have read and what I have experienced, I believe it is a fad of sorts, an interesting one with tremendously good intentions. According to Piko's, California Cuisine is comprised of foods indigenous to California and uses recipes from the State's many ethnic groups. You will find Mexican dishes rubbing plates with Chinese and Japanese entrees.

There are even hamburgers at Piko's. A burger here is a full, 1/3 lb. pattie grilled over 1,000 degree mesquite charcoal. One time I had a cheeseburger and received a huge pattie grilled to a medium degree with a top coat of cheese. The flavors were pure beef, cheese and bread without sauces or condiments to subvert the flavor.

Providing a clear example for the essence of California Cuisine is Piko's Calamari preparation. Unlike the Italianated versions, the tender filets of squid were sauteed in a clean, fresh sauce with tomato, onion, a dash of garlic, and green pepper. The sauce was more refreshing than spicy and the calamari was mouth-watering and right-off-the-boat fresh.

The Japanese influence is very strong at Piko's. You can order such items as sashimi. Thick, pink slices are decoratively displayed and served with the appropriate condiments of soy and wasabi (green horseradish paste). The Japanese influence was also tasted in Piko's special chicken salad. A bevy of fluffy deep green leaf lettuce served as a pillow for julienne of poached chicken breast. It was lightly dressed with a mixture spirited with sesame seed oil. A side of orange wedges accompany for extra flavor of citrus.

Piko's offers daily blackboard specials, listing fresh fish catches and chef creations. When Coho Salmon is in season the chef here handles it with tender care, presenting the delicious fish, grilled lightly, and served au natural with a colorfully visual garnish.

Piko's Bar and Grill is linked to the San Carlos Bowl. Don't expect typical bowling alley environment. The clunking explosion of bowling pins does not invade this linen-clean environment. The interior is done in China white and tile blue with details of fresh flowers, tasteful artwork, and Japanese lamps. You will forget that San Carlos Bowl is next door. You may even forget you are in San Jose.

THE PINE INN ★★★★   Price Range: Moderate to Expensive
Breakfast – Lunch – Dinner

Carmel-by-the-Sea, Carmel   All Major Credit Cards
Phone: (408) 624-3851   Reservations Required
Hours: Breakfast: 8–11 am, Daily   No Non-Smoking Section
         Lunch: Noon–2:30 pm, Daily Limited Wheelchair Access
         Dinner: 6–9 pm, Daily
Full Bar – Sunday Brunch – Friday Buffet

The Pine Inn, Carmel's famous European Plan Hotel, offers a long line-up of repast alternatives to hotel guests and weekenders looking for a tasty mouthful.

I have always enjoyed breakfast at The Pine Inn under its beautiful gazebo with the morning light filtering softly through the glass dome. In addition to a fine plate of bacon and eggs called the Carmel Breakfast, the Inn serves a millionaire's version of Eggs a la Benedict. Two poached eggs are laid atop toasted and generously buttered English muffins. They are then sheathed in thin slices of ham and covered with a golden, yolk rich Hollandaise. With breakfast, I rarely forget to order a side of sausage links. The Inn's sausages are fat and pork juicy with a popping tight skin and a sweet pork meat stuffing.

When Lunch rolls around, forego the dining room and sit yourself at one of the leather chairs in the lounge, order an ice cold beer, and create a delicious cold cut sandwich. Every noontime, a host of quality meats, condiments and breads are put on display. I particularly cherish the ham which is thinly sliced and folds onto fragrant rye in thick manageable layers. With a spread of spicy mustard, a little horseradish, a comfortable seat, you're on easy street. The Pine Inn's lounge is a perfect place to eat a simple, old-fashioned lunch without all the fanfare and dining room clutter. And don't forget the potato salad.

Though the basic dinner at The Inn is adequate, I find both the Sunday Champagne Brunch and the Seafood Buffet on Friday nights to be worth a sampling. Both the brunch and the buffet are elaborately arranged with several varieties of well prepared dishes from hot roasts to flavorful salads and fresh fruits in season. The seafood buffet offers a host of delicious crustaceans and mollusks at an all-you-can-eat rate. Prawns, fresh crab (when available), clams, and oysters are laid out in dazzling displays. There are crisp salads, condiments, breads, and other dinner items that will keep your plate loaded high.

The Sunday Brunch is an all-the-champagne-you-can-drink affair. In addition to the delicious lunch dishes and salads, there are scrambled eggs, sausages, bacon, fruit cups, and desserts galore. When you're finished with this meal, plan on a brief nap on the beach or in one of Carmel's verduous parks.

THE PLUMED HORSE ★★★★★   Price Range: Expensive
Continental

14555 Big Basin Way, Saratoga   Master Card – Visa
Phone: (408) 867-4711   Reservations Required
Hours: 6–11 pm, Tues.–Sat.   No Non-Smoking Section
Full Bar   Full Wheelchair Access

The Plumed Horse has gleaned quite an entourage of faithful diners. On weekends, patrons jam into this restaurant donning smart evening attire with their eyes asparkle from the soft, flickering candlelight in the dining rooms.

All of the restaurants of Big Basin Way are distinct, each embracing a theme consistent with their personal philosophy of food and ambiance. The Plumed Horse is the rich, red flocked brethren, hosting an atmosphere of bordello elegance with romance astir at every table. The interior is regal with velvet high-backed chairs and ornate Victorian fixtures.

Through the years, the menu has remained simple. In addition to several continental favorites, the management has flavored the dinner ledger with some unique offerings. Lamb Curry still remains, echoing the pungency of East Indian curry.

For a special appetizer, I recommend a slice of Pate Maison, au Truffles. A rich loaf of finely ground goose liver, studded with whole pistachios, is cut into portions from the cart and served with a traditional English Cumberland sauce. Other appetizers of note include Fresh Artichoke 'Facon du Chef' and Prawns Bordelaise for two.

Flambe at The Plumed Horse is conducted with discretion. There is total emphasis on correct preparation and concern for food, not on the flaming theatrics I have endured at bogus establishments. Waiters here are most adept in preparing the flambe specialty, Steak Diane.

After wheeling his cart into place, the waiter sears two medallions of beef tenderloin, then sets them aside momentarily while he concocts the sauce. When complete, the steaks are reset in the pan and sauteed in the sauce of dijon mustard, sour cream and demi-glace. An excellent entree!

The Plumed Horse continues to serve Chicken a la Kiev. I ordered this dish on a past visit and wanted to see if the consistency had remained up to par. Indeed, it had. A large supreme of top grade chicken was filled with butter and herbs, rolled, then lightly breaded and deep fried according to the traditions prescribed by Russian chefs. One incision into the Kiev and a slow oozing of melted butter, herbs, and natural chicken juice came forth, forming a delicious moat.

Vegetable preparations have been inconsistent. Sometimes, the vegetables are perfectly cooked. Other times, they are soft and mushy Zucchini has been consistently overdone.

Service has never been pretentious or unfriendly. Waiters here know their stuff and perform tableside duties with aplomb. They flambe with a careful eye, are meticulous in serving dishes, and make sure tables are cleared and reset with silverware after each course. And most of all, your host, Klaus Pache, performs as a concerned technician, greeting guests, monitoring the kitchen's output, and maintaining a smooth flow in both dining rooms.

QUALITY CAFE ★   Price Range: Bargain
Diner Fare

---

175 East Santa Clara St., San Jose   Cash Only
Phone: (408) 297-0991   No Reservations
Hours: 5:30 am–7:30 pm, Mon.–Fri.   No Non-Smoking Section
        6 am–3 pm, Sat. & Sun.   Limited Wheelchair Access
No Alcoholic Beverages

When I was attending San Jose State University, John Sharp and I would go to the Quality Cafe for breakfast. The prices at that time were tearfully reasonable and the portions so big, we wouldn't have to eat again until the next day. Sharp would always go for the stack of pancakes, two eggs, toast and coffee, delivered to the table by an elderly matron with the flabbiest arms I'd ever seen. She was a princess to us.

Since then, changes have occurred, but the basic operation remains unaltered. You can still eat up a storm and still have money to buy a paperback at the Recycled Bookstore. Breakfasts are still rib sticking and the pancakes as big as inflated Rolling Stone albums.

Dinners are heavenly bargains. For a very low set price, you receive soup, salad, entree, vegetable, potato, bread, butter and dessert. Entrees range from griddle fried pork chops to long-boiled corned beef and cabbage. I won't say the food is exceptional. It isn't. The food is basic, no trick grub that settles well without too much gastrointestinal discussion.

The only drawback still remains the somewhat disheveled clientele. The inebriates still like to come in once and a while for a meal, but so what. The Quality Cafe is a people's diner, not an elite dining establishment.

RIERA'S ★★★
Italian

Price Range: Moderate

1539 Solano Ave., Berkeley
Phone: (415) 527-1467
Hours: Dinner: 5:30–10 pm, M–Sat.
       Closed Sunday
Limited Wine List

Master Card — Visa
Reservations Required
No Non-Smoking Section
Limited Wheelchair Access

Being a restaurant critic and having had the opportunity to visit an unending number of eating establishments, I am often tempted to throw in the pen and open a restaurant myself. I know I am not alone in this intermittent compulsion. In fact, Russ Riera, author of *TWO HUNDRED GOOD RESTAURANTS,* did just that. He opened his own restaurant.

And as I figured, he put together many of the good ideas he had seen working so well in other restaurants that he liked. Of course, these ideas only lend color and interest to Riera's basic concept of what he believes a good restaurant should be. Riera places emphasis on good food, good Northern Italian food.

The decor is somewhat stark, the dining room minimally decorated. A beautiful garden does lie beyond a wall of plate glass windows that make up the rear portion of the dining quarters. The restaurant is small, the tables clustered closely, but not to the point of being distracting. In final analysis, I don't think decor was Riera's main objective. Food was and the product of his kitchen is where he succeeds immensely.

All pastas are made daily on the premises. Being from an Italian family, the pastas we sampled at Riera's reflected his remembrance of what good quality pasta should taste like. I sampled Fettucine alla Ghiotta. Thick ribbon noodles were tossed in a smooth cream based sauce flavored with strips of prosciutto and fresh mushrooms that carried the deep earthy flavor of the Oriental black mushroom. The pasta was boiled al dente. The noodles were hearty and pleasantly chewy. Pastas on the menu number eight, with each highlighting a special sauce.

Veal is worth a sampling here, especially Vitella Bocconini. Milky scallops of baby white veal are presented in a natural sauce accented with pine nuts and pieces of fresh tomatoes. A finish of fresh chopped anise gave the overall flavor an aromatic dimension. All of the sauces I have sampled in Riera's dishes reflected the hand of a methodic culinary technician, Chef Lewis Pasco. They were not too thick or overly seasoned, and always complement the meats or fish they covered.

When mussels, scallops, or prawns are in season and available (they go fast here), they are worth a taste. We settled for Gamberi alla Veneziana. The spotlight here bore down on the preparation of the prawns.

They were succulent and plump with natural juice. A light wine sauce with fresh mushrooms was sparingly applied.

I have even sampled a plate of liver done in the typical Italian-style. Thick cuts of calf's liver were breaded and fried in olive oil and garlic. Very simple.

I must commend Russ Riera. I believe his restaurant serves good, wholesome food. Decor was lacking, but I don't think it matters too much. Riera's is doing a good business.

RONG SHING ★★★　　　　　　　　　　　　Price Range: Moderate
Szechwan / Hunan

10725 N. De Anza Blvd., Cupertino	A.E. – M.C. – Visa
Phone: 252-3393	Reservations Suggested
Hours: Lunch: 11:30–2 pm, M–Fri.	No Non-Smoking Section
Dinner: 5–9 pm, Daily	Wheelchair Access
Sunday Brunch: 10–2 pm	
Full Bar	

Rong Shing translates the "Glorious Star." Like a star, it shines brightly on occasion. Other times, it dims and sputters. I have been here on several eating visits and have met with mainly quality Chinese cuisine with intermittent inconsistencies. For example, one visit, I sampled a fine recipe of Rong Shing Tea Smoked Chicken, considered the specialty of the House.

Carefully hacked segments of chicken were fried skin crisp, then served with four plump, sweet-dough Chinese buns. We were instructed to remove the bones from the chicken piece and lay the moist meat onto the bun. A touch of hoison sauce, served on the side, brought the simple flavors of chicken and bread into harmony.

Another sampling proved quite disappointing, the most salient problem being the gamey flavor of the chicken.

I have always been impressed with the Szechwan specialty, Beef with Spicy Tea Sauce. Prepared tableside in a flurry of sizzles, pops and crackles was a mix of beef tenderloin slices, fresh-cut broccoli and bamboo shoots seasoned with the aromatic essence of 5 Spices, a house blend of spicy seasonings, similar to curry in preparation. The juiciness of the beef was sustained in the quick-fry process, while the tingling spiciness of the sauce well imbued the tenderloin slices.

Rong Shing's Mongolian Beef will activate the palate. This recipe is traditionally hot and spicy. Most restaurants employ the hot pepper to unmouthable extremes. However, we found Rong Shing's version to be pleasingly hot without burning the tastebuds into uselessness. Garlic, hot peppers and tender beef medallions found balance in an evenly textured brown sauce. This lightly sweet, zesty blend was thin though adhesive, and coated the ingredients like a glaze.

With both the Scallops with Garlic Sauce and Prawns in Chili Sauce, I have experienced highs and lows. My first taste of the scallops was doubtless a haute preparation, the fish fresh and full-bodied and braised in a well balanced garlic laced glaze . . . My second taste was a haphazard construction. The sauce displayed little integration of spice with fish.

Rong Shing is a good Chinese restaurant, specializing in Szechwan cuisine. Unfortunately, I do not consider it one of the best Chinese restaurants in California as *California Magazine* classified it in one of their extensively researched pieces.

ROYAL MOROCCO ★★★★
Moroccan

Price Range: Expensive

14510 Big Basin Way, Saratoga	Master Card – Visa
Phone: 867-7442	Reservations Required
Hours: Lunch: 11:30–2 pm, M–Fri.	No Non-Smoking Section
Dinner: 6–9:30 pm, Daily	Private Banquet Room
Beer and Wine	Clumsy Wheelchair Access

Most of us don't really know what good Moroccan food is, so we go to one of these dream weavers and think it's great because we sit on the floor, eat with our hands and spend a night of cultural disintegration where fantasies are totally indulged. But to me, quality is the essence of any restaurant fantasy, the most inspiring element being good food.

Royal Morocco is perhaps one of the first Moroccan restaurants in the South Bay to serve quality Moroccan cuisine. The food is delicate, well-made, nutritious and isn't hazardous to your gastronomic anatomy.

Of course, the restaurant is well endowed with all the Moroccan trappings. You enter into a single room outfitted in the fabric tent regalia known to many of these establishments. As in most Moroccan restaurants, you sit on the floor with pillows or along velvety benches. You eat with your hands and are entertained by hand-washing rituals, *prix fixe* five-course meals and a continuous show of belly dancers, who, by the way, are well-trained and do not debauch the art.

My one complaint with Royal Morocco is the lack of room. The seating arrangements are somewhat uncomfortable. Too many tables are lined up in close proximity to each other. If you are a communal sort, new friendships and interesting conversation can be initiated. If not, you may feel like people are staring at you, which, in fact, they are.

Our meal began with the hand-washing ceremony. Situated at the table is a brass apparatus, over which you place your hands. Warm water is then poured over them. A towel is supplied.

After a brief interlude of wide-eyed expectation, your first course is served. In most Moroccan restaurants, this first course is often called *harrira*, but here is called *soup aux lentilles*. It was carmel-hued lentil soup with a chunky consistency and a distant aftertaste of cumin.

Next comes Salad Maison. This colorful palette of diced tomatoes in a vinegar-tart salsa-style salad joins a cumin-laced eggplant puree, a portion of carrot slices and fresh cucumber slices. Each offering is served in a crisp lettuce leaf which enhances the visual freshness as well as retaining natural texture and flavor. A basket of unleavened Moroccan bread is served for scooping up the liquidy salads.

After the salad comes an exquisite manifestation of quality Moroccan cooking, *La B'Stilla*. Wrapped snuggly in layers of light, crisp filo was a juicy assemblage of freshly shredded chicken and almonds. The pie was dusted heavily with powdered sugar and served piping hot. Be careful not to burn your fingers on this one.

If you seek the apex of authenticity in Moroccan cooking, you must sample *Cous Cous a L'agneau*. Cous Cous is steamed wheat semolina. In this dish, a tidy portion of braised lamb shanks rests atop a bed of these fluffy grains which are deliciously moist with a deep wheat flavor. With the lamb and semolina a wide variety of steamed vegetables is served. Here, the flavors are very light and rely almost entirely on the natural assimilation of juices without seasonings.

To test the chef's ability at making sauces, dispense with your prejudices and order *Lapin aux paprika*. Though the rabbit, according to our waiter, wasn't taken fresh from the field that day, it was nonetheless fresh-tasting without the slightest hint of gaminess. The rabbit was braised in a paprika broth that was intense in flavor and very spicy, yet the sauce did not obliterate the flavor of the white, fatless meat. Like the lamb and the chicken, the meat pulled from the bones without a struggle.

One of my favorite Moroccan entrees is Paulet aux Citrons et Olives. A whole game hen is slowly simmered with lemons and black pitted olives until the meat disengaged effortlessly. The zesty lemon essence penetrates the meat thoroughly, but does not dominate the natural flavor.

Before dessert, our fingers were washed with a sweetly scented rose water that left us perfumed well into the following day. With a platter of buttery rich wedges of baklava, we were poured cups of tantalizing mint tea. The tea is poured from an unnerving height to aerate the tea, giving the sweet libation a fresh, invigorating quality. A delicious conclusion to an intoxicating meal.

Service at Royal Morocco was performed according to prescribed tenets of the culinary ritual by waiters wearing fezzes. Not all of the waiters were North African, but they still understood the complexity of their duties and executed them well. Our courses were delivered promptly and rituals performed with sincerity.

R.S.V.P. ★★★   Price Range: Expensive
French / Italian

---

106 East Campbell Ave., Campbell	**A.E. – M.C. – Visa**
Phone: 866-8466	**Reservations Required**
Hours: Dinner: 6–9 pm, Tues.-Sat.	**Non-Smoking Section**
Extensive Wine List	**Limited Wheelchair Access**

R.S.V.P. has a warm, endearing quality that draws you helplessly into its culinary embrace. The chef, who is also the proprietor, displays a rough hewn style, one I have encountered nowhere else. He shows little finesse in his Italian/French dishes. Flavors are strong and bracing, heavy cream is used liberally, and garlic, when applied, announces itself with a trumpet blast.

The restaurant resides in a quaint, tranquil little house in Campbell. Elegance is introduced by clean white linen and fresh flowers set against the austere whitewash of the bordered walls in the dining rooms. Unfortunately, parking is terrible. If the small back lot is full, you will be forced to seek parking in other, more inconvenient locations.

The menu is small and manageable. Nightly specials are offered and number only four, as a rule. One appetizer, one entree, one salad, and one dessert.

On one visit, we sampled the chef's version of Rouladen as an appetizer. Scallops of lamb were rolled around a portion of ground lamb, then finished with a potent dijon mustard embodied with heavy cream. Sadly enough, a muttony aftertaste pervaded the inherent flavor, forcing the attributes of the French mustard into submission.

Salad courses have always been excellent, emphasizing the attractive visual appeal typified by nouveau cuisine. A special artichoke salad, delivered a fully ripened artichoke trimmed down to the edible, fleshy leaves and heart. The center was filled with fresh Bay shrimp, and set in a fluff of red leaf lettuce, then dressed with a zesty, mustard cream blend.

Two pasta dishes are offered on the menu, Linguine Con Vongole and Tortellini. I've sampled the Linguini dish and found new definition in R.S.V.P.'s version. The strands of semolina were starchless and separate, yet slightly overcooked. The lemon-butter based sauce was exceedingly pungent with fresh crushed garlic and shallots. The flavor of the tender baby clams was defeated by the strength of the garlic.

Of the five current entrees listed on the menu, I have sampled Escalope of D'agneau Chasseur and the Saltimbocca Alla Romana. The first delivered thinly sliced escalopes of lamb tenderloin in a sauce made from shallots, garlic, Madeira, and demi glace. The lamb was tender, yet its rich, characteristic flavor was not present. The Chasseur, or Hunter's sauce was reduced to an adequate smoothness with all ingredients unified and subtle.

The Saltimbocca was a success. It comprised delicate, milk fed veal scallops rolled around rich Teleme cheese and proscuitto. Covering the three veal rolls was a light, tawny brown sauce spiced with an even application of garlic, shallots and wine.

Vegetables were methodically presented, quite attractive, and deep with natural color and flavor.

Capping off one evening, we lingered over a chocolate mousse with French chestnuts. The custardy nature of this classic chocolate puree was nicely juxtaposed to the crunchiness of the sweet, minced chestnuts. We enjoyed this dessert with strong cups of coffee filtre.

R.S.V.P. is the rebel in a burgeoning society of class eating establishments. The chef here has a courageous style and makes strong commitment to flavor. In some dishes, his excessive doses of herbs and spices succeed deliciously, while tasting heavy-handed in others. R.S.V.P. has flaws, but should not be avoided. It's one of the South Bay's heartthrobs.

THE RUSTY SCUPPER ★★★
Steak & Lobster

Price Range: Moderate

1235 Oakmead Parkway, Sunnyvale
Phone: 245-2911
Hours: Lunch: 11–2 pm, Mon.-Fri.
Dinner: 5:30–10 pm, M–Thurs.
Till 11 pm, Fri. & Sat.
Till 9 pm, Sunday

A.E. − M.C. − Visa
Reservations Taken
No Non-Smoking Section
Full Wheelchair Access

Full Bar

Entertainment

When I consider going out to dinner for pleasure, a place like the Rusty Scupper is rarely my first choice. The planned perfection of its menu, the total kitchen operation, leaves little room for culinary imagination. Nonetheless, I'd be a blithering idiot to deny that The Rusty Scupper isn't a good restaurant. It succeeds brilliantly and must be complimented for constant follow through.

The interior is a split level affair equipped with a luxurious setting of tables and wicker chairs. Many of the tables are situated close to a long bank of picture windows overlooking Hilton Hotel's tranquil grounds. A profusion of blond wood harmonizes with deep rust Spanish tiles.

The menu is predictable and very simple in scope. The Rusty Scupper serves a basic fare with few continental departures. Red meat, fresh fish, and selected varieties of shellfish are offered. Certain fresh fish items are announced tableside as specials. Listen closely. We enjoyed a thick filet of very fresh King Salmon broiled over the coals in a simple manner. I commend the cooks in their handling of the fish. The salmon was cooked to perfection and exuded a delicate natural flavor. The portion was large.

We also sampled The Scupper's Shrimp Scampi. Several large gulf prawns were butterflied then sauteed in lemon, butter and garlic. To me, it was somewhat diluted, a weak rendition of the Bordelaise. Though slightly soupy, it didn't stop my guests and I from dipping bread into the sauce.

For the best of the red meats at The Rusty Scupper, you can't go wrong with either a slab of Prime Rib or a broiled Rib Eye Steak. Unless you are extremely hungry and want to kill yourself on red meat, I suggest you order the basic cut of prime rib. It was large enough and very thick. I found the meat to be of top quality with adequate marbling and little fat around the edges. The Scupper doesn't seem to foul up when it comes to cooking meat. If you order it rare, you will receive it rare.

The Rib Eye Steak was a big cut of meat that took up most of the plate. The meat was fork tender in places, which is unusual for this cut of steak, yet I also did detect some troublesome veins of gristle in spots that made the cutting of the meat a bit tricky.

With all dinner orders, you will receive a tureen of clam chowder, salad and sourdough bread, plus rice or potato with your entree.

The staff at The Rusty Scupper is comprised of young, eager waitresses, waiters, hosts and hostesses, who perform their duties according to the standards set down by the corporate headquarters. They are efficient, friendly, and seem pleased to be working at The Scupper.

SAIGON II ★★★
Vietnamese

Price Range: Bargain

374 East Santa Clara St., San Jose	A.E. – D.C. – M.C. – Visa
Phone: 288-9511	Reservations Taken
Hours: 9 am–9 pm Daily	No Non-Smoking Section
	Wheelchair Access

Beer and Wine

The Vietnamese cuisine at the new Saigon II may not inspire the most productive discussion. Yet, it won't put you to sleep either. The cooks here make definite commitment to flavor, applying hot pepper and garlic as though they were the only two seasonings on hand. The food is mighty powerful stuff, guaranteed to give your breath an aroma that belongs on a mouthwash commercial.

But, so what if nobody will want to talk to you when you get back. Saigon II is still worth a sampling. The food is an education, as well as a perfect way of purging the impurities from your body.

My meal at Saigon II, the third in a series of Vietnamese restaurants, began with a warm-up of Imperial Rolls. These traditional Vietnamese finger nibbles were egg roll in appearance, though the wrapper fried out to a crispier texture that made grating sounds against the teeth. The filling was a garlic potent, nearly pureed mash of spiced meat and vegetables. The rolls were served with the National Vietnamese dipping sauce, Muoc Mam. This clear, highly tangy fish sauce is spiked with garlic, hot pepper and lime juice.

For those who really want to indulge your fancy on authentic Vietnamese fare, it is mandatory to try Nem Nuong, or skewered pork meat balls. This dish is a gastronomic carnival. You are served a large, metal platter laden with stalks of freshly washed leaf lettuce, sprigs of Chinese parsley, pickled veggies of various origins, an expansive wad of rice paper, and two long skewers of grilled pork balls. The pork balls are sausage-like in texture and flavor with a strong garlic back bite.

To eat, you must first peel a thin sheet of rice paper from the thick wad, then swab it down with a special sauce served on the side. From there, you pile on the lettuce, the parsley, the veggies, and the pork balls. Wrap tightly and stuff it in your mouth carefully. The flavors are intense and refreshingly unique.

To counterbalance the spiciness of the former dishes, I ordered a plate entitled Dau Hoa Lan Xao Nam. Very simply this dish presents fresh, crunchy snow peas and three varieties of mushrooms, including the Black Mushroom, sauteed in a mild oyster sauce. This dish tranquilized the heat of the peppers and provided a light, easy-to-digest third course.

A dish I did not like at all was Ga Kho Sa Ot, or Lemon Grass Aromatic Chicken. It was poorly prepared. Several hacked segments of chicken ringed with fat was fixed in an extremely oily sauce that purveyed a singularly sweet flavor. The lemon grass was on furlough.

The service at Saigon II can be slow. I suggest you tell your wait person at the beginning of your meal what kind of time schedule you are on. This way, you won't be delayed. Maybe.

SAL AND LUIGI'S ★★★ Price Range: Moderate
Italian

347 South First St., San Jose	Cash Only
Phone: 297-1136	No Reservations
Hours: 11 am–11 pm, Mon.–Thurs.	No Non-Smoking Section
To Midnight, Fri. & Sat.	Wheelchair Access
Beer and Wine	

Sal and Luigi's has been around for 21 years, enduring the helter skelter of change that has vexed San Jose's downtown renaissance. Amidst the unsavory elements of First Street, this family operation, wedged between the old Fox Theater and Mac's, has boldly competed with monumental Original Joe's.

Sal and Luigi's is a small restaurant with a rich downtown appeal, similar to a New York pizzeria. The owners are warm, family-oriented people who take an active part in their restaurant. It's not uncommon to see them dressed in cook's whites and strolling through the restaurant from front kitchen to rear kitchen, hefting sauce pots and pasta-laden plates.

The food here is not fancy, but displays a home-style brand of Italian cooking with a hearty dedication to olive oil and garlic. Spaghetti with white clam sauce is a good pick. The pasta was boiled firm and twirled onto the fork in long, unbroken strings. Coating the spaghetti evenly was a rich sauce made with clams, broth, a half mix of butter and olive oil, wine and a dash of cream for smooth consistency.

For those who have never had gnocchi, Sal and Luigi's serves a plate of the best in town. Replacing the commonly used potato and flour, the chef here makes his dough with ricotta cheese. These small dumplings were moist and tender, not starchy, like the gnocchi made with potato. Covering the gnocchi was a lively home-brewed tomato blend. Other commendable dishes utilizing this Sunday dinner sauce, are the home-made ravioli. I prefer the ricotta-filled variety. Each ravioli was a large, hand-sized envelope of tender pasta, layered inside with ricotta cheese.

Highly touted is Sal and Luigi's home-ground Italian sausage and bell peppers. The anise-flavored sausage, served in skinless chunks, was simmered in a wine-accented saute of tomato, onion, mushroom and garlic. A glaze of olive oil finished this dish with a subtle Italian flavor.

Dining-room operations are run by one of the proprietors. Julie has been here ever since they opened their doors in 1960. She loves to tell the story of how they had planned on being in business for only two years. But one thing led to another and they never left.

Sal and Luigi's has never really been discovered. It has simply persisted, captivating the palate of a few select diners, mostly students and businessmen in the know. It's certainly a likeable place where you can sit and relax and maybe read the paper while you put down a plate of spaghetti and meat balls.

SAM'S LOG CABIN ★★★   Price Range: Moderate
Lunch Only

---

245 Willow Street, San Jose	Cash Only
Phone: 279-9941	Reservations Taken
Hours: Lunch: 11 am–2 pm, Mon.–Fri.	No Non-Smoking Section
	Limited Wheelchair Access

In 1933, two events transpired that made dramatic impact on San Jose. The abductors of Brooke Hart were lynched in St. James Park by a mob of avenging citizens and Sam's Log Cabin opened its doors for business. The former has become legend, while the latter continues to thrive in the clustered streetscape of Willow St. Sam's is a landmark hangout where people crowd in for the lunch hour, seeking spirited libation and a mouthful of Steak and Beans or The Famous Abalone Sandwich.

Sam's is a small quadrant outfitted with a long whiskey counter (the original) and closely spaced tables and chairs. A few black and white snapshots share wall space with a 1930's pin-up poster. Ambience here is created by the people. At lunch, noise and smoke fill the quarters to the brim. Suit and tie businessmen mingle with blue collar workers. Cowboy hats frequently dot the heads of many lunchers scattered throughout the boisterous throng. If Sam's sounds like a place for just the guys, forget it. I saw as many women as men joining in the festivities.

For lunch, plan on a wait of about ten to fifteen minutes. If you want a table, you'll wait longer, depending, of course, on the crowd. If you don't mind sitting at the bar, you can usually get a seat within five minutes. At Sam's you sit where you can when you can. Don't be picky. To avoid hassles, come early or call ahead for reservations.

At first sight, it appears that Sam's is just a place to bend the elbow with an ice cold brew or a tall scotch on the rocks. Maybe so. But during lunch, which is the only meal served here, there are some special treats that are well worth sinking your teeth into. The number one attraction is the Abalone Sandwich ($6.57). Without question, $6.57 is expensive for a sandwich. However, when you consider that ab is priced so high and is becoming so hard to get and that Sam's is probably the only place in town to procure this pricy seafood, the cost dwindles in proportion.

The abalone sandwich is an experience. The shellfish is pounded thin and tender. I did not detect even one small eraser tough piece. The ab steak is breaded, pan fried carefully, and laid between two pieces of buttered white toast. No condiments are added, though tartar sauce and lemon are provided on the side. With an application of each, the sweet, fresh flavor of abalone was well enhanced. Served with the sandwich was a hulking scoop of dill strong potato salad. It was blended smooth with enough seasoning to give it an old-fashioned potato salad flavor.

For those not partial to abalone, don't fret. Sam's cooks up a great steak sandwich or a bargain plate of steak and beans. Most gratifying was the consistent tenderness of the beef. Usually at a place like this, the steak has at least one strip of gristle or muscle that sinks uncomfortably between your molars. Not here. The steak was trimmed of fat and pan fried over a hot fire so the outside was slightly charred and the inside still a hue of pink.

THE SARDINE FACTORY ★★★★
Continental/Seafood

Price Range: Expensive

---

701 Wave St., Cannery Row, Monterey
Phone: 373-3775
Hours: Lunch: 11:30–2:30 pm, M–Sat.
Dinner: 5–11 pm, Mon.-Sat.
From 2 pm, Sunday
Full Bar — Extensive Wine List

All Major Credit Cards
Reservations Required
Non-Smoking Section —
[Upon Request]
Wheelchair Access

The Sardine Factory is landlocked on Monterey's Wave Street with an elevated view of Cannery Row and the beautiful Monterey Bay. The interior boasts several elegant rooms. The Captain's Room is a marvel of Baroque design with ceiling-high mirrors and a portrait gallery of stern-faced sea captains. The Conservatory Room features a canopy of glass through which diners can view the evening mist as it descends upon the bay. In the center of the room there is a Grecian fountain surrounded by manicured greenery.

Dinner begins with an antipasto of sliced cold cuts, bean salad, marinated octopus, artichoke hearts, olives and other nibbler treats. Sesame-covered breaksticks are served alongside.

Following the antipasto, we received a cup of The Sardine Factory's famous abalone chowder — creamy and not too thick, with an abundance of abalone bits. Next came our salads of romaine lettuce dressed with a caper-tart oil and vinegar.

When available, which it frequently is, the Monterey Bay Prawn is a must-try item for those who have yet to taste this unique crustacean. The Monterey prawn, larger than the usual gulfer, has extra-tender meat and a deep, sweet flavor that permeates any sauce that covers it. The Sardine Factory sautees these prawns in shell with a simple lemon and butter combination. We wandered off course and ordered the prawns with linguine, which proved to be a mistake. The pasta and prawns just couldn't find balance. The noodles were bulky and the fettucine cream sauce was butter heavy and shallow on flavor.

The Sardine Factory has mastered the preparation of abalone. Every ounce of our ab medallions were pounded to a delectable, mouth-watering texture, sauteed in butter and served very simply. A squeeze of lemon brings the unique creamy flavor of the fresh abalone into delicious-harmony.

On our second visit, we sampled the award-winning entree, Vitellon Cardin, the Factory's special creation. The waiter's opening rhetoric has always included the description of this dish. No one will ever tell you that it is the most expensive item on the menu. That's for you to figure out. Nonetheless, the dish displayed three generous slices of exquisite provimi veal and a shelled lobster tail. The scallops of veal were characteristically milky and etheral in texture while the lobster meat was sweet and tender. A choice pick.

The sauce described on the menu as "extraordinaire" was far from being extraordinary. I expected a masterful blend, very delicate and smoothly textured. What I did receive was a sauce commonly found in other continental restaurants. It was apparently concocted from a basic stock with butter and lemon, the citrus tartness most dominant. The lemony flavor did assist in bringing the veal and lobster into the chef's intended balance.

We have also tried The Sardine Factory's popular creation, Lobster Wellington. This dish is very rich and I recommend that you go easy on the pre-entree courses so that you can enjoy it fully. Nestled into a very flaky pastry crust is a luscious, meaty lobster tail, covered with a cream sauce similar to the nantua which highlights the nutty-sweet flavor of the lobster.

All dinners are served with an array of vegetables du jour. We had broccoli and carrots on our last visit. Both were cooked perfectly and seasoned lightly to enhance the natural flavors. With dinner, you are also treated to baskets of The Sardine Factory's famous cheese toast. Eat it when it's hot.

As stated earlier, the service at The Sardine Factory is conducted by what your host will announce as world famous. On our first visit, we were served by world-famous Guiseppe. He was cordial, sincere, prompt and efficient. He never rushed us. On our last visit, our world-famous waiter was a bit forgetful and had a tendency to make excuses for his mistakes.

In my final appraisal, I must say that The Sardine Factory is indeed a fine restaurant. A restaurant this big and world famous will always be the target of cheap shots from critics — anything it does wrong is magnified out of proportion. Overall, the Factory does many more things right. Although the prices are high, I feel it is worth at least one visit. It's a landmark.

SCOTT'S SEAFOOD GRILL ★★★
Seafood   Price Range: Moderate to Expensive

2300 E. Bayshore Rd., Palo Alto	A.E. — M.C. — Visa
Phone: (415) 856-1046	Reservations–Dinner Only
Hours: 11 am–10 pm, Mon.–Thurs.	Non-Smoking Section
Till 11 pm, Fri. & Sat.	Full Wheelchair Access
5–10 pm, Sunday	
Full Bar	

Two things stand out in my mind about Scott's Seafood Grill. The first is high prices. The second is good fish grilled in a simple, careful manner. Though the San Francisco Scott's took a heavy beating at the hands of Stan Sesser, Restaurant critic for San Francisco Magazine, I hold steadfast to my initial impression about this seafood house: I believe the Palo Alto store serves some of the freshest fish I have eaten this side of the San Mateo Bridge. I don't know why the prices have to be so high, but maybe the answer lies in the fact that the fish is prime quality, taken from boat to kitchen in the same morning.

I recall having an exquisite piece of black bass one afternoon as a special of the day. The fish was utterly delectable, its flesh moist and silken, the flavor mild and clean. Black bass is definitely a rarity. It is almost impossible to procure on a daily commercial basis. Yet, once and a great while, Scott's will offer it as a special when other seafood restaurants are groping for gulf prawns. To me, this says something about the shrewd talent of the head chef who does all the buying early in the A.M.

Don't count on having black bass when you come to Scott's. But do count on having other fresh fish favorites like King Salmon, Halibut, Swordfish, Red Snapper, Schrod, Trout, and many other varieties that rear their scales several times throughout the year. On a dinner visit, I recall forking into a thick slab of firm, juicy swordfish, grilled over charcoal with only a glistening swab of butter over its ashen white meat. The flavor of the fish unified with a thorough, yet mild flavor of the grill.

King Crab Legs have been good and bad. On one occasion they were characteristically moist and supple, tearing from the deep red shells with the slightest tug. Drawn butter was superfluous in accentuating the richness of the sweet white crab meat. On another occasion, the legs were overcooked and dry, the meat tasting more like smoky squid, than quality crab. Inconsistencies do vex the shell fish here. I have met with problems with the prawns and scallops, also.

Service, too, has its problems. The staff of waitpeople are young collegiates who have a tendency to rush you through a meal. However, I have also been served well on an occasion or two. One waitress was exceptionally well versed in her knowledge of seafood, its seasons of availability, and current weather conditions.

Palo Alto Scott's serves fresh fish at high prices. I would certainly stick to the blackboard items when seeking the best here. The freshest catch is usually the best buy.

SHADOWBROOK ★★★   Price Range: Expensive
Seafood/Continental

1750 Wharf Road, Capitola   A.E. − M.C. − Visa
Phone: (408) 475-1511   Reservations Required Far
Hours: Dinner: 5−10 pm, Mon.-Thurs.   In Advance
       Till 10:30 pm, Friday   No Non-Smoking Section
       From 4 pm, Sat. & Sun.   Limited Wheelchair Access
Full Bar − Saturday & Sunday Brunch

The Shadowbrook is probably one of the most beautiful restaurants in which to dine. This truly romantic site rests in a tangle of greenery on the banks of the lazy flowing San Lorenzo River. You can either descend to the restaurant in a six passenger cable car, or you can walk through the hillside gardens down to restaurant level. Either way, you will embrace the scenic flora that surrounds you on all sides. The Shadowbrook is ideal for the tourist seeking to return home with a soft, tranquil memory.

As for cuisine, The Shadowbrook remains pretty much average. Atmosphere overshadows the culinary performance of the chefs on station here. The menu is basic with a strong fish influence. When Salmon is in season, it is probably the best fish item on the menu. The King Salmon is said to be caught by the troller "Vega II," which fishes specifically for the Shadowbrook. The freshness was outstanding, the flesh firm and pink, the flavor mild. It comes with either a rich, eggy Hollandaise or drawn butter. I prefer it with drawn butter, though the Hollandaise here is light enough not to detract from the fresh fish flavor.

Prime Rib is a failsafe item, but is not always available. When the kitchen is cutting rib, it will be delivered to the table in a large slice surrounded by a pool of natural juice. The flavor of the beef has always been rich and unmasked by seasonings and herbs.

I do recommend that you avoid Shadowbrook's rendition of Canneloni. These pasta tubes are filled with sauteed chicken, beef, mushrooms, and spinach, all of which do not assimilate in flavor. On one visit, the canneloni were overcooked and breaking apart. Even the accompanying rice pilaf was tasteless, the rice kernels dry and stuck together.

An average entree that will not offend your sense of good eating has always been the Chicken Teriyaki. Two meaty breasts are simply char-broiled. The teriyaki marination is mild and not cloyingly sweet.

Once again, I repeat. The Shadowbrook is a beautiful restaurant. The scenic splendor of the decor, the verduous grounds, the view of the river will inspire great romance. The food is adequate. It will not dazzle you, but it will not disappoint you either. Don't expect great cuisine when you come here and your experience will be fully realized.

SIAM ★★★★   Price Range: Bargain
Thai

5140 Stevens Creek Blvd., San Jose   Master Card — Visa
Phone: 243-5549   Reservations Taken
Hours: 10:30 am–10 pm, Sun.–Thurs.   Non-Smoking Section
       Open till 11 pm, Fri. & Sat.   Limited Wheelchair Access
Beer and Wine

Siam exists amidst the hustling thud of the Futurama Bowling Alley. In my experiences as a restaurant critic, I have found bowling alleys and restaurants to be quite compatible.

At Siam, there are two Bangkok chefs, one of which is the master chef, Nam, who speaks not a word of English. In her dishes, she has exhibited a subtle blending of sauces used in her Sate, Curries, and fiery hot Tom Yum soups. Thai cuisine brings elements of Chinese, Indian, Vietnamese, and Indonesian cuisines into a harmonious art of cookery. Liberal applications of garlic, hot red and green peppers, corriander, lemon grass, mint, peanuts, ginger and coconut milk are found in many dishes.

To begin a meal at Siam, it is necessary to sample a plate of sate. The sate consists of grilled strips of beef served with a mildly sweet, smoothly textured peanut butter sauce and a chilled, tartly sweet cucumber marinade spiked with hot green pepper. The synthesis of flavors and spices opens the palate.

One of my favorite dishes here is the Pad-pet pla-muk. Tender ringlets of squid are braised in a clear sauce made from garlic, chili pepper, onion and whole basil leaf. The color balance was striking.

For a taste of a blazing Thai dish, the Kang-kai or nor-mai will send you off on a sudden orbit. Strips of boned chicken are wok sauteed with bamboo shoots, coconut milk and red curry. Thai curry relies on an organic blend of hot pepper, lemon grass, scallion, garlic, and corriander. With this dish a special tray of condiments is presented. On this tray were pure red pepper, a diluted red pepper sauce, sugar and fish sauce. The sugar is used to cut the hotness of the pepper.

Nur Num-tok brings a new variety of seasonings into play. Grilled beef is first marinated in lemon juice and tossed with minced mint leaves, hot chili pepper and crispy rice. Yoo-Moo Yang is similar, yet replaces the beef with tender pork slices.

If you really want to purge all impurities from your body and soul Tom Yum king is your confessor. Several simmered prawns, straw mushrooms, corriander, lemon grass, ginger, and tomato pulp, plus hot pepper come steaming in a blazingly spicy hot and sour soup. It will send needles of pleasure along your lips. The Thais use this soup to cure sore throats.

Whenever I visit Siam, I always order bottles of Singha, the number one Thai beer. It is called a stout, but has the light, bubbly attributes of a lager. Don't miss it. You may need plenty of Singha to cool your mouth and keep it from melting away.

SOUSA'S CAFE ★★★   Price Range: Moderate
Portuguese

1614 E. Santa Clara St., San Jose   Cash and Checks Only
Phone: 926-9075   Reservations Taken
Hours: 7 am–9 pm, Daily   No Non-Smoking Section
Beer   Limited Wheelchair Access

If I were to be sent to the front lines in the dead of winter, I'd want to stop off at Sousa's for one of their hearty meals before facing my destiny. Portuguese cooking is heavy, basic and ascribes to little culinary subtlety. It is difficult to classify Sousa's brand of cookery as fine cuisine, because it's not. It is the food of a humble folk who are able to create interesting dishes out of basic ingredients.

Sousa's Cafe is located in a Portuguese enclave along an obscure strip of Santa Clara Street. Soft strains of Portuguese spoken among customers and employees attest to the authentic nature of this place. The atmosphere is cozy and inviting to all.

We started our meal with the most commonly known Portuguese dish, Linguica. Sousa's Portuguese sausage is homemade and ground by the chef himself. It was served in a sunken dish, pre-cut diagonally into slanted wedges. The titillating, spicy flavor combined the deep smoke of the grill with a heavy dose of fresh garlic. The meat was firm and had the texture of pork butt, not cast off tidbits. With the sausage, we received a basket of Portuguese-style rolls, baked at the Alves Bakery, another Portguese establishment located next door. The rolls are round like a ball, with a dry, airy texture.

Next, we sampled a plate of Bacalhau a Gomes Sa, or Codfish. This is considered a truly authentic Portuguese dish. And you'd better be geared up for the uncommonly strong flavor of codfish. If you haven't had it before, it may put you off. The fish was cut into morsels and cooked with potatoes. Other than the flavor of the cod, it had a briny bite that brought potato and fish into a heavy balance.

All entrees are served with your choice of soup or salad. With these two items, Sousa's must improve. Both the soup and the salad were mundane offerings that showed little expertise. The soup was watery, with grease beads floating on the surface. Though the greens of the salad were crisp, the bleu-cheese dressing had that sweet, bottled flavor.

An entree I recommend for first-timers is Carne de Porco Salteada. This pork dish celebrates the heartiness of Portuguese cooking, forcing you to hunker down with elbows propped on the table and a fork tightly clenced in a big first. Large chunks of quality pork and equally large chunks of potatoes were pan-roasted until golden brown and crispy on the outside. The ingredients were fixed in a slightly salty sauce made primarily of the rich, natural pan juices.

Our last entree for that visit was another house specialty, Carne Asada a Portuguese. Cast aside any notions you might have had about carne asada. At Sousa's it is slices of well-done roast beef served with a dark-brown gravy. The gravy had a strong bottom-of-the-pan flavor with an infusion of red wine that made my ears draw back.

All entrees are served with vegetables. Here again, Sousa's needs to improve. The vegetables appeared to be nothing more than boiled and buttery frozen-style peas and carrots. They added nothing to the meal.

I suggest for dessert you order something light to counter-balance the heavy entrees. The lightest is the only Portuguese dessert on the menu, Pudim Flam. This sweet egg custard goes fast, so make it known that you want some when ordering.

Our waitress for that evening was most accommodating. She was very kind and had a sincere smile that made us feel totally at home. Though not well-versed on some of the dishes, she made it a point to ask the chef and returned with the information. She never tried to bamboozle us and make excuses for not knowing.

THE SPUR ★★
Down–Home Cooking

Price Range: Bargain

3378 Monterey Road, San Jose
Phone: (408) 225-4381
Hours: 6 am–10 pm, Daily

Cash Only
No Reservations
No Non-Smoking Section
Limited Wheelchair Access

Long before Highway 101 was built, the truckers used Monterey Road as their commercial thoroughfare. Along that route was a small, brave truck stop called The Spur. It was there to feed the weary and hungry truckers, refueling them for their long drive to the South.

Despite the opening of 101, The Spur has prevailed and still keeps its leather booths and stools occupied with the hungry and weary. The food is basic, down-home style. No tricks. No cute stuff. Just good food that sticks to the ribs.

Breakfast meals are typical in scope with only a few interesting departures like the Linguica and Eggs or the Italian Sausage and Eggs. Both sausage renditions are spicy and blend extremely well with the creamy farm fresh eggs served in a variety of ways. Occasional breakfast specials are also offered. The most notable includes a large waffle, one egg, and two slices of bacon.

Lunch and Dinner meals are, again, basic, country style compositions. Daily specials are worth a look see. Corned beef and cabbage, Short ribs, Swiss Steak, and, my favorite, Ham Hocks and Lima Beans rotate throughout the week. Sandwiches are less impressive, as are the mundane hamburgers. I suggest you stick to the hot plates.

STEAMER'S SEAFOOD CAFE ★★★★   Price Range: Moderate
Seafood

---

40 North Santa Cruz, Los Gatos	Master Card – Visa
Phone: (408) 395-3474	No Reservations
Hours: Lunch: 11:30 am–2 pm, Tu.-Fri.	Non-Smoking Section
Noon–3 pm, Saturday	Very Limited Wheelchair
Dinner: 5–10 pm, Mon.-Thurs.	Access
Till 11 pm, Fri. & Sat.	
4:30–9:30 pm, Sunday	

Beer and Wine

During peak business hours, Steamer's Seafood Cafe transforms into a chaotic stew of hungry fish eaters. Those afflicted with claustrophobia beware. In two out of my three visits, I have been elbowed in the head and had my bread basket knocked to the deck by a passerby. God forbid if you happen to have a broken leg or are in a wheelchair. Brace yourself for some hair raising maneuvering. To avoid this insanity, come to Steamer's during the slow hours. Give them a call and find out when the crowds are the smallest.

Despite the war zone conditions, Steamer's ranks high as a quality fish house. The proprietors maintain integrity in serving fresh fish. Steamer's chalkboard follows the seasons, listing the best the sea has to offer throughout the year. What I admire most about Steamer's is the kitchen's simplistic approach to preparing fish. Nothing I have sampled has been overcooked, oversauced, overdone in any way. To me, Steamer's follows the best policy for a seafood restaurant: The less done to the fish, the better.

My favorite fish items are usually those listed on the chalkboard. I have enjoyed beautiful slabs of mesquite grilled King Salmon when in season, halibut, and red snapper. When swordfish is offered, by all means, go for it. It has always been a generous thick cut and very fresh. I love the texture of swordfish, the way it remains firm and juicy under almost any cooking conditions.

Shellfish is almost always present on the regular menu. Prawns, scallops, and crab can be ordered just about any time. I've had the Atlantic Sea Scallops on two occasions. Each time, they were served on a skewer with bell peppers, onions and bacon. The last time I ordered this dish, I found the portion to be diminished, and in turn, the price to be rather steep.

Steamer's also serves a tempura style Prawn dish. The batter is crisp and very light with little grease residue. As in the Japanese restaurants, the prawns beneath the batter remain juicy and sleek.

The service at Steamer's is commendable considering the unending succession of tables they attend without dropping from battle fatigue. The waitresses, especially, have shown tremendous ability at dodging protruding elbows and long, aisle-blocking legs.

If you like crowds and you like to wait, sometimes, up to an hour and a half to get a table, then come during the rush. If you don't, then come to Steamer's during the off time when you can sit down in relative quiet and enjoy quality seafood without people breathing down your neck as they wait for your table.

The Steamer's enterprise has recently opened a new restaurant called **STEAMER'S SEAFOOD AND PASTA, TOO,** *located in Old Town, Los Gatos. Pastas are made fresh daily and hung to dry on pasta racks visible to the patron. It's worth a try, if you can't get into the original store.*

STICKNEY'S HICKORY HOUSE ★★★★
BBQ/American Fare   Price Range: Bargain to Moderate

Stevens Creek Plaza, Santa Clara   A.E. − M.C. − Visa
Phone: (408) 241-2500   No Reservations
Hours: 9 am−10:30 pm, Mon.−Thurs.   Non-Smoking Section
        Till 11 pm, Fri. & Sat.   Limited Wheelchair Access
        10:30 am−9 pm, Sunday
Full Bar: Silver Spur Lounge

One day while hot-footing it down Stevens Creek Boulevard with breakfast heavy on my mind, I happened upon an old diehard restaurant called Stickney's. I stopped off to cool myself while digging into a plate of bacon and eggs. As I rested at the counter, exchanging glances with the elderly folk assembled at the stools to my right, it dawned on me what I had been missing. It took the happy face of a senior eating her pineapple-bran muffin to remind me: Stickney's is a veritable emporium of good eating.

Stickney's does just about everything from baking quality pastries to smoking the finest meats over a trademark hickory blaze. Stickney welcomes all to partake of his victuals. Businesspeople, seniors, children, students, and passers by share space amidst the elegant Western motif.

One of Stickney's favorite dishes is the Rib Plate. The ribs here are easily jockeyed with the fingers and do not entail a messy eating ordeal. Each bone is plump with meat tender enough to gnaw easily from the bone shaft. To clean the bone, you will have to exercise a little more effort. The hickory flavor is present, but not striking. With the ribs, a side of Stickney's, either-you-like-it-either-you-don't, BBQ Sauce is served. It is a mild, zesty sauce with a carmel color and a semi-thick consistency.

I have also indulged on Stickney's patented, Fourth of July style Fried Chicken. Four meaty pieces of chicken are coated in a secret batter recipe, then deep fried to a crackling golden brown. The chicken meat squirts juice upon impact with teeth. It was very succulent.

Other sure bets include the steak sandwich, Stickney's highly regarded cheeseburger made on homemade buns, barbecued leg of pork, and a wide assortment of breakfast plates served throughout the day.

For dessert, you can pick from just about any form of pastry you crave. My favorites are the brownies, the Danish rolls, and the huge pineapple bran muffins.

Service is executed by a veteran staff of ladies who know their stuff. They are very friendly, but rarely have time to waste on frivolous conversations unless you have a really good joke to tell. It better have a rollicking punch line, or you might not get another cup of coffee.

For those of you who seek quiet seclusion where a business transaction can be followed through with little interruption, Stickney's offers the Silver Spur room located at the rear of the Hickory House. The decor is elegant and the many banquettes are sequestered and private. There is a full bar in this room.

*Stickney's has three other locations in the South Bay and along the Peninsula: Palo Alto at **Town & Country Village**; the **Flamingo Hotel** location in Palo Alto; the **Redwood City** location.*

THE SZECHWAN ★★★
Szechwan/Chinese

Price Range: Bargain

1075 S. Saratoga-Sunnyvale Rd., San Jose
Phone: 996-7797
Hours: Lunch: 11:30 am–2 pm, Tu.-Fri.
        Dinner: 5–8:30 pm, Tues. thru
         Thurs. & Sunday
        Till 9 pm, Fri. & Sat.
Beer and Wine

Visa
Reservations Advised for
  Large Parties
No Non-Smoking Section
Wheelchair Access

When the little storefronts on Murphy were razed to make way for the TownCenter Mall, the Szechwan Restaurant packed up its wok and peppers and moved to a new location on Saratoga-Sunnyvale Road.

Upon getting out of my car, I was pleased to detect the stout aromas wafting around the parking lot as they used to do on South Murphy. Overall, the dishes served here were exceptionally prepared, the original flare and savor still implicit in the spicier Szechwanese dishes. What I like most about this restaurant is its stark commitment to flavor. The chefs here don't hold back on the pepper power, but apply it generously along with doses of garlic, ginger and other inspiring ingredients.

The Szechwan's claim to fame is the Szechwan Shredded Beef. Even though I have sampled better, I still use the rendition here as a measure stick for judging this famous peasant dish of China's Western pepper-eating province. The beef is cut into long thin strips and toss fried with shreds of carrot, onion, long dry pepper pods and a slightly sweet and spicy brown sauce. The physical appearance of this dish was an alluring sight, the bright orange of the carrot contributing a beautiful splash of color. Although it was spicy, the heat of the pepper was not truly felt unless eaten whole.

Kung Pao Beef was equally fiery. This dish offered less eye appeal, but was heavy on nose appeal. We could smell it approaching several tables away. The composition of this item brought tender medallions of beef together with the Kung Pao trademark: peanuts, garlic, scallion and black hot pepper. With this one, you didn't have to bite into the pepper to burn the mouth. The fire was harmoniously interwoven into the flavor which relied on the cohesion of its natural ingredients, not on a sauce or additive.

I was most impressed with the Yu-Shiang Broccoli found under the "Vegetables and Meat" heading on the menu. Sprigs of fresh, deep-green broccoli, cooked to the perfect crunch, joined shreds of pork in an adhesive, sweet and garlicy sauce that did not congeal through the cooling process. Peppers were added, but their heat was not as implicit as in the beef dishes.

The one thorough disappointment my guest and I encountered was the Shrimp with Cashew, one of the dishes we ordered to counterbalance the blaze of the pepper. The shrimps were plump enough, but the flavor was blatantly fishy tasting and the texture unappetizingly slippery. The cashews were abundant, but after a couple fishy mouthfuls of shrimp, we decided to push the plate to the side with the soy sauce cruet. It was better forgotten.

Service at The Szechwan was adequate. Our dishes were brought out promptly and our beverages were served upon request. As far as beverages were concerned, I was disappointed. Coors is the only beer served and it wasn't very cold.

TACO AL PASTOR ★★   Price Range: **Bargain**
Burritos Al Pastor

---

375 So. Bascom Ave., San Jose	Cash Only
Phone: 275-1619	No Reservations
Hours: 10 am–8 pm, Tues.-Fri.	No Non-Smoking Section
From 8 am, Sat.	Clumsy Wheelchair Access
8 am–6 pm, Sunday	

A friend of mine once said in defense of her pint-sized boyfriend that "Dynamite comes in little packages." This statement applies directly to a dingy little windowbox located on Bascom Ave. called Taco al Pastor. This glass eruption from the earth is definitely nothing to look at. It is small, cramped, run down, and geared primarily for fast food service. Taco al Pastor is a great place to stop when you're hungry for a Mexican tasty, in a hurry, and low on money.

The specialty of the House is the "taco al pastor." According to a magazine clipping taped onto the order window, a special method of preparation is employed to make this recipe. Beef is packed onto a spindle, then cooked slowly over a charcoal fire. As the meat is cooked, it is cut away and served hot and fresh. When applied to a tortilla, the morsels of barbecued beef are combined with pieces of thick bacon and spicy seasonings. I detected the addition of the potent Mexican sausage, Chorizo. Though greasy, the marriage of flavors forms a remarkable blend that was by far the most popular offering sampled.

This filling can be used to stuff the taco or the burrito. The tacos are unusual creations. Instead of shells made from oil fried tortillas, the meat fillings are rolled around two, hearth-warmed corn tortillas. This cuts down on the intake of grease, brings out the flavor of the corn, and makes a perfect pocket for the meat.

Carne Asada is also a savory filling for either the taco or the burrito. It is seasoned grilled steak cut into thin strips. In the burrito, the steak joins a helping of fresh pinto beans and an ample splash of pulpy tomato salsa.

The salsa at Taco al Pastor is a hot, spicy brew, packed with pepper seeds, fresh cilantro and minced onion in a loose, natural tomato juice base. While waiting for your order, you can crunch into a basket of chips with a side of this fiery salsa.

Service at Taco al Pastor is almost non-existent. You order at a tiled counter. A lady or man who speak a halting tenor of English will then go to work fixing your food. You are mostly accountable for the success or failure of your table service. Listen for your order to come up. Every once and a while a busboy appears from the back to wipe down tables and clear debris.

No alcoholic beverages are served, so figure on an ice cold soft drink or a cup of coffee with your lunch.

Taco al Pastor is a fast, casual lunch stop-off. The tacos and burritos are well made, moderately spicy, and reasonably priced. For a combination lunch of one taco and one burrito, plus two cokes, you will pay about $3.50 and change.

TADICH GRILL ★★★★
Seafood   Price Range: Moderate to Expensive

240 California St., San Francisco	Cash Only
Phone: (415) 391-2373	No Reservations
Hours: 11:30 am–8:30 pm, Mon.–Sat.	No Non-Smoking Section
Full Bar	Limited Wheelchair Access

San Francisco's Tadich Grill was established in 1849, soon after gold was discovered by James Marshall at Sutter's Mill. As you can guess, this eating establishment is thoroughly seasoned. Tadich is a true culinary veteran and has earned its reputation as one of San Francisco's finest seafood restaurants.

The Tadich Grill is almost always busy. No reservations are taken, so you'll have to leave your name at the cash register and wait your turn. Time passes quickly, however, so don't fret. You'll certainly have enough to do watching the people and absorbing the classic fish-house atmosphere. If you want to avoid the crowds, come at around 3 p.m.; however, being able to avoid crowds even at this hour is not guaranteed.

Tadich's kitchen employs several styles of preparing fresh fish and shellfish. Charcoal broiling is one of its specialties. Tadich has been using the ever-popular mesquite charcoal for many years, long before the fad swept through the restaurant business. All dishes here are presented in a simple, basic manner without heavy garnish or overbearing sauces.

At first glance, the prices may strike you as high. You must consider, however, that the quality is top-notch and portions are large – so large, you may be pressed to finish. I was, and I am a big eater.

On a recent visit, we commenced with a half dozen Eastern oysters on the half shell. I found the oysters to have a mild sea-fresh flavor and a rich, slurpy texture. They were delicious.

After our appetizer, my guest and I enjoyed one of the best crab-leg salads we have had in the Bay Area. Meticulous care was taken to present each Dungeoness crab leg whole and unbroken. These sweet, firm crab legs were served on a bed of crisp lettuce. Topping the salad was Tadich's house dressing; it is similar to a Louie dressing, but without the relishy sweetness.

Next, I ordered one of the specials boxed in red on Tadich's menu. Fried Calamari Steak, Bordelaise. Fresh squids are formed into large steaks, lightly breaded, then fried until the breading is sizzling crisp and the squids moist and sweet. Melting into the breading is rich butter, applied generously. Served on the side is a small portion of Bordelaise sauce. Tadich's rendition was garlic-potent and somewhat masked the delicate flavor of the squids. Next time, I would prefer a side of Tadich's tartar sauce.

Other fresh fish favorites include sand dabs, swordfish, flounder, filet of English sole and red snapper. Though Tadich has based its name on serving fresh fish, it is also known for fine broiled meats. Salisbury steak, calves' liver, Filet Tips, plus baked shoulder of lamb after 5 pm are among the red meats listed.

Service at Tadich is as seasoned as the restaurant itself. Our waiter was well versed in his knowledge of fish, in many preparations, and was quite helpful in guiding us to the recommended selections.

TAIWAN ★★
Chinese

Price Range: Bargain

1306 Lincoln Ave., San Jose
Phone: 289-8800
Hours: Lunch: 11 am–3 pm, Mon.–Fri.
         Dinner: 5–9 pm, Daily
Beer and Wine

Master Card – Visa
Reservations Taken
No Non-Smoking Section
Limited Wheelchair Access

Most people use Lincoln Avenue as a route from home to work and back. But now as one drives down Lincoln, the spicy aromas of Szechwan, Mandarin, and Taiwanese cuisines fill the air, tantalizing the nostrils of Willow Glen's bustling residents. The Taiwan Restaurant has arrived.

Though Szechwan and Mandarin cuisines are highlighted on Taiwan's menu, I highly recommend that you sample at least one Taiwanese specialty. On one visit, I had two Taiwan dishes: Tender Turnip Roll and Fishman's Delight. The tender turnip rolls were excellent. Large, slightly weighty wedges of deep fried pastry shells were presented. Inside of the crackling crisp pastry exterior were layers of moist turnips highly accented with spices and herbs. A dipping marinade of Chinese greens was served on the side.

The Fishman's Delight promised much, but delivered a plate of disappointment. The menu describes this dish as "Monterey squids sauteed with sliced pork and celery." Indeed, all of these ingredients were present; however, the squids were old and fishy tasting, the texture rubbery and very hard to chew. Unfortunately, the fishy flavor invaded the entire dish, destroying the sauce.

Kung Pao Beef was an honorable rendition. A generous portion of beef slices were tossed fried with the characteristic Kung Pao ingredients of peanuts and roasted hot chili peppers. The meat was cooked succulent in a spicy-hot, ginger zesty sauce that was not burdened with heavy thickening agents.

Following our beef dish, we tasted a waitress suggestion, Da-Chien Chicken. Tender, fully boned cubes of chicken breast were prepared in a slightly sweet sauce flecked with hot peppers and whole roasted peppers. The sauce had a similar flavor to the Kung Pao Beef with green pepper offering the only real flavor departure. Portion was large and enough to divide four ways.

A local favorite at Taiwan is the Mu-Shu Pork. A fresh, crisp toss of pork shreds, bamboo shoots, egg, lettuce, and seasonings were presented in a light natural sauce. The pork mixture was served with the traditional pancakes for wrapping the meat and vegetables, plus a side of hoison sauce.

One of my favorite dishes on the menu was the Pot Stickers. Taiwan's version of these Mandarin dumplings were very light in texture without that often oily residue that I find in other Chinese restaurants. The dumplings were filled with a puree of pork and vegetables spiked with ginger and garlic. Cruets of white vinegar and hot pepper oil are presented as condiments.

Though I cannot classify Taiwan an exquisite Chinese restaurant, it is certainly a good one, serving some authentic Chinese dishes that were well prepared and spicy, Taiwan is definitely a gastronomic boon to the Willow Glen area.

THREE FLAMES ★★★　　　　　　　　　　　Price Range: Moderate
Continental/American

1547 Meridian Ave., San Jose　　　　　Master Card — Visa
Phone:　(408) 269-3133　　　　　　　　Reservations for Large
Hours:　Lunch: 11 am–3 pm, Mon.-Fri.　　Parties
　　　　Dinner: 4–10 pm, Sun.-Tues.　　No Non-Smoking Section
　　　　4–11 pm, Wed.-Sat.　　　　　　Limited Wheelchair Access
Full Bar

Three Flames is a better place for lunch than it is for dinner. During the noon hour bargain specials abound and quality of cooking has always been more memorable. One of my favorite dishes for lunch is a special item, Lamb Shanks. Unfortunately, it only comes around once a week, if that often. But it's definitely worth planning for. The shanks are always laden with stewed lamb done in a thick, hearty gravy laced with wine and herbs. What I like most about this dish is the marrow packed into the shank holes. I savor this delicious finale.

Lunch and dinner are both highlighted by juicy cuts of prime rib. Of course, the lunch cut is reduced in size and may be called a sandwich. But the meat is quality, very tender, and not chewy. Steaks are broiled to order and come in various sizes and cuts. A good red meat buy here is the London Broil. It is served in thick slices and topped with a beef stock gravy.

Lunch and dinner entrees include your choice of soup or salad, vegetables du jour (I had overcooked zucchini on one occasion), rice, bread and butter. If you are a bread eater, the waitresses here will keep the breads coming all night. Your basket will never be empty at the Three Flames. Portions for every entree have always been generous. You'll get your money's worth here.

Three Flames presents a dining room where red-flocked, casino elegance dominates. High backed wrap around booths line the perimeter of the spacious dining room while comfortably spaced tables and chairs comprise central seating. I recommend a booth for the total comfort and privacy you may want for a special business discussion or a quiet dinner argument involving very personal insights to your life. Crowds seem to come all at once here, so plan ahead for lunch and dinner. If you come early, you'll have a better chance getting the seat and table you desire.

TOM AND JERRY'S ★   Price Range: Bargain
Fish & Chips

2108 Story Road, San Jose	Cash Only
Phone: 259-4636	No Reservations
Hours: 11 am–9 pm, Daily	No Non-Smoking Section
	Limited Wheelchair Access

Tom and Jerry's Fish and Chip Restaurant doesn't belong to a chain. It is a family-style establishment, tailor made for the low budget diner. The owners are usually on station, taking orders, frying fish, and bantering with local business clientele I felt a keen sense of personal involvement here.

The best item on the menu is the straight fish and chip entree. There are four sizes, ranging from the Superfish, which includes four fish filets, to the Mini, which includes only one fish filet. The Scotty offers two fish filets and fries. This middle portion is well suited for the average-sized appetite.

Each filet contains a thick cut of white fish well secured beneath Tom and Jerry's special batter recipe. The batter is thick and cohesive and fries out to a very bubbly, very crisp exterior, so crisp each bite rings out a loud, embarrassing crunch. I found the batter to contribute a milky attribute to the flavor of the fish.

Of course, the fish retains its inherent firmness and moist texture through the deep fry process. The filet didn't shrink in size either, but stayed full and juicy. Typically, the fried fish filets were slightly greasy, though less than most I have sampled.

With your fish and chips, I highly recommend a serving of tartar sauce. The recipe here is tart and dill in flavor with a greenish tint. The owners don't skimp on the tartar. They spoon it up in generous amounts, enough to last through your meal.

TONY ROMA'S ★★★ Price Range: Moderate
Ribs

4233 Moorpark, San Jose | A.E. — M.C. — Visa
Phone: (408) 253-4900 | No Reservations
Hours: 11–1:30 am, Daily | No Non-Smoking Section
Full Bar — Entertainment | Full Wheelchair Access
| Take-Out

I don't know if suffering the communal frenzy of Tony Roma's is worth eating those exquisite baby back ribs. When this place gets busy, there is no hope for peace and quiet. Voices assault on all sides. Worsening matters is the absurd policy of closely crammed tables. I don't understand why the Tony Roma management thinks this is neat. I have been to two of Tony Roma's other California locations (Palm Springs and Encino) and both of them have tables pushed close together. Geezz, give me some elbow room.

But, there is hope. You don't have to eat inside Tony Roma's anymore. You can order from a take-out window accessible from the outside. This might be the best way to enjoy these delicious ribs.

What makes Tony Roma's ribs so special is the incredibly tender, sweet pork meat clinging to the neatly butchered bone shafts. Your teeth will glide through the meat like a hot knife through butter. I love baby back ribs. They are the best for my money. At Roma's, they are barbecued over a wood fire which infuses the meat with a deep smoke flavor.

Aside from the regular side dishes of French fries and cole slaw (baked potato after 5 pm), you can order Tony Roma's world famous onion rings. Though the masses find these rings a valuable commodity, I have yet to see the reason behind them. An ugly tangle of stringy, greasy, batter-coated onions are served in a heap. They are difficult to pry apart and are basically limp. I find them ridiculous.

There are other items on the menu like Barbecued Chicken, and other red meat selections, but the ribs are the best Tony Roma's can offer. And that's good enough. Dig in and forget the chortling fool to your left.

TRE KRONOR ★★★
Swedish

Price Range: Bargain

1765 Winchester Blvd., Campbell
Phone: 374-6882
Hours: 6 am–6 pm, Mon.–Sat.
      9 am–4 pm, Sun.
Beer and Wine

Cash Only
Reservations Taken
No Non-Smoking Section
Limited Wheelchair Access

Tre Kronor is the South Bay's most authentic Swedish Restaurant and Bakery. Having lunch here was a satisfying experience that left me happy and well fed.

The main focus of this restaurant is its bakery where authentic Swedish petits-fours (fancy bite-sized cakes), breads, and morning rolls are taken from the ovens daily. The air is fragrant with the sweet aromas of hot pastries.

Aside from the pastries, Tre Kronor offers a brief lunch menu listing some intriguing noon comestibles, plus a rotating daily special which may include Swedish meatballs or seafood quiche.

Offered everyday is homemade Swedish Pea Soup. Tre Kronor's brew dispels any notion that pea soup must be thick to be good. Their pea soup is exactly that, soup, made according to a true Swedish recipe. The sweet peas remain whole and plump in the natural broth like stock. Defining the flavor are tender chunks of fresh ham.

Another traditional Swedish entree offered daily is the Swedish Pancake. A rich, foamy batter is griddle fried with butter, creating crepe-light pancakes that are airy and fork tender. Each serving delivers two pancakes plied together and topped with a large scoop of whipped cream and strawberry preserve. This may sound like a lot of calories, but it's not. The pancakes settle like a feather.

Sandwiches are few, but well prepared, especially the Ham. A morning baked Swedish roll is layered with thin folds of ham with a spread of mayo and mustard and tomato and lettuce for garnish. The roll was most noteworthy. It was soft and firm and flexed gently inward to the press of fingertips.

Dessert here is mandatory. Any one of Tre Kronor's Petits-fours offers the perfect conclusion to any meal. I closed my eyes and fell into sudden dream over the chocolate and almond finger cake. Chewy almond pastry was topped with a solid cone of rich dark chocolate. I ate four different varieties that day, including a light, eggy Swedish Morning Roll.

Ambience is bright and tranquil, punctuated with a deep blue and red color motif. Service is conducted by Swedish ladies who also cook, bake, and maintain the cleanliness of the dining room.

TRINE'S CAFE #3 ★★

Mexican

Price Range: Bargain

---

995 South 1st Street, San Jose
Phone: 998-9018
Hours: Breakfast, Lunch & Dinner
      Served 7 am–11 pm, Sun.–Th.
      To 4 am, Fri. & Sat.
Beer and Wine

Cash Only
No Reservations
No Non-Smoking Section
Clumsy Wheelchair Access

Trine's is a small, converted coffeeshop. There is a counter to the right and a flimsy line-up of tables and chairs to the left. Looking down upon this skeletal assemblage of tables and chairs are imposing wall cartoons, depicting Aztec heroes saving distressed Aztec maidens. Other than the fake brick walls, these pictures are perhaps the only other color that Trine's can muster. Otherwise, the interior is smoky and always buzzing with passionate jukebox Mexican songs.

For those who have never experienced Cocido, it is simply beef soup. At Trine's, it becomes a feast and is the dish most customers come here to have. It is served in a large bowl brim with hulking chunks of fresh, bright orange carrot, potato, cabbage, and other vegetables. I spooned several oddly cut pieces of zucchini. Adrift in the center of the vegetables and the hearty broth are three meaty knuckles of stewed beef. No bones. If you have a cold, this dish will exterminate the germs instantly. Like the chicken soup to the Jewish mother, Cocido is the Mexican cure all.

Another soup dish that wasn't nearly as good as the cocido was the Albondigas De Res, a favorite Mexican standard. It consists of meatballs rolled with beef and rice simmered in broth with plenty of vegetables. In this dish, I found a long, cooked stalk of celery floating in the liquid. The other vegetables were equally large and unwieldy. My complaint lies in the off flavor of the soup and in the strange color of the meat. The flavor did not assimilate the vegetables and the meat at all. It tasted old with a chili powder dominance. The beef remained red through the cooking process. I have never seen beef stay red after simmering for a long time, especially in soup. Also, a beady oil surface made the soup ugly in appearance.

The Chile Verde de Puerco was very well made, following a family recipe down to the last ingredient. This stew was packed with plenty of pork pieces that carried a strong flavor of the grill. It added an interesting dimension to the green chile gravy that was smooth and thick in consistency.

Be advised that the salsa at Trine's is extremely hot, guaranteed to raise beads of sweat on the brow. It is a deep rust-colored liquid thick with red pepper seeds. Our mouths burned so much, we drank down our first round of beers in a hurry. Whatever we spooned it onto, the penetrating pepper heat became the first stimulus to the mouth.

If you come to Trine's order the Cocido. It is delicious and worth a sampling. It's Trine's specialty.

TRUFFLES AND CREAM ★★★   Price Range: Bargain
Brie and Croissants

1145 Lincoln Avenue, San Jose	Master Card — Visa
Phone: 947-1588	No Reservations
Hours: 10 am–5:30 pm, Tues.–Sat.	No Non-Smoking Section
Beer and Wine	Limited Wheelchair Access

Truffles and Cream is an ambitious storefront restaurant that brings a taste of provencial Europe to Willow Glen. Refocus your meal time expectations when you come here. The food is different, light, and very European.

The most inspiring item I have sampled has been the Stuffed Croissant. This is truly a viable sandwich alternative. A large, freshly baked croissant with a delicately flaky outer crust and an airy, almost wispy inside was cut in half lengthwise. It is layered with thin slices of smoked ham, white cheese, and sprinkled with flecks of dill. After being heated, the melted cheese bonded the subtle flavors together. If you want, you can apply a touch of dijon mustard which gives this creation a piquant aspect.

A delightful selection is the anti-pasto salad and croissant plate. The anti-pasto salad was a mix of juicy, marinated artichoke hearts, button mushrooms, pickled eggplant, and Julienne of salami. All ingredients are soaked in a highly tart dressing. The buttery flavor of the croissant helped to balance the striking tartness of the salad marination.

Truffles and Cream presents tiny finger sandwiches called Arams. Swirls of smoked ham and creamy, smooth brie form a circular sandwich wrapped in Armenian cracker bread. Arams consist of about two or three bites at most and would make a great warm-up appetizer or side dish to a salad.

Also offered here are freshly baked baguettes. If you really want to simplify your lunch, purchase a baguette and a portion of French brie. To eat, just spread the rich brie over pieces of fresh, crusty bread. The flavors are simple, though extremely appetizing, especially if you enjoy it with a glass of chilled white wine.

Truffles and Cream is fairly new. The management is still in the process of working out the kinks and learning the ins and outs. Nonetheless, the idea works well and is quickly taking shape. Prices are reasonable and portions adequate.

THE TRUKADERO ★★
Truck Stop Specials

Price Range: Bargain

2018 North 1st Street, San Jose	Cash Only
Phone: (408) 294-5119	No Reservations
Hours: Open 24 hours	No Non-Smoking Section
	Limited Wheelchair Access

For one of those unforgettable breakfasts, follow a hungry trucker, and five times out of ten, he'll lead you right to the Trukadero. The parking lot of this 24-hour truck stop heaven is a veritable convention center for truck drivers. During the morning hours, they converge at The Trukadero en masse. Even the view from an inside table is blocked by the huge front ends of their behemoth vehicles.

The Trukadero draws its gastronomic charm strictly from the grub it serves. Big portions and gobs of melted butter are mandatory here. You'll eat hearty, or you won't eat at all. The Trukadero's griddle masters are versatile and fix omelets, waffles, hash browns, pork chops, burgers, and eggs with tremendous down home savor.

Super breakfast specials are offered daily, including a rib eye steak and three eggs with three hot cakes or biscuits and gravy. If you want to dance a jig, you can do it with a special Greek omelet made with rich feta cheese. On my first visit, I filled my bucket on a paw-sized spread of Virginia ham steak and two eggs. The ham was thick, lean, and well-smoked.

On a lunch visit one day, I had a plate of pork chops. Unlike so many restaurants that only serve two chops on a plate, The Trukadero serves three, browned and griddled without a lot of fanfare. The chops were escorted by a bed of mashed potatoes with an eye of melting butter, and a scoop of frozen style peas and carrots.

The ambience here is cigarette smoke, loud guaffaws, and burly undertones. Come to eat and leave. And if the tables are taken, the counter isn't a bad spot to raise a fork.

T. S. MONTGOMERY ★★★
Continental / American

Price Range: Expensive

Cor. of Market St. & San Carlos, San Jose	A.E. – M.C. – Visa
Phone: (408) 295-2000	Reservations Required
Hours: Lunch: 11:30 am–2:30 pm, Daily	No Non-Smoking Section
Dinner: 5:30–10 pm, Daily	Full Wheelchair Access
After Theater Hours: 10–Midnight	
Full Bar	

T.S. Montgomery has provided Downtown San Jose with a needed upthrust of class and elegance. Located on the first floor of the newly refurbished Sainte Claire Hotel, this restaurant is the perfect setting for lunch, dinner, or after theater repast for those who work and play in the downtown area.

Though the interior is a vision of unmitigated beauty with its regal appointments, its plush velvet furniture, its white linen and napery, its paneled walls, and its refreshing potted palms, the kitchen output and service are still working out their kinks. Waiters have been forgetful on three occasions and the food has been inconsistent in quality. Any new restaurant must first get settled, firmly established before realization is achieved.

The menu lists several continental entrees and a few red meat offerings like Prime Rib and Steaks. The prime rib has, on two visits, been an adequate cut with a nice marbling and with plenty of natural juice which kept the meat moist throughout the dinner. It wasn't particularly a large cut and I found the price not to be commensurate with the portion.

I have also sampled the Rack of Lamb. This was a total disappointment. A rack of lamb must be served in a whole rack to be considered a true rack. T.S. Montgomery's rack was served already cut into chops. The meat sat in its juices and actually continued to cook until the degree of rare was a medium rare going on medium. There is a world of difference between a rack of lamb and lamb chops.

For lunch I have enjoyed the Melange of Sea Fruits. Displayed on a bed of crisp Romaine Lettuce were three rolls of smoked fish, two, small salmon steaks, and approximately two tablespoons of crabmeat. The seafood shared a garnish of fresh lime halves and a whole slice cooked egg. The visuals were very colorful and eye appealing and the fish notably fresh and light. A complete success.

Most entrees for both lunch and dinner are served with perhaps the best premise baked breads I have eaten in the South Bay. I have enjoyed fresh, buttery croissants and mouthwatering cinnamon rolls. They are served in generous amounts.

In final analysis, I will safely say that T.S. Montgomery is rising and has yet to reach its full potential. I am glad it has come to the Downtown area. San Jose needed a classy restaurant of this caliber.

VAHL'S ★★★   Price Range: Moderate
Continental/Seafood

El Dorado & Taylor, Alviso   Cash & Personal Checks
Phone: 262-0731   Reservations Advised
Hours: 11 am–11 pm, Wed.–Sat.   No Non-Smoking Section
        Dinner only on Sunday   Limited Wheelchair Access
Full Bar

Many years ago when duck hunters sculled across the shallows, stalking their limit of game birds, Vahl's was there to replenish their spirits with food and drink when their hunting was finished. The duck hunters and locals still color this place with their gab and laughter. In fact, laughter is the most striking remembrance I have of my visits here. It can't be denied that Vahl's patrons come here for good times and resounding fun. My guests and I were swept up in the festivities, even though the food was generally mediocre.

Within seconds after being seated for dinner, we were presented with salads and hors d'oeuvre trays. Dinners here are complete and include salad, soup, entree, spaghetti and dessert. Vahl's also offers a la carte dishes for those who do not want to eat too much. Our salads were covered with a creamy dressing that was tart and oniony.

The hors d'oeuvres were somewhat unusual. There was a plate of salami, pickles, celery, radishes and olives, a plate of over-fried, fishy-tasting mackerel and a selection of cracker spreads that ranged from strong bleu cheese, to a creamy baked-crab dish, to a slice of red jello. With these dishes, Vahl's served a basket of lukewarm, oil-soaked garlic bread. Shortly after, we received bowls of a very watery chowder with some gritty clam bits at the bottom of the bowl.

Heading the lineup of entrees for that evening was a broiled Australian lobster tail, one of Vahl's specialties. I have sampled lobster here three times. The first sampling, I found this ritzy crustacean to uphold its royal stature. It was succulent, sweet, and juicy. Unfortunately, my following two lobsters here were far less in quality. The worst was stringy and flat.

The best offering for my most recent visit was the squab made according to Vahl's special recipe. The delicate, tiny-boned bird was roasted to a turn with a stuffing of rice. Before being served, it was cut tableside by the waitress into four meaty sections. The squab meat was tawny and delicately sweet with a moist tender texture that melted in the mouth. A wine-spiked brown sauce added an interesting dimension to the overall flavor of the bird.

Another one of Vahl's perennial favorites is abalone brought in from Half Moon Bay. For the inflated price, I was disappointed with the preparation of this shellfish. The abalone was pounded to a flat, expansive piece that could be tender if not overcooked. As a result, it was a little dry and toothy. The egg jacket covering the fish had a strong, overcooked egg taste which further diminished the quality of this expensive seafood.

Dinners are served with vegetables du jour, buttered potatoes and/or rice. One of the vegetables was green peas that suffered from the deep freeze. The potatoes, on the other hand, were deeply buttered and cooked tender. The dinner also includes a communal plate of spaghetti with meat sauce.

Service at Vahl's is as charismatic as the restaurant itself. Most of the waitresses are elderly veterans who have been with Vahl's for many, many years. Our waitress was a true character. When we asked to see a wine list, she replied matter-of-factly, "Honey, I am the wine list."

VANESSI'S ★★★   Price Range: Moderate
Italian/Grill

---

498 Broadway, San Francisco   All Major Credit Cards
Phone: (415) 421-0890   Reservations Advised
Hours: 11:30 am–1 am, Mon.-Sat.   No Non-Smoking Section
         4:30 pm–Midnight, Sunday   Limited Wheelchair Access
Full Bar — Extensive Wine List

Vanessi's sits on Broadway in the rainbow neon of North Beach's world famous porno clubs. Parking is typically nettlesome, unless you don't mind spending a goodly sum for a protected slot. The interior is comprised of three dining rooms, one of which shares space with the bar. The front room is equipped with Vanessi's famous counter where patrons can sit and watch the chefs, flanked by tins of olive oil and cooking wine, perform gastronomic pyrotechnics. The aromas are strong and invigorating, the saute dishes marvelous.

Vanessi's menu is long and well versed with Italian dishes, plus a host of excellent red meat offerings. One of the best steaks in town can be purchased at Vanessi's.

If you are going to spend an entire dinner here, I recommend starting with an hors d'oeuvre wheel laden with proscuitto, headcheese, salami, scallions, radishes, black olives, fresh celery stalks, and a row of fresh, unshelled prawns. Served with this anti-pasto is cocktail sauce and a cup of garbanzo bean salad. Other appetizers are offered, but not as refreshing as this one.

Delicious anti-pasto followups include Vanessi's famous minestrone soup, a thick brew with beans, vegetables, macaroni, and sausage, or whatever else the kitchen throws into the pot. Also, a fine Caesar salad is offered in place of the typical salad of greens with Italian dressing.

In my visits here, I have had problems with the entrees. Linguini with clams has consistently been made with a thick, glutinous sauce that buried the essence of the pasta. It was too creamy. Likewise, Gnocchi Bolognese was heavy and bready with a much too meaty sauce.

Veal dishes are made with quality milk fed provimi, but, on some visits, have been haphazardly prepared. Veal Parmigiana, for example, appeared as though the cook splashed on the sauce and cheese as the waiter was carrying the plate out of the kitchen. I know it gets busy here, but there's no excuse for dishes wearing the marks of a rushed chef.

Despite all the contrary reports, I have always found the service to be friendly and efficient, considering the war-time conditions. I do find the host to be a bit cold and unwelcoming, handling his guests as though they were cut from a crude mold.

VICTORIAN HOUSE ANTIQUES & GARDEN RESTAURANT ★★★★
Continental/Italian   Price Range: Expensive

476 South First St., San Jose	All Major Credit Cards
Phone: 286-1770; 286-6187	Reserv. Recommended
Hours: Lunch: 11 am–3 pm, M–Fri.	No Non-Smoking Section
Dinner: 5–10 pm, Mon.-Thurs.	Limited Wheelchair Access
To 11 pm, Fri. & Sat.	
From 3 pm, Sunday	
Sunday Brunch: 11 am–3 pm	
Full Bar	

The Victorian House has remained true to its original concept, which was based on a unique idea. The owners have put together an antique shop and a continental restaurant, blending them into a beautifully continuous theme. A bower of Tiffany-style lamps and glossy philodendrons hang from the ceiling. A profusion of old brick, stained-glass partitions and windows, oak tables and chairs, and an unending montage of antiques, both useful and decorative, dazzle the eye. If you look closely at the antiques, you'll see price tags. Just about everything is for sale and nothing is cheap.

In addition to a small intimate bar, the Victorian House offers its guests a spring and summertime retreat in its courtyard patio. When it's warm this area provides the perfect romantic setting.

The menu here is continental with Italian leanings. If you like mussels, I suggest you try a serving of Black Mussels Fra Diable for an appetizer, or if you are here for lunch, have them over linguine. This particular variety of mussel is large and juicy with a sleek, silky, soft body that melts in the mouth.

We also sampled a plate of Linguine with White Clam Sauce and divided it up as an appetizer. I commend the chef on knowing how to boil pasta. The noodles were al dente, offering a pleasant resistance to the bite. Spooned over the pasta was a brothy sauce, light in garlic, and deep in natural clam flavor. Clam bits seasoned with aromatic oregano covered the tender strands of pasta, while whole clams in shell surrounded the plate.

If you like scampi, this is the place to order it. The menu lists more than four variations. We sampled Scampi Remey. Oversized scampi were simmered to a moist, succulent sleekness in a cohesive butter-based sauce, strong with garlic and chives, with a distinct sherry sweetness.

Our second entree was a masterful dish, Chicken a la Francaise. Three fully skinned, meaty supremes of quality chicken were dipped in a light batter of egg and flour then sauteed with mushrooms in a mild sauce of butter and sherry. The natural juiciness of the chicken was most impressive. With one stroke of the knife the juice trickled out, blending its natural flavor into the butter and sherry sauce.

I sampled Veal Milanese for lunch one day. I was pleased to see that it is also offered on the dinner menu. The Milanese-style is a very simple one, performed according to traditional standards here. A slice of milk-fed veal is breaded and pan-fried in olive oil and garlic until the breading is crisp. It is served with a wedge of lemon, a drizzle of which completes the marriage of simple flavors.

One dish that has raised question is the Homemade Sausage and Peppers. This preparation has been on the Victorian House's menu ever since it opened. On one visit, my guest complained that the sausage was dry and mealy, the sauce too thick and unevenly flavored with green pepper. After several mouthfuls, I agreed that the sausage wasn't at its best.

The service at the Victorian House has always been efficient, but occasionally aloof. Our waiter rarely smiled, though he always appeared on the verge of saying something profound. I wish he had. But he managed our table with professional dispatch.

The Victorian House Antiques and Garden Restaurant can join the ranks of San Jose's best. It has become a downtown standard along with Emile's, Original Joe's and Paolo's.

THE VILLAGE ★★
Italian

Price Range: Moderate

4996 Stevens Creek Blvd., San Jose
Phone: 248-7191
Hours: Lunch: 11–2:30 pm, Tues.-Fri.
Dinner: 5–10 pm, Tues.-Sun.
Beer and Wine

Master Card — Visa
Reservations Taken
No Non-Smoking Section
Limited Wheelchair Access

For approximately 23 years, The Village has been serving Italian food in one form or another. Though the store has remained steadfast at the convergent borders of San Jose, Santa Clara, and Cupertino, the proprietorship has changed aprons three times. According to the waitress, the new owners have been with the Village for over a year now.

In my opinion, The Village excels in pizza making. Ever since I can remember, it's been a place to fill up on finely crafted pizzas. The Village's honorable pie is made with a sturdy bread dough crust that has a light yeasty flavor and a supple texture. When fresh from the oven, the bottom surface of the crust is a crispy golden that offers a thin crackle to the bite. Cheese is adequately applied over the crust and the meatless, very tangy tomato sauce. Many variations are offered from the plain cheese to the large everything.

Outside of pizza, you might encounter some dishes at The Village that will leave you less than satisfied. The Spaghetti and Meatballs couldn't find balance. The meat sauce that covered the pasta was a cohesive blend of tomato, spices and hamburger. It was very tangy with tomato flavor and clung to the strands of spaghetti without falling off and forming a watery puddle at the plate's bottom. It was the meatballs that threw a monkey wrench into the works. They were very hard and rubbery and took a burst of strength to cut through. The flavor was strongly influenced by garlic.

The Village's dinner menu lists a wide variety of pasta dishes, ranging from a long list of spaghetti assortments to manicotti, ravioli, linguini, fettuccine, lasagna, rigatoni, and a few others. We met with disaster at the hands of Ravioli Alla Inglese. The ricotta-filled pasta envelopes were nearly raw, several degrees from the al dente state. The ravioli were gummy and, towards the center, had a taste of raw dough. Yucking up the works was an over application of melted butter compounded by a top covering of melted cheese. By the time the plate arrived to our table, the cheese was an elastic mat.

We also ordered Veal Milanese. The breaded veal cutlet presented in this dish utilized what appeared and tasted to be an aged cut of veal. It was very dark in color with an inherent toughness that was not particularly unpleasant. I am not adverse to tough cuts of veal. I grew up with it and enjoy it with a fine breading and fried in olive oil and garlic.

200

The cooks at The Village did a good job with this dish, presenting it attractively with a row of freshly sliced lemon and a combination of garden fresh vegetables.

All dinners come with both minestrone soup and salad.

Service at The Village was excellent. Our waitress was very patient with our demands and went out of her way to accommodate. The hostess is also a fine lady who makes it a point to greet her customers with a warm smile and an inviting attitude.

WARBURTON'S TAMALE PARLOR ★★★
Early Californian   Price Range: Bargain

1370 Franklin St., Santa Clara	M.C. — Visa — Gold Card
Phone: 248-7041	
Hours: 9 am–6 pm Daily	Wheelchair Access
Closed Sunday	
Take Out Only	

Warburton's Tamale Parlor dates to 1904 when Henry J. Warburton made his first tamale and went into business. At first, he operated a small sit-down eatery, equipped with a few tables and chairs. It was a cubbyhole business and lasted until 1914, when he moved to the basement of the Koehle residence.

He survived at this location for 48 years. In 1962, he moved again to another basement at the corner of Franklin and Alviso Streets. Poor Henry died in 1962 about the time Warburton's made its move. But his spirit was embraced by the foster family he raised; they took hold of the reins and kept going.

What makes Warburton's special transcends Henry J. himself. His famous tamales, tailored after a secret recipe revealed to him by Santos Lagos, are the commodities that have laced the Warburton history with flavor and delicious interest. It must be noted a Warburton tamale or enchilada is not Mexican, but Early California. The difference is implicit in the manner of preparation and the ingredients used.

Dry corn is ground by hand every day to insure the right texture and moistness of the *masa*. This "on premises" production has been the trademark of Warburton's ever since Henry made his first tamale. Customers are invited to view the operation through a convenient window set up along the rear kitchen.

Once the *masa* is made, the crafting begins. First, the *masa* is spread onto each corn husk, which traps in the moistness, insuring a character-istic juiciness not found in other tamales around town. The beef, trim-med and cubed by hand, shares the center body with a spicy hot chili sauce and an old-fashioned unpitted black olive.

The texture of the sauce is very smooth and evenly blended, the spiciness robust, yet not overpowering. The final result is a large, fistu-lar tamale, tied at both ends. The only way to eat this tamale is with a spoon, because the ingredients are soft and saucy and cannot be jock-eyed with the hands.

Two varieties of enchiladas are offered: cheese and onion, and meat and cheese. Both are long, solid construction made with flour tortillas and filled generously. The cheese and onion offers a strong bite of freshly chopped onions in a pleasantly sharp cheese filling, melted in a smooth layer inside the tortilla wrap.

The beef enchilada is packed with a spiced ground beef blended with ample melted cheese. Topping both enchiladas is Warburton's famous chili sauce.

Warburton's is not a restaurant, but it will accommodate large parties. Just call ahead.

THE WHITE HOUSE ★   Price Range: Bargain
Steak Sandwich

---

116 E. Campbell Ave., Campbell   Cash Only
Phone: 378-6767   No Reservations
Hours: 11 am–10 pm, Mon.–Wed.   No Non-Smoking Section
         11 am–Midnight, Thurs.   Clumsy Wheelchair Access
         Till 1 am, Fri. & Sat.
         Till 10 pm, Sunday   Take Out & Delivery
Soft Drinks Only

What is an American dream steak sandwich? For over a decade now, The White House in Campbell has been frying them up on a steady basis. As far as I am concerned, there was nothing patriotic about these unwieldy sandwiches. They were large, juicy, and freshly made, but not one bite struck up a note of Stars and Stripes Forever. So what is an American dream steak sandwich?

According to The White House menu, the steak sandwich here is the answer to the hamburger, hot dog syndrome. To begin, they are built on a foundation of sweet dough French rolls. I was impressed with the supple, springy texture of the bread. It was chewy, yet soft and did well soaking up the juices of the various meats and miscel-laneous sandwich packings.

There are ten steak sandwich varieties to choose from. For the proper initiation, I suggest you go for either the Combo Steak or the Super Steak. Both offer a tasty variety of dressings and toppings that made the sandwich quite intriguing, maybe even dream inspiring. The combo is packed with thinly sliced strips of griddle fried sirloin, with cooked onions and green peppers, plus a layer of cheese. By the time you bite into the sandwich the cheese is melted into a creamy ooze. The final result was a tubular, fist-sized sandwich that was plump and juicy. The flavors were simple with a sauteed aftertaste. For additional taste enhancing, The White House brews up its own special steak sauce. It was on the spicy side.

The Super Steak Sandwich brings you all the ingredients of the combo, plus mushrooms and avocado. The avocado is guacamole-like and gives the flavor of the meat a creaminess that is somewhat unusual.

You can eat at The White House, take out, or have them deliver to your office or place of work. If you plan on eating there, you will sit in a room painted red, white and blue, and plastered with American History regalia. Cigarette smoke has a tendency to linger long after it's been puffed into the atmosphere. I recommend that non-smokers take-out.

YU SHAN ★★★★   **Price Range: Moderate**
Hunan/Szechwan

1330 S. Mary Ave., Sunnyvale	M.C. – Visa – No Checks
Phone: 245-1222	Reserv. Recommended
Hours: 11:30 am–9:30 pm, Sun.-Thu.	No Non-Smoking Section
To 10 pm, Fri. & Sat.	Wheelchair Access
Beer and Wine	

After chopsticking my way through just about every Chinese restaurant in the South Bay, I have finally come to a steadfast conclusion: One of the top three is undeniably Yu Shan in Sunnyvale, a Hunan-Szechwan dinner house where gourmet finesse blazes with the spirit of the pepper pod. Chef Wang has been at the wok for more than 40 years and has become a venerable master of Chinese haute cuisine. Balance, color, texture and spice embrace Buddhist harmony in Wang's inspiring meat, fish and vegetable presentations.

Unlike Cantonese, Mandarin or Peking cuisine, Szechwan and Hunan dishes are almost always spicy hot, employing such palate stimulators as the hot black-bean sauce. The people of China's Western provinces are known for their love of pepper.

Although the Western provinces represent a large segment of China's peasantry, Chef Wang refines these homeland dishes with touches of wine and personal gourmet secrets. Most of his sauces are thickened naturally without the use of gooey agents.

For a sauce extraordinaire, Lamb Hunan Style provided a perfect example. Sensuously moist, all meat slices of lamb were sauteed in a velutinous brown sauce, springing with a divine application of white wine. Scallions and hot pepper were added, the pepper distinctively hot without burning. Similarly, the Double Sauteed Sliced Pork displayed a bountiful array of thinly sliced pork tenderloin in a heady, satiny-smooth brown sauce with pepper pods, garlic and freshly chopped cabbage. The sauce in this dish was a tad more spirited than in the lamb, offering a spicy robustness that left a slight tingle on the lips.

Another pork dish that is a must for first timers here is the Yu Shan Pork. Because of this dish, Chef Wang was written up in Sunset Magazine several years back. Tender pork shreds with bamboo shoots and scallions were toss-fried in a saute of wine, pepper and a mild bean sauce. Highlighted here were two etheral sesame Chinese bisquits, freshly baked on the premises, in which the pork mixture is applied and eaten like a sandwich.

We reveled in the Kun Pao Scallops. The Kun Pao method employs a quick stir-fry over a sizzling hot wok with a dash of oil. The process traps in the inherent moistness of the provender it sizzles. Such was the case with the platter of sliced sea scallops explosively fired with roasted peanuts, chopped scallions, water chestnuts, and again those beautiful flecks of hot red pepper. The sauce was an adhesive glaze that drew the rich, creamy essence of the scallops into a gleeful balance.

A beef dish that exhibited creativity on Chef Wang's part was the Shredded Beef Dry Sauteed Szechwan Style. A crispy fried scramble of golden bronze beef shreds with onions, garlic, green peppers and carrots dazzled the eye with color as well as the tongue with excellent flavor. The sauce here tended to be a bit overbearingly peppery which may eliminate the greenhorn from the taste experience. It is definitely different, so be advised, but don't turn away.

On to fowl. We ordered a half Szechwan Tea Smoked Duck with four steamed rolls. Splayed on a bed of crisp lettuce was a well fatted, crispy skinned duckling hacked into several chopstickable wedges. On first bite, I thought how similar it tasted to smoked butt ham, a tad salty with a scent of woodsiness. However, the flavor became more complex than just butt ham, presenting a unique smoky flavor. We gnawed the bones until the plate was a skeleton heap.

When the choosing comes, I'll always choose Yu Shan over the rest. Quite frankly, good food is the No. 1 consideration; all else follows behind.

ZAKI'S ★★★   Price Range: Expensive
Steak

---

258 Union Ave., Los Gatos   A.E. − M.C. − Visa
Phone: 371-2094   Reservations Accepted
Hours: 5:30–9:30 pm, Mon.–Thurs.   No Non-Smoking Section
       Till 11 pm, Fri. & Sat.   Limited Wheelchair Access
       From 4:30 pm, Sunday
Full Bar − Entertainment

Even though red meat has taken a nose dive with public opinion, Zaki's bucks the odds, serving a limited menu, dripping with thick cuts of Kansas corn-fed beef.

The fare is absolutely basic. The cook is a real straight-shooter and does a fine job char-broiling steaks and cutting prime rib. And speaking of prime rib, it doesn't last long. When I tried to order it, I was told that only medium cuts were left. Well, I don't care for medium-cooked beef, so I went for one of the steaks. Several are listed, with the Shogun Steak, a sake-marinated slab of New York, being the most risque. I settled for a simple New York steak without the frills.

My meat was fired to the degree of doneness that I asked for, medium rare. It tapered from hues of pink to a juicy red at the very center. The large cut is about 2½ fingers thick with little fat around the edges.

As with most basic steakhouses, Zaki's offers a few shellfish items. A separate menu located on the table lists such catches as lobster, king crab legs, and prawns. Our waiter suggested that we sample the prawns scampi. I was surprised by the quality of the prawn preparation. Five jumbo gulfers were sauteed in a well-crafted butter, lemon and garlic sauce.

The cook at Zaki's gave evidence that he is indeed an aspiring chef by his side-dish presentations. Our vegetables could have shared space with fine veal at any one of the finer continental or French restaurants in the area. The carrots and zucchini were cooked al dente and sparingly buttered. I was also impressed by a side of mushrooms. They weren't your typical button mushrooms drowned in a beefy, soupy, ill-tasting swill. They were thoughtfully sliced and sauteed in butter, garlic and sherry. The sherry was strongly evident, yet it did not bespeak a haphazard application.

Zaki's success will be determined by the number of people who still hanker after a good 'ol steak and baked potato. I'm sure the proprietors were well aware of the fact that steak has lost much of its popularity since the health-food craze put a bug in everybody's ear. But, Zaki's is there, a restaurant to be reckoned with whenever the urge for a supercharge of animal protein knocks on the walls of your gastronomic consciousness.

ZORBA'S ★
Greek/American

Price Range: Moderate

1350 So. Bascom Ave., San Jose
Phone: (408) 293-7170
Hours: Lunch: 11:30 am–3 pm, M–Fri.
Dinner: 5–11 pm, Daily
To Midnight, Fri. & Sat.
Full Bar — Entertainment: Belly Dancing

A.E. — M.C. — Visa
Reserv. Recommended
No Non-Smoking Section
Limited Wheelchair Access

The interior of Zorba's stirs memories of Ricky Ricardo's Tropicana Club. There's a long, serpentine, leather tufted bar enwrapped with stools constantly occupied with shady characters mixing their cocktails with bejeweled forefingers. The dining room is large, open and drafty, decorated with bas-relief wall pieces of quasi-Greek scenes. Corinthian columns, year round Christmas decorations and a bandstand and dance floor round out Zorba's aging supper club milieu.

As a restaurant, Zorba's has improved somewhat since my earlier appraisals. Unfortunately, it has yet to convince me that its kitchen is sincere in pleasing the public with quality Greek cuisine. Zorba's should be our Greek jewel, a place where Greek food is a glorious presentation. But it's not. And that's a damn shame. Prime rib and American style steak dinners are much better offerings.

On two of my visits, I have begun with an appetizer of Saganaki. This traditional Greek dish is a plate of kefalotiri (Greek cheese) baked until the outer surface is crisp and golden. Before serving it is flamed in rum and drizzled with fresh lemon juice. It is important to eat this appetizer quickly. It has a tendency to congeal into a chewy, rubbery clump. Other Greek appetizers include an excellent plate of feta cheese dressed with olive oil and oregano. The flavors were plain, simple, and direct.

Greek entrees at Zorba's include the house specialty, Lamb Kapama. A large, meaty lamb shank, laden with tender, stewed meat, is served in a tomato-based sauce. It has been the sauce that has vexed this dish. It is mundane and thick with little herb accent.

Avoid, at all costs, the trip around Greece. This is a trip you may not return from. It includes the Greek commonalities: dolmades (stuffed grape leaf), Keftethes (Greek meatballs), Pastitso, and a shank of lamb. None of the items in this dish have ever shown a great deal of expertise. The food on this trip has been heavy and hard on the digestive tract.

All dinners are served with a cup of avgolemomo (lemon soup), salad, and baklava for dessert. These dishes have been quite good.

Though my criticisms of Zorba's have been harsh, I still believe San Jose needs this veteran Greek dining establishment. Maybe someday, we will all be surprised by a sudden change that will bring a quality Greek chef to Zorba's kitchen.

GLOSSARY – MENU TERMS

–A–

Aglio, It.: Garlic.

Agneau, Fr.: Lamb.

Al Dente: "To the tooth"; cooked to the point at which pasta or vegetable offers a slight, enjoyable resistance to the bite.

Alfredo, It.: A style of making Fettuccine which is mixed with butter; grated Parmesan cheese and heavy cream.

Allumettes, Fr.: Thin, matchstick French fries.

Almandine: Prepared with almonds.

Antipasto, It.: Literally, before the meat, an appetizer.

Aromates, Fr.: Prepared with aromatic herbs (parsley, thyme, bay leaf, rosemary, tarragon, garlic, onion, shallots, chives and celery).

Arreganata, It.: Prepared with oregano.

Artichaut, Fr.: Artichoke.

Aspic: Jellied broth.

Augolemono, Gr.: The smooth soup of Greece highlighted by lemon.

–B–

Baked Alaska: A thick slice of ice cream on a slice of sponge cake, sprinkled with liqueur, encased in meringue (whipped egg whites and sugar).

Bayonne Ham, Fr.: French raw ham.

Bearnaise, Fr.: A rich sauce of beaten egg yolks, butter and white wine, flavored with shallots and both fresh and dried tarragons. Goes well with fish and red meat.

Benedict, Eggs: Poached eggs on slices of ham on toasted English muffin, capped with Hollandaise.

Bercy, Fr.: A sauce concocted from shallots cooked in butter, white wine, fish broth, with a touch of lemon juice.

Beurre, Fr.: Butter.

Bigarade, Fr.: An orange sauce for duck.

Bisque, Fr.: A thick soup made from shellfish, fish broth, often white wine, and perhaps a dash of brandy or sherry.

Bistecca, It.: Beefsteak.

Blanc, Fr.: White.

Blue Points: Oysters cultivated in special beds off Blue Point, Long Island.

GLOSSARY – MENU TERMS

–B–

Boeuf, Fr.: Beef.

Bolognese, It.: In the style of Bologna where the cooking is rich. Meats are breaded or floured, sauteed in butter, and perhaps topped with a slice of prosciutto and Parmesan cheese, and cooked in white wine or broth.

Bordelaise, Fr.: A red wine sauce seasoned with shallots or onions and browned in butter, tomato, beef marrow, broth, parsley, a little thyme, nutmeg and chopped mushrooms.

Borscht, Ru.: A hearty beef soup served hot or cold with sour cream.

Bouillabaisse, Fr.: The famous Mediterranean fish stew made with an assortment of fish and shellfish. The broth is made from fish broth, onions, garlic, olive oil, fennel, thyme, rosemary, tomatoes, bay leaf and parsley.

Bouillon, Fr.: Clear broth from meat, fish, or vegetables.

Bourguignonne, Fr.: A red wine sauce seasoned with shallots, thyme, bay leaf, parsley, a touch of hot pepper, and thickened with a butter and flour paste.

Bretonne, Fr.: In the style of Brittany, Sauce Bretonne is made with butter, onions, carrots, celery, leeks in white wine, meat or fish broth, and perhaps cream.

Brioche, Fr.: A light, puffed pastry made with flour, yeast, butter, eggs and possibly milk and sugar.

Brochette, Fr.: Spitted on a skewer and grilled or broiled.

Burro, Al, It.: With butter.

–C–

Cacciatore, It.: Hunter style. This almost always includes chicken sauteed in oil and cooked in a sauce of tomatoes, mushrooms, onions, green peppers, garlic, red wine, and spices such as bay leaf, basil and parsley.

Caesar Salad: A salad prepared tableside from romaine lettuce tossed with olive oil, raw egg, lemon juice, anchovies, grated Parmesan, croutons, and freshly ground black pepper.

Cafe, Fr.: Coffee.

Caille, Fr.: Quail.

Calamari, It.: Squid.

Calde, It.: Hot, warm.

Calvados, Fr.: Apple brandy. Very strong!

—C—

Canape, Fr.: Tiny open-faced appetizer sandwich.

Canard, Fr.: Duck.

Cannelloni, It.: "Big tubes" of rolled pasta squares stuffed with chopped meat and spices, baked in a tomato and/or cream sauce and sprinkled with grated Parmesan cheese.

Cannoli, It.: Pipes of crispy pastry filled with Ricotta cheese, cream, flavored with Marsala or vanilla, chocolate, candied fruit and dusted with powdered sugar.

Caper: Marinated buds from the caper bush.

Cappuccino, It.: A coffee specialty made with hot milk forced into black coffee.

Carbonara, It.: A sauce for spaghetti made tableside with diced unsmoked bacon, sauteed in butter, olive oil, and garlic. Raw eggs are added just before serving.

Cardinal, Fr.: A sauce made from fish broth and bits of lobster, a touch of hot pepper, and an optional truffle mixed into a white sauce of flour, butter and cream.

Carne, It.: Meat.

Carre, Fr.: Rack, rib roast.

Casa, alla, It.: In the style of the house.

Casino, Oysters or Clams: Served in the half-shell sprinkled with chopped green pepper, onion or shallots, chives, pimento, parsley, lemon juice, pieces of bacon, then baked.

Caviar: The eggs, or roe, of the sturgeon.

Cervella, It.: Brains.

Chantilly, Fr.: Unsweetened whipped cream flavored with vanilla.

Chasseur, Fr.: Hunter's Sauce made with mushrooms, sauteed in butter with shallots, white wine, and tomato.

Chateaubriand, Fr.: A thick cut of steak from the tenderloin.

Chaud, Fr.: Hot, warm.

Cherrystones: Hard shelled clams.

Choron, Fr.: A sauce made with egg yolks, butter, and tomato puree flavored with shallots and tarragon.

Chutney: A sweet and sour relish of chopped vegetables, fruits and spices.

Cioppino: A San Francisco seafood stew made with onion, garlic, green pepper, scallion, tomato cooked in olive oil and wine seasoned with basil, bay leaf.

GLOSSARY – MENU TERMS

–C–

Citron, Fr.: A citrus fruit in the lemon family.

Coq Au Vin, Fr.: Chicken cooked in wine.

Coquilles De Fruits De Mer, Fr.: Mixed Seafood prepared in a wine and herb sauce enriched with butter, flour, cream and egg yolks.

Cordon Bleu, Sw.: Veal cutlets stuffed with a slice of Swiss cheese and ham, breaded and sauteed.

Creole, Fr.: A tomato sauce seasoned with onions, shallots, green peppers, pimentos, garlic, hot pepper and wine.

Crepes, Fr.: Thin, light French pancakes.

Crepes Suzette, Fr.: Crepes prepared tableside in caramelized sugar and butter, lemon or orange juice, then flamed with Cognac and Grand Marnier.

Crevettes, Fr.: Shrimp.

Croissants, Fr.: Flaky, delicate, buttery crescent-shaped pastry rolls.

Croute, Fr.: In a crust.

Cumberland Sauce, Br.: A traditional English sauce made with red currant jelly, Port, chopped cherries, orange and lemon rind, a dash of vinegar, and a touch of hot pepper.

–D–

Demi, Fr.: Half.

Diane, Steak: Steak sauteed in butter and shallots, then flamed with Cognac. Many variations exist.

Diavola, Alal, It.: A dish prepared with hot pepper.

Dijonnaise, Fr.: A sauce made with Dijon mustard.

Dolce, It.: Sweet.

Duxelles, Fr.: Chopped mushrooms sauteed in butter with shallots and onions used as a stuffing.

–E–

Entre Cote, Fr.: A cut of steak.

Escalope, Fr.: A boneless, flattened piece of meat.

Escargots, Fr.: Snail.

Escoffier, Fr.: Famous French Chef (1846–1935).

Espresso, It.: A very strong, highly caffeinated coffee.

–F–

Facon, A La, Fr.: In the fashion, in the style of.

Fettuccine, It.: Ribbon noodles of Rome.

Financiere, Fr.: A rich sauce of Madeira, meat broth, mushrooms, truffles, chicken livers and olives optional.

Flambe, Fr.: Flamed with brandy or optional liqueur.

Flan, Sp.: Egg custard.

Florentine, A La, It.: Meat, fish and poultry are served on bed of spinach and topped with cream sauce.

Foie, Fr.: Liver.

Foie Gras, Fr.: Liver of a fattened duck or goose.

Forestiere, A La, Fr.: A style of cooking made with diced lean bacon, mushrooms, and potatoes in butter.

Fraises, Fr.: Strawberries.

Fresco, It.: Cool, fresh.

Fricassee, Fr.: A method of stewing white meat or chicken.

Fritto Misto, It.: Mixed fry of meat, poultry or vegetables.

Froid, Fr.: Cold.

Fromage, Fr.: Cheese.

Fruits De Mer, Fr.: Seafood.

Fume, Fr.: Smoked.

–G–

Garni, Fr.: Garnished with the trimmings.

Gazpacho, Sp.: A cold soup made from raw tomatoes, cucumbers, sweet peppers, onions, garlic, pepper, a dash of vinegar, olive oil and a touch of cumin.

Gelato, It.: Ice cream.

Genovese, Alla, It.: A style of cooking, highlighted by the use of aromatic herbs.

Gnocchi, It.: Thumbprint dumpling made of flour, potato or ricotta cheese.

Grand Marnier: Orange brandy.

Gratin, Au, Fr.: Baked with a crust of breadcrumbs.

GLOSSARY — MENU TERMS

—H—

Hasenpfeffer, Gm.: Hare stew.

Helene Poire: Poached pears served over vanilla ice cream and topped with chocolate sauce.

Hofbrau, Gm.: Beer Cellar with open food buffet.

Homard, Fr.: Lobster.

Hors d'Oeuvre, Fr.: An appetizer.

—I—

Insalata, It.: Salad.

Imperiale, A L': Served with the delicacies of truffles, liver, kidneys.

—J—

Jambon, Fr.: Ham.

Hardiniere, Fr.: A fresh vegetable garnish.

Joe's Special: Invented by the famous North Beach band leader, Fortune Nelson "Bunny" Burson. It is a scramble of eggs, spinach and hamburger.

Jour, Du, Fr.: Of the day.

Jubilee, Fr.: A preparation of cherries.

Julienne, Fr.: The style of cutting vegetables and meat into matchstick shape.

Jus, Au, Fr.: In natural juice.

—K—

Kasseler Rippchen, Gm.: Smoked pork chops.

Kiev, A La, Rs.: A chicken breast preparation.

Kipper: Smoked processed herring.

Kirsch: Black cherry brandy.

—L—

Laid, Fr.: Milk.

Langouste, Fr.: Spring Lobster.

GLOSSARY – MENU TERMS

–L–

Langoustines, Fr.: Saltwater crayfish.

Lapin, Fr.: Rabbit.

Lasagne, It.: Squares of pasta baked with ricotta cheese tomato sauce and topped with mozzarella. Many styles prevail.

Legumes, Fr.: Vegetables.

Limone, It.: Lemon.

Linguine, It.: Narrow ribbon pasta.

Little Neck: Small, hard shell clams.

Livornese, It.: Prepared in style of Livorno. Usually seafood cooked in oil, tomato, garlic and celery.

Lyonnaise, Fr.: A dish made with onions.

–M–

Madeira: A Portuguese wine used in cooking.

Madere, Fr.: A sauce made with meat broth and Madeira.

Maison: Prepared in the style of the House.

Maire D'Hotel, Fr.: A sauce of butter creamed with egg yolks and flavored with lemon juice, parsley and pepper.

Manicotti, It.: Pasta tubes rolled around a stuffing of meat or cheese.

Marble: Fat veins in meat.

Marchand De Vin, Fr.: A sauce of shallots cooked in red wine and meat broth.

Marengo: Chicken or veal is sauteed in olive oil, then cooked in a sauce of white wine, tomatoes, garlic, Cognac, mushrooms, black olives, onions and topped with crayfish or shrimp.

Marsala, It.: Sicilian sweet wine.

Medallion, Fr.: Small, round, thick slices of meat, fish or pate.

Meuniere, Fr.: A style of cooking seafood. The fish is dusted with flour and then fried in butter until golden.

Milanese, It.: The style of cooking found in Milano. The dishes of this Northern Italian city are rather hearty.

Minestrone, It.: A vegetable soup with pasta or rice.

Morilles, Fr.: The wild morel mushroom.

Mornay, Fr.: A cream sauce made with butter, and flour cooked with milk, broth, cream, egg yolks, and grated cheese.

GLOSSARY — MENU TERMS

—M—

Mousse, Fr.: This is an airy dish made of puree of meat, poultry, fish, or of vegetables, fruit or sweets.

Moutarde, Fr.: Mustard.

—N—

Nantua, Fr.: A sauce made from crayfish butter, crayfish broth, white wine, brandy, egg yolk, tomato, and a touch of hot pepper.

Napoleon, Fr.: A flaky puffy pastry in layers filled with a light custard or pastry cream.

Nicoise, Fr.: Features seafood and vegetables made with tomatoes, garlic, olive oil, anchovies and ripe olives.

Noisettes, Fr.: A small, thick boneless cut of meat, often from the loin.

Normande, Fr.: Dishes in the Normand-style are characterized by the use of apples and Calvados (apple brandy).

—O—

Oignon, Fr.: Onion.

Olio, It.: Oil, olive oil.

Oreganata, It.: Prepared with oregano.

Osso Buco, It.: Braised veal shanks cooked in wine and tomatoes. Bone marrow is intact.

—P—

Paella, Sp.: The famous rice dish of Spain, named for the large, shallow two-handled pan in which this dish is cooked.

Parmigiana, Alla, It.: A dish that uses the famous cheese of Parma, Italy. Parmesan cheese.

Pate, Fr.: Rich loaves of puree of meat, poultry, liver, or game mixed with pork fat. They are baked, cooled and served sliced with a garnish of gherkins.

Pesto, It.: Fresh basil is crushed and mixed with garlic, Parmesan cheese, olive oil and pine nuts. The sauce is applied to pasta.

Piccata, It.: A style of preparing veal cutlets that are sauteed in butter and drizzled with lemon juice.

Pignoli, It.: Pine nuts.

–P–

Pizzaiola, It.: A widely varied sauce made from tomatoes, olive oil, garlic, oregano, black pepper.

Poires, Fr.: Pears.

Poisson, Fr.: Fish.

Poivre, Fr.: Pepper.

Pollo, It.: Chicken.

Pomme, Fr.: Apple.

Potage, Fr.: Soup.

Poularde, Fr.: Chicken.

Prix Fixe, Fr.: At a fixed price.

Prosciutto, It.: Italian ham cured by salting.

Provencale, A la, Fr.: In the style of Provence where the cuisine is typified by its liberal use of garlic, tomatoes, olive oil and herbs.

–Q–

Quenelles, Fr.: Light, airy dumplings of fish, poultry, or meat puree.

–R–

Rau, It.: The rich meat sauce of Bologna, Italy.

Ratatouille, Fr.: Diced eggplant, zucchini, tomatoes, green peppers and onions stewed in olive oil, garlic and tomato.

Renzo: A waiter who is also a tableside chef. Flambe is considered their specialty.

Ris, Fr.: Sweetbreads.

Risotto, It.: The spicy rice dish of Northern Italy.

Rockefeller Oysters: Oysters on the half-shell topped with a puree of spinach, chopped green onion, celery cooked in butter with chopped parsley, breadcrumbs with a dash of Pernod.

Romanoff, Fr.: A style of preparing fresh fruit which has been soaked in orange juice and Curacao or Grand Marnier and served over ice cream.

Rouladen, Gm.: A German specialty of beef slices rolled around a stuffing of chopped meat or bacon, then simmered in wine.

−S−

Saddle: A roast of meat comprised of both loins and kidneys.

Saison, Fr.: In season.

Saltimbocca, It.: Pounded veal slices topped with prosciutto and sage leaf. They are sauteed in butter, wine and pan juices.

Satay, Ind.: Indonesian skewer specialties.

Sauerbraten, Gm.: A pot roast of beef marinated in vinegar and seasoned water.

Saute: Flip fry or pan fry with little fat.

Scaloppine, It.: Thin slices of veal pounded flat.

Scampi, It.: Large shrimp or prawns of the Adriatic.

Schnitzel, Gm.: A breaded veal cutlet sauteed in butter.

Scungilli, It.: Conch.

Semolina, It.: Pasta flour made from durum wheat.

Shish Kebab, Arm.: Lamb brochette.

Sorbet, Fr.: A frozen dessert made with pureed fruit.

Souffle, Fr.: A light, airy egg dish made from the frothed white of eggs. Souffles can be eaten as an entree course or as a dessert − the most famous being the Grand Marnier Souffle.

Spiedini, It.: Spitted; Broiled or grilled on skewers.

Spumone, It.: Neapolitan ice cream.

Squab: A fledgling pigeon.

Stroganoff, Rs.: A beef preparation where the meat is cut into thin strips, sauteed in butter with onion, mushrooms and mixed with a sauce of sour cream and meat broth.

Supreme, Fr.: The skinned and deboned breast of chicken.

Sweetbread: The thymus or pancreas of either the calf or the lamb.

−T−

Tartare, Fr.: A raw beef dish garnished with raw onions, parsley, capers, and raw egg.

Tarte, Fr.: An open, single-crust pie.

Tortellini, It.: Rings of egg pasta stuffed with ground meat, cheese and spices.

Tournedos, Fr.: A thick slice of beef from the filet usually sauteed in oil or butter.

GLOSSARY – MENU TERMS

–T–

Tournedos Rossini: Tournedos are sauteed in butter and served on a piece of crustless toast and topped with a slice of goose liver.

Truffles: Truffles are a variety of underground fungus that come in white from Piedmont, Italy or in black from Perigord region in So. France.

–U–

Under Glass: Food is cooked under a glass bell which steams in the natural juices.

–V–

Veau, Fr.: Veal.

Veloute, Fr.: A velvety sauce made with flour, butter and broth.

Verde, It.: Green.

Vermicelli, It.: Extra thin spaghetti.

Veronique, It.: Dishes prepared in this style call for the garnish of grapes.

Vichyssoise: A French leek and potato soup served chilled.

Vin Blanc, Fr.: Made simply in white wine.

Vinaigrette, Fr.: A vinegar dressing for cold foods, particularly salads.

Vitello, It.: Veal.

Vongole, It.: The little clams of Rome and Southern Italy.

–W–

Waldorf Salad: A combination of chopped apples, celery, walnuts and tossed with a mayonnaise dressing.

Wellington, Beef, Br.: A whole tenderloin of beef, roasted, then spread with pate and wrapped in pastry crust and baked.

–Z–

Zabaglione, It.: A Marsala wine custard pudding.

Zuppa, It.: Soup.

GLOSSARY OF WINES

AURORA (Aurore): A recent white wine made from American-French hybrid grapes; semi-sweet. Good with seafood.

BACO NOIR: Rich full-bodied red wine; made from American-French hybrid grapes; comparable to Cabernet Sauvignon when aged several years. Good with hearty meats and cheese.

BARBERA: Popular in California coastal regions, this hearty red wine made from Italian grapes is tart but excellent with beef and hearty meats.

BURGUNDY: Refers to blended red table wine in the U.S. If the wine is from the Burgundy area of France, it refers to white wine made from Chardonnay grapes or red wine from Pinot Noir grapes; dry but easily palatable; good with daily meals.

CABERNET SAUVIGNON: Made from red grapes of Bordeaux, France, this wine is highly respected for its longevity and quality. Longer aging (8–10 years) enhances the bouquet and flavor and is excellent with hearty red meats or fowl.

CHABLIS: Refers to a blend of white grapes in the U.S. If French, it refers to the White Burgundy made from Chardonnay grapes. Taste varies greatly, but is often semi-sweet; good with fish and lighter foods.

CHAMPAGNE: Sparkling white wine that may appear as pink, red or shades in between and referred to as sparkling burgundy or cold duck. "Brut" refers to the driest of the champagnes and "extra dry" or "sec" to the sweeter ones.

CHARDONNAY (Pinot Chardonnay): A dry, full-bodied white wine made from the Chardonnay grapes. Often aged in oak to enhance the drier, sublter qualities of this excellent wine. Superb with veal and seafood.

CHENIN BLANC: A popular white table wine made from grapes originally of the French Loire Valley, this often fruity wine is aromatic and good with everyday meals or alone.

CHIANTI: Although Italian chianti is a dry, smooth full-bodied red wine, American chianti can be sweeter or blander. Excellent with hearty meals or tomato-based Italian cuisine.

EMERALD RIESLING: Developed in California from a variety of white grapes, this wine is crisp and excellent as an appetizer wine, with seafood, or with other light dishes. Depending on makes, it can be sweet.

GLOSSARY OF WINES

FRENCH COLOMBARD: Made from the white grapes of Central Valley in California. It's light and slightly tart taste is excellent with light foods or with an appetizer.

FRUIT WINES: Made from fruits such as peaches, loganberries, strawberries, apples, cherries. Sweet, easily perishable, good as dessert wines or over fruit.

FUME BLANC (Napa Fume, Sauvignon Blanc, Blanc Fume): In France this wine carries a smoky taste, but in the U.S. we have instead a simple dry white wine, sometimes fruity, that is excellent with seafood, fish, or light meats.

GAMAY (Gamay Noir or Napa Gamay): Red Gamay grapes originally from the Beaujolais area of France comprise this light, fruity wine that is best served when young with such items as lamb or pork.

GAMAY BEAUJOLAIS: Made traditionally from Pinot Noir grapes, this red wine is best consumed when young, and if labeled "nouveau" is good with light food items. Otherwise, good with heartier foods such as red meat or ham.

GEWURZTRAMINER: This crisp, spicy, aromatic white wine is made from the grapes of the Alsace region in France or the west coast of the U.S. Although often dry in France, the taste can be quite sweet here in the U.S. Good with cheeses, chicken, sausage.

GREEN HUNGARIAN: Fruity white wine which varies from dry to sweet tasting, and is good with light food items and fruit.

GRENACHE: A light fruity red wine made originally from the grapes of Spain or the Provence area of France. Good with light food items.

JOHANNESBURG RIESLING (White Riesling): Made from a variety of grapes, this fruity, semi-dry wine is very good with light foods.

MERLOT: Dry red wine grape similar to Cabernet and often used for blending. Richness improves with oak aging and sometimes has an herb taste. Excellent with red meat and game.

MUSCAT (Muscatel or Moscato): Predominately sweet white wine, very fragrant. Good with desserts or as an appetizer wine.

PETITE SIRAH: Pungent when aged well, this earthy deep red wine may have a peppery flavor. Good with hearty red meats and stews.

PINOT BLANC: An excellent white grape comprises this dry, rich wine, similar in taste to Chardonnay. Excellent with shellfish and fowl.

GLOSSARY OF WINES

PINOT NOIR: An excellent deep-colored grape comprises this red wine, best served when aged well. Excellent with red meats.

POUILLY-FUISSE: One of the best dry wines of the Macon region of France. Excellent with veal, fish and other light items.

RHINE: Generally refers to fruity white table wine that can be served with light dishes.

ROSE: Refers to a wide variety of pale red wines that can be dry or sweet. Best served young with light meat dishes.

RUBY CABERNET: Developed at U.C. Davis, this fruity dry red wine is a cross of Cabernet and Carignane and is an unpretentious wine that can be served with simple meals.

SEMILLON: Fruity wine grape vine ranging from dry to sweet, sometimes accompanied by an herbal scent. Good with fish, fruit, light dishes.

SHERRY: Includes a dry sherry, a rich, nutty tasting before-meal wine; and cream sherry, a sweet dessert wine.

VERMOUTH: Includes two kinds: dry (white) and sweet (red). They can be enjoyed alone or in cocktails.

ZINFANDEL: Considered California's own red table wine that can be served as a young fruity, raspberry-tasting wine, or as an aged spicier, smooth wine, or as a late-harvest Zinfandel, high in alcohol and also enhanced with aging. Excellent with cheese, pasta, and meats.

GENERAL INDEX

GENERAL INDEX

PRICE INDEX

BARGAIN

Adam's Rib
Aldo's
Angelo's
Australian Restaurant
The Big Yellow House
Birdcage Wok
A Bit of Wyoming
C.B. Hannegan's
Central China
China Delight
Col. Lee's
Crepe Shoppe
Day and Night
El Faro
El Pariso
Falafel Drive-In
Guadalajara Bakery & Market #3
Harry's Hofbrau
Henry's
Jalisco's
Jersey's
La Margarita
Las Palmas
La Taqueria
La Tarantella
Le Cafe
Lexington House
Lien's Cafe
Mama Tried
Mekong
Meyberg's
Minato Sushi
Mini Gourmet
19th Hole
Noodle Palace
Okayama
Paradiso's
Quality Cafe
Saigon II
Siam
The Spur
Stickney's
Szechwan
Taco Al Pastor
Taiwan
Tom and Jerry's

BARGAIN

Tre Kronor
Trine's Cafe #3
The Trukadero
Warburton's Tamale Parlor
The White House

MODERATE

Acapulco
Andy's BBQ
Armenian Gourmet
Au Bon Vivant
Azuma
Black Forest Inn
The Bold Knight
Buy The Bucket
Cathay
The Cat's
Chef Chu's
Chez Yvonne
Chuck E. Cheese
Crow's Nest
D & G BBQ
Di Cicco's
Dinah's Shack
Don The Beachcomber
Durkee's Seafood Mama
El Burro
El Charro
El Torito
Eulipia
Famous Pacific Fish Co.
The Fish Market
Florentine
Flying Lady
Foo Loo Soo
Frankie, Johnny, Luigi
Galano's

PRICE INDEX

MODERATE

Gasthaus Adler
Germania
Gifu
Giorgio's
Golden Flower
Grand China
Guido's
Hakone Sukiyaki
Hamasushi
Harvest Time
Henry's Hi-Life
Ida's Fireside Inn
Inaka
India Joze
Jasmine
Jose's
Kikyo's
Kokeshi
Komatsu
Korean Gardens
Loon Wah
Los Pericos
Main St.
Manny's Cellar
Mother Lode
Original Joe's
Patisserie Boissiere
Pedro's
Piko's Bar and Grill
The Pine Inn
Riera's
Rong Shing
The Rusty Scupper
Sal and Luigi's
Sam's Log Cabin
Scott's Seafood Grill
Sousa's
Steamer's Seafood Cafe
Tadich Grill
Three Flames
Tony Roma's
Vahl's
Vanessi's
The Village
Yu Shan
Zorba's

EXPENSIVE

Adriatic
Anthony's Pier 9
Au Chambertin
Benihana
Che Panisse (Downstairs)
Dartanian's
Domenico's
Emile's
Ernie's
Fung Lum
Gaylord India Restaurant
Gervais
The Hungry Tiger
La Batonville
La Belle Helene
La Chaumiere
La Foret
La Hacienda Inn
La Mere Michelle
La Terrasse
Le Concorde
Le Mouton Noir
Le Papillon
Maddalena's
Maxwell's Plum
Menara
Nicolino's Garden Cafe
Paolo's
Pear Williams
The Plumed Horse
Royal Morocco
R.S.V.P.
Sardine Factory
Shadowbrook
T.S. Montgomery
Victorian House
Zaki's

CITY AND TOWN INDEX

CITY AND TOWN INDEX

MOUNTAIN VIEW

PALO ALTO

SAN FRANCISCO

SAN JOSE

SAN JOSE

CITY AND TOWN INDEX

CUISINE INDEX

AMERICAN

The Big Yellow House
A Bit of Wyoming
The Greenhouse
Mini Gourmet
Mother Lode
The Pine Inn
Quality Cafe
The Spur
Stickney's
Three Flames
Trukadero

ARMENIAN

The Armenian Gourmet

AUSTRALIAN

The Australian Restaurant

BARBECUE

Adam's Rib
Andy's
The Cat's
Day and Night
D & G
Henry's Hi-Life
Jose's
Tony Roma's

CALIFORNIA CUISINE

Piko's Bar and Grill
Warburton's Tamale Factory

CHINESE

The Bird Cage Wok
Cathay
Central China
Chef Chu's
China Delight
Foo Loo Soo
Fung Lum
Golden Flower

CHINESE

Grand China
Henry's
Jasmine
Loon Wah
Rong Shing
Szechwan
Taiwan
Yu Shan

CONTINENTAL

Adriatic
Anthony's Pier 9
Dartanian's
Eulipia
Flying Lady
The Greenhouse
Harvest Time
Ida's Fireside Inn
Le Concorde
Le Papillon
Maddalena's
Maxwell's Plum
Paolo's
The Plumed Horse
Sardine Factory
Three Flames
T.S. Montgomery
Vahl's
Victorian House

CUBAN

Jose's

EATERIES

Aldo's
C.B. Hannegan's
Crepe Shoppe
Jersey's
La Tarantella
Le Cafe
Lexington House
Mama Tried
Meyberg's Deli

CUISINE INDEX

CUISINE INDEX

MEXICAN

Guadalajara Bakery & Market #3
Jalisco's
La Margarita
Las Palmas
La Taqueria
Pedro's
Taco Al Pastor
Trine's Cafe #3

MIDDLE EASTERN

Falafel Drive-In

MONGOLIAN BBQ

Col. Lee's

MOROCCAN

Menara
Royal Morocco

NATURAL FOODS

The Good Earth

PIZZA

Angelo's
Buy The Bucket
Che Panisse (cafe)
Chuck E. Cheese
Frankie, Johnny, Luigi
Guido's
Jose's
The Village

POLYNESIAN

Don The Beachcomber

PORTUGESE

Sousa's Cafe

SALVADOREAN

Los Pericos

SEAFOOD

Anthony's Pier 9
Buy The Bucket
Domenico's
Durkee's Seafood Mama
Famous Pacific Fish Co.
The Fish Market
The Hungry Tiger
Main St.
Sardine Factory
Scott's Seafood Grill
Shadowbrook
Steamer's Seafood Cafe
Tadich Grill
Tom and Jerry's
Vahl's

SMORGASBORD

Dinah's Shack

STEAK, PRIME RIB, LOBSTER

Andy's
Bold Knight
The Cat's
The Crow's Nest
Henry's Hi-Life
Ida's Fireside Inn
Main St.
The Rusty Scupper
Zaki's

SWEDISH

Tre Kronor

SWISS

Emile's Swiss Affair

THAI

Siam

VIETNAMESE

Lien's Cafe
Mekong
Saigon II